GROWING UP IN AUSTRALIA

GROWING UP IN AUSTRALIA

With an introduction
by ALICE PUNG

Black Inc.

Published by Black Inc.,
an imprint of Schwartz Books Pty Ltd
22–24 Northumberland Street
Collingwood VIC 3066, Australia
enquiries@blackincbooks.com
www.blackincbooks.com

9781760643188 (paperback)
9781743822074 (ebook)

A catalogue record for this
book is available from the
National Library of Australia

Cover design by Akiko Chan
Text design and typesetting by Marilyn de Castro

CONTENTS

INTRODUCTION

Erik Jensen said that 'We spend our whole lives trying to work out what happened in the first fourteen years.' Why are our 'growing up' stories so urgent, no matter where or when we live? What is it that makes us dive again and again into this period of our lives?

Perhaps it is a combination of two things that make these experiences so indelible: time and power. When we are children, time moves differently; an hour can seem like a day, a week, a month. We also experience the greatest number of 'firsts' during our childhood and adolescence. And as children we are entirely subject to the decisions of adults – your family might move country, your government might exclude you (or worse, remove you from your family), your teachers might not understand you, your friends might suddenly shun you.

It's no wonder, then, that the combination of powerlessness and having a surfeit of time to reflect on first-time events tattoos these experiences on our memory. Our childhood often shapes our ingrained adult aspirations, reactions and fears.

In these thirty-two pieces, spanning states (geographical as well as internal), eras and even continents, something specific and seismic has happened to each author, as they seek to find their place in that mysterious chimera 'The Great Australian

Childhood'. You know: the sort of childhood you see on television commercials about daily-use domestic products – toilet paper, tinned peaches and Vegemite – mostly featuring middle-class nuclear families living in clean white interiors with a pet.

Many of these authors looked to literature to rectify this false portrayal, to make their lives seem real and genuine, to say to their adult selves, 'I exist too!' You don't always need to see someone like you in literature for books to be enlightening, relevant, relatable or life-changing, as Tim Winton's piece about the power of reading and living attests. But *never* to see someone like you depicted as a three-dimensional human being, always to be the disempowered object-of-charity (but never subject-of-agency), the only gay in town, the 'Scary Spice' of the quintet, or the noble savage, is disheartening. 'That's all? … That's not me,' Tara June Winch realises.

These younger selves of celebrated Australians did not see themselves reflected in their culture. Candy Bowers writes that 'the authors I was looking for didn't exist in Australian bookshops.' It's no wonder there is anger in these stories: 'Australia, you stole years as I tried to be smaller and whiter and less bold.' Stan Grant writes, 'exclusion and difference: these were the abiding lessons of my early school years … We were a footnote, a prehistoric relic.' 'All I can hear is gay static,' writes Natalie Macken, 'No gay people in my orbit, no gay news, no gay dogs even.' Phoebe Hart writes: 'All I knew was that I was different. Very, very different. It was a profound feeling that shaped my adolescence and my life for a long time to come.' And Thinesh Thillainadarajah wonders: 'Will I be ground into dust, waiting for someone else to speak?'

In these stories, you'll find children uniting with each other against power, as Benjamin Law and Vanessa Woods did with their siblings when navigating the adult landmine of a divorce, or dealing with a school bully, as portrayed by Aditi Gouvernel in 'Wei-Li and Me'. You'll find lonely teenagers confounded by the nonchalant, self-possessed power of their peers, as Joo-Inn Chew,

Carly Findlay, Miranda Tapsell, Natalie Macken and Oliver Reeson did, wondering 'why what was happening in me didn't match exactly what was happening in almost everybody else.'

As a result of all this alienation, many of our authors, like Carly Findlay, spent a lot of time alone, 'reading and being creative'. Similarly, Gayle Kennedy's periods of hospitalisation meant that she 'formed a rich inner life'. Andy Jackson writes about how becoming a poet changed his life.

The great American short-story author Grace Paley wrote: 'There isn't a story written that isn't about blood and money. People and their relationship to each other is the blood, the family. And how they live, the money of it.' Katie Bryan tells a heartbreaking-hilarious story of how class and race collided in her childhood, and Lech Blaine similarly writes unabashedly and self-deprecatingly about 'real' battlers, as well as 'smug pricks … jerking each other off at university.'

The heartbeat of many of these stories is family and kinship. Faustina Agolley finds her late father and a sense of identity: 'hearing that I am from a lineage of an actual tribe makes me feel like the coolest kid on the planet', and Joo-Inn Chew writes of her triumph at finally finding a 'tribe' for her own family. Nyadol Nyuon discovers that her mother was 'treated with a level of honour I had never seen before' on a trip to Ethiopia, while Olivia Muscat ends her epistles with a beautiful ode to her mother's legacy.

Anna Goldsworthy writes tenderly about how a teacher can be life-changing, while Alistair Baldwin writes with wry humour about the surprising joy of horse-riding. Hope Mathumbu writes about the 'power' of suburban faith, and Olivia Muscat writes searing letters to people who do not understand her disability. There's wonderful humour in Sara El Sayed's family trying to avoid haram things in their new home, while Uyen Loewald's poem satirises the infantilisation of immigrants.

For many of our authors, including Kerry Reed-Gilbert, Tim Winton, Stan Grant, Magda Szubanski, Tara June Winch,

Nyadol Nyuon, and Rafeif Ismail, childhood evokes a strong sense of place, if not belonging.

The Growing Up series was conceived by Black Inc., with the very first book, *Growing Up Asian in Australia*, coming out over fifteen years ago. Editing that book gave me the rare privilege of meeting a community of Asian-Australian legends, some of whom feature in this anthology. There is now *Growing Up Aboriginal in Australia*, *Growing Up African in Australia*, *Growing up Queer in Australia*, *Growing up Disabled in Australia* and the soon-to-be published *Growing Up in Country Australia.* Each one of these books distils the political events, cultural tags and defining experiences common to an identity, but also showcases the individual experiences unique to each author.

Growing Up in Australia continues this great tradition of countering the 'proper' childhoods propagated by *Neighbours*, *The Saddle Club* and American television. The stories in this anthology are true Australian childhoods, and they are as beautiful, as brutal and as varied as good literature should be, from voices familiar and new. As Oliver Reeson writes, 'You can't choose to opt out. If you don't tell the story, others will fill in the gaps for you.'

Alice Pung

TALKING TO MY COUNTRY

Stan Grant

I was born into what anthropologist W.E.H. Stanner called the 'great Australian silence'. It was the period of forgetting. The myths we created fed Australia's lie: that no blood had stained the wattle. We were told a story of peace and bravery and the conquest of a continent. This was the inevitable push into the interior, a land opening up before the explorers. It was empty; tamed and claimed.

These were the myths of my childhood, the myths of my education. In this telling, Australia was discovered by Captain James Cook. The *Endeavour* was a ship of destiny that led to the First Fleet. On 13 May 1787 eleven ships set sail with a cargo of prisoners to found a penal colony in New South Wales – but the true first fleet landed here 60,000 years earlier. I was told Lawson, Blaxland and Wentworth were the first people to cross the Blue Mountains.

There were people standing on the shore as Cook weighed anchor. Smoke from campfires trailed the white men who trekked over the great mountains west of Sydney; black people watched these people who appeared like ghosts. But that story wasn't told in my classroom. The lesson I learned was that we didn't matter. In fact we didn't even exist.

I was young when I began to question all of this. Even through the eyes of a boy the glory of Australia did not match with the reality of our lives. Something was rotten here. Each morning at school I would stand in line to recite the pledge: I honour my God, I serve my Queen, I salute the flag. And then, in the evening I would return home to where this flag had deposited us. Home was wherever we could find it. It was a home on the margins, outside of town, outside looking in.

Here, was my place, among the detritus of the frontier: the huddled remnants of the hundreds of nations who formed here as the continent formed around them. Two thousand generations of civilisation and culture, all of it now smashed against the reality of white settlement, a people whose land was taken because the people themselves were not legally here.

School told me we faded from the frontier. The dying pillow was smoothed to soften our inevitable extinction.

It need not have been this way. The birth of Australia was meant to be so different. For a brief moment there was hope. Captain Arthur Phillip founded a penal colony with instructions from the crown to protect the lives and livelihoods of Aboriginal people and forge friendly relations with the natives. There were reports of blacks and whites dancing together with joy in the early days of the settlement. The local people began teaching their language to the newcomers. Here's what we could have been. In this moment there was a glimpse of a better Australia, and we failed.

Within a matter of years violence had broken out on both sides and Phillip would now instruct raiding parties to bring back the severed heads of the local warriors. Within a generation the heads of Aborigines were shipped back to Britain in glass cases, to be studied as relics of a doomed race.

Enlightened people throughout the world were wrestling with ideas of humanity and civilisation. The notion that all men are created equal was alive in the world. The 'immortal declaration' – as it was known – had been penned by Thomas Jefferson at the birth of America's independence a decade before the First Fleet arrived on these shores.

Yet, such lofty ideals had no place here. Not for us. We were dismissed as brutes. We were deemed to be the living example of what seventeenth century philosopher Thomas Hobbes meant when he spoke of the natural state as being 'solitary, poor, nasty, brutish and short'.

At best to some we were the 'noble savage'. We belonged to those so-called primitive people uncorrupted by civilisation. Yet such relics were seen to have no place in a modern world. The great writer of his age Charles Dickens spoke for many when he described such peoples as cruel, bloodthirsty and murderous. In Dickens' words we were whistling, clucking, tearing savages that he wished civilised off the face of the earth.

Charles Darwin – the father of the theory of evolution – visited Australia and despaired at the impact of colonisation. There was some 'mysterious agency', he said, that meant that 'wherever the European has trod, death seems to pursue the aboriginal [sic]'. There was of course nothing mysterious at all in the theft of land and the disease and violence that followed. Yet to Darwin – as sad as our passing may be – this was unavoidable, inevitable. His theories were born out of a belief in our common humanity but his name was linked to a popular acceptance of a hierarchy of races where the stronger trumps the weaker: 'Social Darwinism'.

How easy it can be in the sweep of history to stop seeing the individual lives. These were my ancestors they were speaking of, my great-great-grandparents. Such views formed a powerful logic that was unshakeable. It provided the moral blindfold through which people could no longer even see the atrocities perpetrated on my people. Even those people, whose eyes were opened to this suffering, accepted that our fate was doomed.

My ancestors were driven to the brink of extinction. We survived – the half-white remnants of the first nations herded onto Christian missions. We were told this would save us from the brutality of the frontier. But we often lived like inmates, roped and tied if we dared escape.

Now, I was a confused young boy at school, ashamed of what I was. I would cringe against the black and white ethnographic films: the snot-smeared faces of the little 'piccaninnies', the fly-blown women grinding seed into flour, the bedraggled, bearded men gripping a spear, one leg resting against a knee. I remember there was always a narrator with perfectly rounded vowels telling of the 'once proud tribes of Aborigines'. Each head turned to look at me, and I felt anything but pride.

I saw my reflection in Australia and felt diminished. Everything told me I wasn't equal. The whites told the story of this land now; there was no glory in us. There was nothing that redeemed my ancestors. In books proudly titled *The Making of Australia* – a key school text of the 1960s – we were dismissed as the 'dark-skinned wandering tribes who hurled boomerangs and ate snakes' not fit to be counted in the glorious tale of white men and women who found the land, explored it, and made it a nation.

Back then no one wrote of our great deeds. If we existed at all, we were a footnote, a prehistoric relic. I was told the tragic story of the original Tasmanians and how they supposedly vanished from the earth.

My school history books carried photos of Truganini. At first she was young, proud and defiant and then older, grey, in a white woman's clothes. It was this later image that illustrated the fate of her people; how in one lifetime – I was taught – they had faded from the landscape. Of course that too was a lie, a tragic convenient version of history where guilt could be buried with the 'last Tasmanian'.

The Tasmanian blacks, just like us were clinging onto life, regrouping and replenishing on sparsely inhabited islands, the mixed offspring of whalers and Aboriginal women, with facial features that merged both and lighter skin, but outcast all the same and now told they were extinct.

*

Exclusion and difference: these were the abiding lessons of my early school years. They could be days marked with ritual humiliation. I can still hear the roll call of our names. One by one the black kids were pulled out of class. We'd be searched for head lice, our teeth examined. Our fingernails examined for signs of dirt. We were questioned about what we'd had for dinner the previous night. We would have to open our bags to show what we had for lunch.

I remember my teacher looking on and smiling as the government officers continued their interrogation. I recall grasping for answers. I did not know if I could satisfy them. These people likely thought themselves well meaning. But they scared me. My family – like any Aboriginal family – had seen children taken. It could just as easily be me. I remember after school, peering around my street corner looking for the tell-tale white cars of the welfare men, as we called them. Any sign of them and I'd hide out for hours. I would wait until dark then creep back home.

This is where I met white people. I met them in their imaginations. I was introduced in the snickering glances of my classmates, in the interrogation and implicit threat of the deceptively kind welfare officers and the complicit smiles of a kindergarten teacher who asked me to sing Cat Stevens songs for my class but was herself trapped in the prism of racism in 1960s Australia and could not see that morning had not broken for us.

I had no illusions of equality. We were another class of people. Our poverty branded on us as clearly as our colour. I wore the hand-me-down clothes of other people, pulled from cardboard boxes in second-hand bins. There were frayed, ill-fitting shirts, and jumpers stinking of mothballs with the names of other boys stencilled in the collars.

Like any childhood memories mine are sketchy. There are flashes of faces, perhaps a smell or a sound. Petula Clark's 'Downtown' is a blast of musical liberation stuck on permanent rotation in my mind with its promise of forgetting our troubles and cares. I saw the movie *Born Free*, entering the cinema and being transported to Africa, a lion and freedom.

And I remember pineapple juice from a Golden Circle can. I can picture the two triangles punched in the lid to release the taste of a world of possibilities. I was probably five years old, and in one sip all of my senses were jolted to life. My small hands folded around the can. I can still smell that tangy, sticky, sweetness. Then there was the taste: an explosion on my tongue like a bee sting.

I only took one sip. It was my father's juice, his one indulgence. It was the small piece of the world he'd hold for himself, a reward for bending his back to put food on our table. My mother warned us not to touch it. But like any child that only made it more tempting. In one forbidden sip I tasted the promise of a world outside my own; a world of music and movies that shone so brightly but were ultimately counterpoints to a more grim reality. The abiding memories of my childhood remain the things that separated us.

On my seventh birthday my mother threw me a party. It was the only birthday party I ever had as a child. Where she got the idea or imagined we could afford it I don't know. Many meals in our house were rounded out with food begged off charity agencies. My mother and grandmother would make the rounds of the Smith Family or Salvation Army. Along with a 'God is love' sticker would come a food voucher to cover the bare essentials.

But I was a good boy, my mother's helper. She could trust me. I'd help her clean. I would run to the shop, chop wood or help with my younger siblings. I guess she just thought I deserved a little party. She poured some cordial into paper cups and sprinkled some hundreds and thousands onto white bread and made some chocolate crackles. She set it all on a park bench and asked me to invite some kids from school.

I can recall so clearly, how I felt. It is a feeling that has never left me. No amount of education, travel and prosperity can ever erase it. I was sick with fear. I had a headache – as a child I was plagued with sickening headaches – and a pain in my gut. I thought these kids would laugh at me. Worse than that I was afraid that they would laugh at my beautiful, kind, loving mother.

These fears, the fear of being laughed at, the fear of being caught out wearing another boy's cast-off clothes, the fear of the welfare men, all of this marked the territory between the world of Australia and me. This was the space that history had made and the place it had reserved for people like us.

*

I was fourteen when I confronted the world that awaited me. I stood sickened and transfixed, repulsed yet unable or unwilling to look away. Others were ready – eager even – to embrace this world. Violence was where we proved ourselves. There was status and glory here. My friends and I measured ourselves on our ability to fight. But on this day I was shocked and stunned and I have carried that memory with me forever.

I recall this scene with a soundtrack of hissing and spitting and heaving and the crack of bone and the heavy dull thud of a fist sinking into that soft skin below the ribcage. There were other people yelling and cheering and others still entangled in their own swinging fists and pulling of hair. The fight had broken out among rival Aboriginal families after a day of drinking at the local showground. But I watched only two men, both black, one of them my older cousin.

Maybe it was because this was my blood, my kin, that it was so much more horrifying and maybe I saw something that was in me too. My cousin had the other man, a much bigger, heavier set man, against a wall; the only thing that kept the other man upright was the rapid-fire piston-like punches of my cousin. His hands had the power of set cement. In my mind it lasts an eternity but perhaps it was over in minutes. In the end the bigger man was coughing blood from his mouth.

What I saw went beyond violence; it was a rage born of history. The whites had thrown us together, potently mixing family, clan and law and we had turned in on each other. We unleashed a fury on ourselves that came from powerlessness. We often hear the term 'black on black crime': but it is just crime. Our victims are our neighbours and they are black.

I had my own taste of violence around this same time. My local high school was divided into black, white and Italian. It was a self-imposed segregation that defined where we sat, who we ate with and which football team we played for. I would break solidarity and walk home with an Italian boy whose family ran the local pizza shop. Occasionally he would sneak me one.

Some white kids liked to sit with us and befriended us, copying the way we spoke and laughed. We tolerated it, to a point. But when fights broke out we knew which side we were really on. One day it came to me to show my allegiance and I was goaded into brawling with one of the white boys who hung with us. Violence doesn't come naturally to me. Some people are born to it. I have seen that. But as much as it scared me, I realised that day that the rage in my cousin, that I had seen in others in my family, was in me too.

This was a time of coming of age in 1970s Australia. The country town I then lived in was like all the others I'd moved between. Young men with their first cars drove up and down the main street; endless looping laps hour after hour. We would meet at the swimming pool, diving and dunking each other. If we had gathered enough discarded bottles we could cash them in for spare change, enough to buy a bag of lollies at two for a cent. Then we'd sun ourselves on our stomachs on the baked hot cement around the pool.

If we couldn't afford the price of admission to the pool we would make do with cooling off in the many irrigation channels that ran through my town. One of them passed through the Aboriginal mission where my relatives lived. The bridge that crossed it split in three directions and the mission became known as 'the Three Ways'.

Home for me was a government housing commission development just up from the mission, in what had previously been another 'blacks camp' known as Frogs Hollow. We were at the very edge of town; we knew where the town ended because that's where the tar road finished. From the last of our houses a corrugated dirt track ran down to the mission and in all my childhood it was never sealed.

My house was next to my uncle's and our cousin's house was next to his. We were tossed together in a social experiment of blacks and whites bound by being poor. But we filled our time with football games and bike riding and playing marbles and stealing watermelons from the local farmers and floating them down the channels to where we'd boarded up makeshift dams. When everyone is poor you don't know you're poor. My father worked so some of the boys thought I was actually rich.

My father's grandmother – my great-grandmother – lived down at the mission. She was always an old lady to me. Her teeth were gone but she loved to suck the caramel out of the chocolates we would always bring with each visit. She loved to collect the pull tops from soft drink cans and wear them as rings. Nanny Cot, we called her; always surrounded by her grandchildren and now her great-grandchildren like me. Some she had raised herself after their parents had died. Nanny Cot outlived many of her kids.

My great-uncle lived behind her house in a caravan. He was my grandmother's brother and would spend a couple of nights a week with her in her house uptown. My grandfather had some land and he built a tin and fibro house before he died. When life on the mission would get too much my great-uncle could escape to be with his sister.

He would walk the couple of miles past the main irrigation channel to her home. One week he failed to turn up. A few days passed before his body was pulled from the water. Death could touch us at any time; it was random but never unexpected.

We lost many people to the channels; slipping and falling in – some with too much to drink – unable to get out.

Nanny Cot was a living link to Australia's frontier history. She'd been born onto the Warangesda Mission on the banks of the Murrumbidgee River; founded by a crazed Rasputin-like preacher, John Brown Gribble, who had been rescued by Aborigines when he wandered off as a child on the Victorian goldfields. In his mind he would repay the debt by saving us from what he saw as the ravages of the colonial whites. Gribble described the blacks of the Murrumbidgee as 'a wretched focus of iniquity'.

But if Warangesda – meaning home of mercy – was meant to be our salvation it failed. It collapsed into a living hell and when the blacks would try to flee, the pastor would round them up on horseback and tie them together with rope and drag them back again. Gribble himself went slowly insane before the church shipped him to England, broken and tormented. He penned a book aptly titled *Dark Deeds in a Sunny Land.*

My great-grandmother now lived out her days on the Three Ways. We would visit each weekend and my grandmother from uptown would attend the mission church. This was a hard place. Barely half a kilometre separated me and where I lived and these houses – but it represented another world, a relic of the frontier. We were the lowest step on the awkward, tentative ladder of assimilation – we were the future; the mission, the past.

We were all blood relatives, but the boys on the mission seemed edgier and darker. The girls had a snarl and an attitude in their walk. Some of them had scratched rough, blue ink tattoos onto their arms: boys' names usually. The dogs looked a bit leaner and meaner, and we kicked the football on a dusty dry oval full of spiky burrs. The tough boys I played footy with eventually torched the church to the ground.

We would all catch the bus to the local high school. The blacks' bus, we called it. It was a time when the government was trying to encourage Aboriginal kids to stay in school. Each term my parents would get a cheque for books and uniforms.

Each fortnight we kids would get a cheque of our own for three dollars. We'd know when it was our payday; all the kids on the blacks' bus would charge out near the school and make a beeline for the local shop to cash in.

Those years from thirteen to fifteen seem now like some sort of reprieve. Just for that time we were boys and girls. The pool was the pool and football was football. Yes, we were blacks and whites and we revelled in our segregation. But in a small town, we all knew each other and we all did the same things. The shade of the prison house had not yet fallen on our lives, but it was looming. Just then though, for that moment, potential and ambition did not seem so fanciful.

For those years from thirteen to fifteen we were invincible. Never again would we as black people be better than everyone else, be tougher than everyone else. There was status and pride in being Aborigines – Kooris – we could strut and laugh loudly.

White kids wanted to be us – not just with us – they wanted to talk like us and act like us. For that brief time we made the rules, we'd scoff how they thought they were blackfellas but they weren't. We didn't doubt who we were, we didn't have to justify it, we didn't even have to think about it. We were on land that was ours; we were blood our families weaved in and out of each other in intricate kinship. I have never known that certainty since.

These were untapped lives, kids full of cheek and wit. I didn't stand out at all as someone especially capable let alone remarkable. I was happy to go along, playing football, messing up in class, going to the pool. But I always watched and thought and wondered why our lives were so different from the whites' lives.

I would sit in the tree behind my grandmother's house just thinking of what else might be out there. Other boys were more handsome, better footballers, brighter students. Many of the girls were absolutely fearless and they gave off sparks of energy. These kids could have powered their communities. But the tyranny of low expectations smothered them.

When I was fifteen, the principal of our high school called some of us Aboriginal kids to his office. He wanted us gone. By law we were no longer required to attend school. He suggested it might be time we looked at other options. We could pick fruit or work on the local council. Some of us might get an apprenticeship, he said, but higher education was clearly not an option.

The government was paying us to try to keep us in school, but the headmaster was doing what missionaries, welfare officers and the police had been doing for two hundred years: he was handcuffing us to our history, reminding us that if we did have a place in Australia it would be on the margins. Here was my early taste of how official policy – well intended – could shatter against a wall of entrenched racism.

It is these moments – minutes in our lives but repeated over and over – which poison our souls and kill us as sure as the waterholes poisoned on the frontier killed our ancestors. It hasn't changed; laws can outlaw discrimination but they can also harden the bigotry in the minds of some people.

The light went out of the eyes of my cousins and schoolmates as they later limped from the classroom. Their bravado wouldn't allow them to show vulnerability. They flaunted their imagined freedom, adding another layer of defiance to their already hardened exterior. But quietly and inevitably whatever fire and spark had existed, now extinguished.

Their lives became like stagnant pools of water. With nowhere to run they were slowly polluted. It isn't that there is no joy. But it gets harder to find, until drink and drugs and violence fill those empty spaces. Not everyone suffers in this way; some find a rhythm of work and family and enough love to push out the confines of their lives. But those who don't make it die.

Funerals call me home far too often. My mother and father seem always to be telling me of another person who has passed away. For indigenous people, life can be a nearly constant state of mourning. If I walk through the graveyard of my hometown I see so many lives cut short. Kids I grew up with, cousins and uncles and aunts whose smiles are still fresh in my mind now lie beneath crosses marking their birth dates, people who would be only in their forties or fifties.

My cousin Lex lies here. As a boy I looked up to him. He had lost his parents – my grandmother's brother and his wife – when he was only young. My uncle and aunt took him in and raised him as theirs. I can remember sitting on his bed as he showed me his school Army Cadets uniform and his rifle. Big Lex, we called him. He always seemed stronger, more grown up even though he was no more than five years older than me. I was living in Beijing when my mother called to tell me he had died.

There is one funeral that has stayed in my mind. It was for another cousin, another man dead at just fifty years old. We sang 'The Old Rugged Cross' that day as we always do: 'On a hill far away stood an old rugged cross, the emblem of suffering and shame.' Our church was always big on sin and redemption: a church of the fallen. They were all there, my old friends and family. I looked at one man, studying his face. He was so familiar but changed. He was hard and lean; there were scars around his eyes. He was hollowed out and looked ten years older than me.

I had seen this man as a boy, curled up on his bed reading comic books. We had played football together, pairing up to gang tackle our opponents so hard they would break. There was one game where we took aim at a big boy on the other side. We smacked our hands together and looked at each other and zeroed in, one high one low. As the ball reached his hands we struck a perfect collision of bone on bone and we felt the air leave his body as he folded into the ground.

This boy I played football with and laughed with; this boy who was tricky and fast and smart; this boy made one false move. He listened when the principal told us to leave school. That man, thin and mean, who loved caning us especially in winter when it stung or bled. He didn't see our potential; he saw our colour. He set my friend on a path of mistakes that led to drugs and jail. Now he sat there barely recognisable to me. This is what Australia can do to black lives.

For that instant, maybe I was unrecognisable to him too. What plans we had made had never been expected to lead us to here. The boys that met as friends were strangers now. We were each left to our own mistakes. It is the conceit of success that the world of our childhood will remain suspended, just waiting for us to reconnect. We can return, laugh and remember and then move on, away from the world that made us to the new one we'd created.

Those who stay behind we expect to remain as we knew them, locked in a photo frame, a reflection of our simpler selves. But their lives turned too and for my friend it had turned hard. We did recognise each other after a minute, we hugged as boyhood friends do but we would never be those boys again.

A different fate beckoned me too. Somewhere in a parallel universe, maybe there were drugs and crime and jail, A sliding door into another life, a life measured in the grim statistics that can define my people: disease, unemployment, death. This life would never have taken me far from the limits of my hometown.

There are those who stayed and still lived quiet lives of dignity; perhaps that would have been me. But I will never know. Part of me is always there, but a greater part of me left. I cheated the odds and it all turned on luck and timing.

My father's restlessness took us away again. We left town, left my friends and family and moved to Canberra. My father had a job on a sawmill that paid a little more money. This was our way: we moved, we stopped then we moved again.

I don't know what drove Dad but I suspect it was the gambler in him. He would place his bet then double it again, hoping to cash in at the next town. He was a saw miller, a tree feller, a fruit picker; he laid concrete, detonated explosives and built dams. He was sinew and muscle, and that bought us shelter and food.

He was hard on me, or so I thought. He wouldn't spare the belt. These were lessons taught by his father and passed to me. Black men who knew the price black men could pay in this country. It felt like I was always in the corner of his eye and I wondered if I was also in his heart. If I strayed too far from view or looked to be nearing the dangerous edges of our world he would corral me and keep me in line; give me a taste of the consequences that might be waiting for me.

He knew the world better than me and he was preparing me for that world. It was a world where men settled arguments with their fists. He taught me how to fight too, moves and combinations he'd perfected in the travelling boxing tents.

We'd put on the gloves, he would put his hands up in front of me and show me how to throw a jab and snap it back straight to guard my face, how to crouch and dig my elbows into my midriff. He'd watch my feet and teach me to keep them just the right distance apart; too wide, he said, and I'd lose power and balance. He'd warn me to keep my eyes trained on my opponent. He showed me how to roll my shoulders to take the sting out of blows. But above all, he said, relax and breathe; a tense fighter is a fighter who has lost.

This was Marquess of Queensberry rules. The real battles when they came would be in the street, and he taught me those lessons too: how never to grab another man's shirt and lose the advantage of two hands. He told me if I was ever outnumbered to get in front of a wall so I could not be surrounded, and never, he said, allow myself to go to the ground or I would get a kicking.

My father couldn't refine my golf swing or show me how to set a sail or strengthen my backhand; he had no need of these things. Those lessons would count for nothing in the world he laid out for me.

I looked on my father's world with a mix of fear and love. I loved the tangy smell of him when he'd come home from the mill, how the sawdust would tickle my nose. I would go to the mill and see big men with muscles carved from hard work and heaving logs twice their size.

They'd break for smoko and twist the lids off flasks of sweet tea; heads bowed and shoulders slumped, beads of sweat tracing unshaven skins. They wouldn't speak much, maybe offer a cigarette and swish the last sip of tea around the bottom of their mugs before emptying it into the dirt and going back to work.

They were usually white, these hard men, but my father found a place there. He found brotherhood in poverty, in shared struggle, black and white. But for white people, being poor didn't define them in the way our blackness defined us. Poverty itself could be temporary and if by chance or effort they broke its chains, there'd be a white world waiting. But we would be black and that would always pose uncomfortable questions for Australia.

My father had pushed against the boundaries of blackness and knew it was safer living in the cracks. This is where we took refuge and he marked out territory with his body. I was wrong to wonder about my place in this man's heart. There wasn't a lot of room for sentiment but he squared up to the world and he took its hardest blows for us and he saved me from that fear that I felt every time I watched him at the mill, the fear that the world he lived in would crush me.

By the 1970s self-determination became the buzzword for Federal Government policy for Aborigines. Gough Whitlam had established the Department of Aboriginal Affairs. There were programs to try to keep kids in school, create employment and promote home ownership. This was an attempt to level the playing field, create pathways for Aboriginal families to merge more successfully with what we were told was 'mainstream Australia'. In Canberra my parents applied for an Aboriginal housing loan. Dad stashed away a small deposit, working overtime shifts at the mill; Mum earned extra cash cleaning cars in Canberra's frosty winter's mornings. It was work that would leave her red raw, cracked and bleeding. No more though, would we be rootless – no more rundown mill shacks or tiny caravans. My father could now settle on land and call it a home.

Now he had a place: his place. It meant change and it wasn't easy. I went from a school segregated by colour to a school where my sister and I were the only Aboriginal children. There was racism and hurtful taunts but I could reinvent myself and I made friends.

It sounds simple. Some would say this is the answer for us all. Leave, find a new life, work; avoid the clutches of poverty and despair. Former Prime Minister Tony Abbott described this as a lifestyle choice. If only that were all there was to it. When we move we don't just leave family, we leave country. If constantly moving made my family a smaller target, forever dodging racism and the heavy hand of the welfare men, then it also came at a cost. I always felt displaced and it could be lonely. I can't deny that the lure of a new town, a bigger city, gave us new hope but it didn't mean white Australia was not uncomfortable or unwelcoming. I learned that the price of acceptance was to smooth out my differences until I was almost in denial about being Aboriginal.

It is hardly surprising that some of our people prefer to stay where they are. Here is another uncomfortable, confronting question: who says we have to aspire to white Australia's idea of a good life? Sometimes defiance is all we have. We know the cost and have paid it and continue to pay it. While ever our communities are not empowered, without an economic base, the opportunity to build wealth, to strengthen ourselves on our own terms, then we face the daunting, sometimes insurmountable challenge of finding our place in a white world that we know can so easily and brutally reject us.

Alone in Canberra, away from the black cousins and friends who nourished my identity, I needed something to cling to. At school I could be the brown boy who played sport and liked music and never spoke much about being Aboriginal. The other kids knew what I was but no one really wanted to talk about it. But at home I found strength and a sense of moral outrage in the words of James Baldwin. I read *Go Tell It on the Mountain*,

Baldwin's first novel. Here were people I knew, a struggle across the generations; religion and race.

Black America fascinated me. I looked to the Civil Rights movement, the oratory of Martin Luther King, the 'by any means necessary' fire of Malcolm X, the Nation of Islam or 'black Muslims' and the Black Panther Party. I had a poster of Tommie Smith and John Carlos, their gloved hands raised in a black power salute of defiance on the victory podium at the Mexico Olympics in 1968. These were people who stood up, and James Baldwin was their poet laureate.

I think I first borrowed it from the library, this book that would change my life. The name attracted me; I had always loved the song and its plea to 'let my people go'. Here was the story of a family and two brothers: Roy and John. Between them was a history of slavery and brutality. John's birthday triggered a rupture that laid bare the secrets, torment and pain all in the shadow of the cross. The book turned on the Oedipal drama of John's life. He looked for the love of his distant preacher father. Reconciling his own sin he embraced God.

But this was a family of secrets. John's father was not his father. He was the man who married John's mother and never let her forget it. In a final act of devotion John prostrated himself at the feet of the lord. It was an act of desperation and it mocked his father's hypocrisy.

How I loved the drama of these stories: the sweep of family and history. Baldwin's God was the God of redemption and punishment. The people of this book, trapped between sin and salvation, shaking with the force of temptation, inviting the fires of hell. These were the lives I saw around me too. My people had been 'saved' on the missions, delivered from sin and their own blackness.

Like Baldwin's characters we fell and were reborn. We were like John's father, the preacher Gabriel, straightened on the path of righteousness only to become punishingly sanctimonious. *Go Tell It on the Mountain* spoke to me with its story of children born in secret, of a woman banished to die young in shame, and a preacher commanding authority from the pulpit he could never replicate at home.

Go Tell It on the Mountain led to Baldwin's other books. In his essays 'Notes of a Native Son' and 'The Fire Next Time', Baldwin charted a course through the pain and humiliation of racism. He was blunt – brutally at times – and he told me: 'For the State, a Nigger is a Nigger is a Nigger, sometimes Mr. or Mrs. or Dr. Nigger.'

In a letter to his nephew James he warned: 'You can only be destroyed by believing that you really are what the white world calls a *nigger*.' I knew this. I had seen this. Being black – being Aboriginal – was intensely political. Our identities were a political statement; even denial of our identities was political.

Baldwin wrote with fluency and confidence. He did not compromise. There was no doubt. He accused America of the crime of destroying hundreds of thousands of black lives and not knowing it and not wanting to know it.

Later I would gain a deeper understanding of his work. I would learn of his struggle to express himself as a black man, as a gay man in America. I would learn of how he sought exile in Paris and saw his country even more deeply; more clearly, from afar. I had no inkling then that one day I would do the same.

RECKONING

Magda Szubanski

By 1966 we had been in Australia for a year and the Szubańskis were well on the way to becoming Aussies. Still, culturally we were British. Even though we spoke the language, all our references, all of our knowledge of custom and practice, was British or European. We knew nothing of local lore or wisdom or parochial efficiencies. We had no connections. We didn't know the names of streets, towns, birds, trees, famous people. We knew nothing of weather patterns and Warning signs. Of the dangers – bushfires, floods, heatstroke, poison berries and sharks. Or sensible precautions – shaking out your shoes in case of spiders; making loud noise in long grass in case of snakes; lifting the toilet seat to check for redbacks. The myriad survival tips that get passed down passed us by. Everything was jarringly and excitingly new.

It took us years to learn how to holiday – that on this island-continent travel is measured not in distance but in hours. That you can travel for three thousand kilometres without seeing the sea or the border of another country. That Sunday drives were potentially life-threatening expeditions on which a carelessly tossed cigarette butt could unleash the fires of Gehenna. My parents tried to grapple with this new reality. My father would get ideas into his head. Ideas like 'beating the heat' and 'feathering the brakes'. Which is how we came to be yanked from our beds at two in the morning and bundled into the pre-packed Holden. 'Come on. We need to get on the road. We need to beat the heat.' We were terrified of the heat. My sister and brother and I would try to recover our lost sleep in the back seat as Dad herky-jerked the car to a stop at every set of lights, pumping the pedal in the belief that this would prolong the life of the brake pads.

We holidayed as if we were still in England. We drove for eight tedious hours along the utterly featureless Calder Highway to Mildura. We took a ride on a paddleboat and the captain let me steer, which was great fun. But after that we couldn't think of anything else to do so straight back home again. Another time we went for a long and windy Sunday drive around the Dandenong Ranges, stopping constantly for my carsick friend Izabella to vomit. We got all the way round and it looked like Izabella's ordeal might finally be over when Dad took a wrong turn and we did the whole circuit again.

'Well,' Dad tried to put a positive spin on things, 'at least you have seen the Dandenongs,'

'Yes,' Izabella groaned. 'Twice.'

There was the time Mum and Dad and I drove to Lakes Entrance and they decided to pick up a hitchhiker – a young man who claimed to be a soldier on his way back to barracks in Puckapunyal – only to regret the decision moments later. Mum was adamant. 'She cannot sit in the back with him!' she whispered furiously when we stopped for petrol. So I was made to sit on the console between the front bucket seats for three uncomfortable hours. Clueless.

But there was one British road-trip tradition that still worked. We sang. My father had a fine Volga-boatmen kind of baritone, my mother a rich and pleasant alto. My brother and sister and I would sing harmonies. Every time we were all in the car together there would be a joyous cacophony of voices. It wasn't some kind of regimented Von Trapp Family awfulness – it was spontaneous, riotous fun. We all still do it. We did it just yesterday on the way to the Chinese restaurant for my niece's birthday.

As part of his contract, the firm my father worked for had given us a house, an old plain weatherboard in Bayswater, about thirty kilometres east of the city. But Dad wanted something new, so we bought a block of land in North Croydon, about half an hour away on the same thirty-kilometre radius, and began to build a brick-veneer house on it. Our house was next door to the Vincent's, Harry with his gingery hair and Maureen with her glamorous, Ann-Margaret shade of red. I remember the excitement of visiting the block, teetering on top of a steep hill. Of seeing our new home emerge from nothing. All around, the landscape was bristling with the skeletons of such new homes. One of our favourite pastimes was to use the raw planks as a jungle gym.

Croydon was an outrider suburb, the wild east. All bush, farmlands and orchards. It had been settled in about 1840. Before that, it would have been forested with eucalypts. The early pioneers had scraped as much of it clean as they could. Long before we arrived teams of bullocks dragged heavy chains across the land, clearing away the dense bush. And of course it wasn't just the bush they got rid of. By the time we got there the original inhabitants, the Wurundjeri people, were long gone. All that remained now were the place names that hinted at their existence – Wonga Park, Mooroolbark, Maroondah, Yarra River. In fact they were so spectacularly absent that I never even saw an Indigenous person until I was about nine. I went to a birthday party and the family had a little adopted girl, who I now realise must have been one of the Stolen Generation. I felt awkward around her, not knowing what to say or do. It was many more years before I even met another Aboriginal person. At school I never learned a single thing about Indigenous history. I was never told of the brave and gallant Simon Wonga, after whom Wonga Park was named. Or his cousin William Barak, one of the first Aboriginal artists and a great statesman of the Kulin nation, called King of the Yarra. Barak was born just down the road from our school at Brushy Creek. It was all within a stone's throw, and we were taught none of it.

Whenever we watched cowboy and Indian films, my father would shake his head and mutter, 'Poor bloody Indians.' I was too little to understand. He knew what it felt like to be an Indian. The cruel irony was that here he was on Aboriginal land – in a sense, an Indian dispossessing another Indian.

Not everything was new. There were pockets of oldness. The Flynns had lived on our street the longest and, unlike the clinky brick-veneer houses we all lived in, their old weatherboard house had an outside dunny – the nightsoil man still came to empty their loo. The house was a haven for redbacks and big fat huntsman spiders. One day Mrs Flynn found a two-metre brown snake coiled up in a kitchen cupboard. Mr Flynn chopped it in half with a shovel, sending the head and tail slithering off in opposite directions.

Their house would have witnessed an awful lot in its day. Ours was brand new and had seen nothing. It was a modest little place with three small bedrooms and thin walls that gave little privacy. The lounge room was separated off with the mandatory frosted-glass sliding doors and the whole place was carpeted throughout with a bilious blue nylon job-lot Dad got cheap from work. The outside was decorated with what looked like quirky, misshapen statuettes but were in fact hardened piles of dross from the extrusion process at the lab. My parents thought this was an ingenious repurposing. Every stick of furniture was new except for the beds, so it was like living in a model home. I felt very groovy.

The land around Croydon had little softness in it. Beneath the grey sagging gum trees the ground was hardscrabble, the grass sharp as burnt matchsticks. Even so, on Saturday mornings the dawn chorus of lawnmowers would start. The low, rumbling hum would be punctuated with the sound of blades crunching on granite and the zing of blinding stone chips flying through the air. A cloud of two-stroke fumes hung over the houses, wafted down the chimneys and into the kitchen and finally settled on your Weet-Bix.

In the distance the roiling hills were rarely green. Mostly they were sundried beyond brown or even yellow. Dried to white or burned black. Far away, on the other side of the highway, long-dead gum trees stood waist deep in the bony grass, their arms outstretched, their twiggy fingers splayed.

But across the valley, on the rise of the opposite hill, was a field of emerald green. Our house was at the top of the hill and our veranda was built high up on top of the garage, like a lookout. I would sit cross-legged on the hard concrete, picking at the bubbles of paint in the corners of the white iron safety railings while I gazed out through the bars and across the valley and dreamed of lying in that lush, gentle grass. The green, green grass of home.

One day when I was about eight the Pommie kids next door and I decided to walk to that field. I got up early and packed my schoolbag with a plastic bottle of frozen orange cordial and a leftover sandwich from my lunch box. We assembled on the nature strip to determine our route and then set off down the steep hill full of intrepid confidence. But once we had crossed Maroondah Highway there were no roads or signposts to guide us to our Shangri La. Overwhelmed by the nearness of things, we soon lost our way. Our resolve stalled in the baking head. Like the early explorers we had not planned well and did not have adequate provisions. We had furious debates about which way to go. Finally we settled on what we thought was the right path and our high spirits returned. For hours we trudged across pocked, rocky paddocks. We trekked along fire-breaks and across cow-shit meadows and shinnied across the slimy water pipe that spanned the stagnant creek. We braved bees and bulls and barbed-wire fences. Finally we arrived at what must have been our field. There were no other candidates. Our hearts sank. Close up, the field was not much greener or softer than on our side. It had the same sharp stones. The same bull-ant nests. We sat for a small while and then went home, having learned the hard way about the false promise of greener grass.

What the landscape lacked in comfort it made up for in space. Our block was a good deal larger than the standard quarter acre. It was irregular and sloped steeply upwards, with unpredictable dips and bumps and no foliage. It was bare and a bastard to mow. My father was forever trying to tame this lumpen block, buttressing it with rock gardens and rock walls garlanded with pigface, courtesy of my mother. Great truckloads of volcanic rocks would arrive periodically and my father would set about arranging them. A rented cement mixer would churn into action and we would be marshalled into shovelling spadefuls of sand and gravel into the porridgy grey maelstrom. He always gave us the shitty, boring jobs. He was not a natural handyman and from my bedroom I could hear the hiss of muttered curses as he blackened yet another finger under a twenty-kilo igneous ornamental feature. I admired his application to something he clearly loathed. Whatever he started he always finished. 'Once your father took something on,' Mum said, 'he would spear the backside out of it.'

Behind the house, way up the top of the back garden, was a huge, unkempt wall of quince bushes and blackberries that loomed forward like a frozen wave in a Japanese woodblock print. This marked the end of civilisation. Behind that everything ran wild with bushland and chicken farms and foxes. There were ramshackle orchards, their trees garlanded with crisp red apples and gaudy lemons like the sleeves of Peter Allen's Rio costume.

In the height of summer the winds blew down from the centre of the continent where they gathered up the dry desert heat before unleashing it on us. The heat was unrelenting and everything felt combustible. Your fingers throbbed and swelled with your own broiling blood and you feared that if you brushed them against the tinder-dry flakes of a paperbark tree the bush would burst into flame. Deadly brown snakes twined themselves through the hot, singing grass; their shed skins lay in the long grass like used prophylactics.

Up behind our back fence was the mythological bush, where the wild things were. It was vast. It didn't care if you lived or died. Our cricket balls disappeared into it, never to be seen again. It was not far from here that Frederick McCubbin had found the inspiration for his famous painting *Lost*, in which a girl stands alone, crying in the bush. This painting embodies the fear that stalked the early settlers – being lost in the vertiginous, agoraphobic immensity of it all. *Picnic at Hanging Rock* without end.

But for me, the freedom of space and open air loosened my limbs and filled my soul with possibilities, I became a frontierswoman. I was Daniel Boone. With a marauding posse of the neighbourhood kids I would be up until all hours playing hide and seek, running through the bush and from house to house. In the eerie black night we would terrify one another and run screaming across Old Man Chandler's place, clambering over fences, getting the seat of our pants caught, skinning our knees. Pretending not to hear our parents who stood at the back door yelling for us to come home.

The roads were unmade and there were no kerbs. Packs of gum trees loitered about the streets like old hobos. The dirt was pale grey and talcum soft under your bare feet. I remember one night running up to the top of the hill and there, at the end of the silver dirt road, perfectly framed between the trees, was the biggest, fattest full moon I have ever seen. It was pale, watery gold and completely filled the frame. And I ran towards it believing, with all the conviction that an eight-year-old heart can carry, that I could touch that moon.

PIANO LESSONS

Anna Goldsworthy

'Do you want to hear "Moonlight" Sonata?' I asked visitors, in preparation for Young Talent Time. I played this broken chord over and over again, faster and faster, my hand cramped in a spasm of effort. B—E—G, B—E—G, B-E-G, BEG, BEG-BEGBEGBEG.

'The "Moonlight" Sonata is a cinch,' I said modestly. 'It's just B-E-G, or in other words *beg*.'

This was my knowledge base. This was what I took to my first lessons with Mrs Sivan. At the Leningrad Conservatorium, she had been preparing students for international competitions; before coming to Adelaide, she had never taught children. During our second lesson, I began telling her my story about the zoo.

'This is where the little girl sees a chimpanzee,' I said, pointing to a chromatic embellishment. My voice faltered. Even I did not believe it.

She took my hand: 'My darling, we must sit and work.'

*

After my first few lessons, my parents swapped shifts at their doctors' surgery so that my father could take me to Mrs Sivan's house. For the next eight years, he accompanied me to my lessons every Tuesday afternoon, listening, day-dreaming, taking notes. Mrs Sivan was a born performer, and enjoyed having him there. I feel it myself now as a teacher: the extra voltage an audience lends to a room.

'Let us talk about the fingers,' Mrs Sivan said. 'This finger, the pointer finger, is good student. This third finger, it is very – what you say – reliable. But this finger … oy.' She shook her head. 'Fourth finger very lazy!

Her words were picturesque but to me entirely abstract. Over the years, my body came to understand them for me.

'It is the thumb that makes a pianist,' she said, and showed me what the thumb can do, her hands fluttering over the keyboard, kneading at it, producing sounds of striking intensity. Over time, I learnt that the thumb is the key to the hand's relaxation, its checkpoint, navigator and conductor. There is an instinct to grab with the thumb, which turns it into a brake; pianistic fluency depends on letting it go, on trusting the hand.

Then she took my little finger into her hand: 'It is the little finger that makes an artist.' She winked her little finger at me, demonstrating its independence. 'Like waving to a friend: *bye bye*.' I imitated her movement and waved back to her, but at the piano I still used my little finger as an approximate edge to my hand. It took me a decade to understand its possibilities: the tiny candle-lights it sets at the top of a melody, its sleigh-bells, its *coloratura*, its left-hand foundations and invitations.

We began work on Bach's small preludes.

'Bach basically is father of all music,' she told me. 'He has *huge* influence on everybody. He was educator of Chopin, of Beethoven, of Schumann. And even all modern jazz already here. You can try anything, and Bach already do it. Of course, Bach never knew piano.'

'Why not?'

'Piano not yet invented.'

I glanced dubiously at my father, who gave an emphatic nod.

'But piano absolutely instrument of imagination, and we

can create anything on it. Clear organ here.' She demonstrated a small prelude. 'Remember always that Bach represents God in this world, with his wisdom, his acceptance, his forgiveness. Like he always bless you.'

'I've already learnt that prelude,' I told her, imagining it was possible to complete a piece. 'I finished it with my old teacher.' 'Bach is never finished. Life in this music *endless*.' She took my finger and dived with it into the key; it plunged to the bottom with the precise weight of a ball bearing. 'And here, very harpsichord touch. What Bach gives? Peace, of course, and bells.'

The evenness she demanded went well beyond the physical handicaps of a lazy fourth finger or attention-seeking thumb. It was an evenness of thought, a spiritual discipline. 'We play with our ears,' she reminded me. 'Seeing ears, hearing eyes. Clever heart, warm brain.'

My hands, brown with the Australian sun, tripped across the keyboard beside hers, as pink and round as starfish. 'Not,' she said, as I guessed at a sound, and then she took my hand and guided my fingers to the right attack. Often I didn't even register the precise spins she put on every sound; I was as tone-deaf to inflexion as a person speaking a foreign tongue. To me the keys of the piano were still on–off buttons, which could be played loud, or soft, or somewhere in between.

*

At home, I was not yet practising two hours a day, but I told my friends that I was. On one camping trip with our neighbours, around the fire, I gave a self-aggrandising account of my life as a junior concert pianist. As we drove home the following day, my brother and baby sister dozed beside me.

I closed my eyes and pretended to be asleep too, so that I could listen to my parents speaking *sotto voce* in the front.

'Lizzie thinks we're pushing Anna,' said my mother. 'That she's missing out on a childhood.'

'That's bullshit,' said my father. 'Did you tell her how much she enjoyed the piano?'

'I told her about the little stories she makes up for her pieces. But Lizzie said that this only proved her point. That this was her way of getting the childhood she was missing out on. She said it was one of the most tragic things she had ever heard.'

I lay in the backseat and rehearsed this in my mind. *Tragic. Me. Missing out on a childhood.* The melodrama of it delighted me; a tear of the most exquisite self-pity formed in my eye and then rushed down my cheek. I let it dry on my skin. If I wiped it away, they would know I had been eavesdropping.

In fact my parents rarely pushed me to practise. 'Practice makes perfect,' my mother said occasionally. I was not sure that I believed her, but I took it on faith, like so much in childhood. Sometimes my father sat beside me when I practised; sometimes he sat behind me in the study and wrote poetry.

Usually, I was glad to play the piano. I was an uncoordinated child, and playing an instrument offered me purchase on the physical world: a small realm of possible mastery. Each night, my parents took me out the back for remedial ball skills.

'Hands ready,' my mother coached, as my father lobbed a soccer ball at me. It approached with the precision of a heat-seeking missile, its black and white hexagons swirling towards my face.

'Catch!' they cried out, in unison.

I always lost my nerve at the key moment.

'You'll never catch it if you don't *look at it*,' my mother repeated, running inside to fetch a flannel. I waited for my nose to stop bleeding, and then returned to the piano.

Every now and then I resented it, and Lizzie's words echoed in my head. One Saturday morning, I rallied the neighbourhood children in a new business venture. We sifted the neighbours' driveway, searching for pieces of gravel of the utmost beauty and rarity, which we painted in watercolours – sapphire, amethyst, ruby and emerald – and marketed to passers-by as 'precious stones'. We had sold four bundles before lunch-time, including one to a stranger, clearing twelve cents in profit, when I had to return home to practise Bach. My father sat behind me in the study, typing a short story; behind him, three windows framed a Saturday sky. It was a sky that was blue with possibility: a sky that contained my missing childhood.

I slammed the piano lid shut: 'I hate Bach.' The words felt blasphemous in my mouth: I knew immediately that this was a much greater sin than hating Stevie Wonder.

At my piano lesson the following Tuesday, my father gave me a mischievous look and turned to Mrs Sivan. 'Anna said she hated Bach.'

'No, I didn't!'

*

Mrs Sivan remained very calm. 'Of course you did not. It is impossible. Bach chooses himself who he will like, and who he will not.'

At the end of the year, there was to be a concert in Elder Hall at the University of Adelaide.

'We have excellent name,' Mrs Sivan said. She collected English words like small coins, and her cache was overtaking mine. '*A Spectrum of Piano Music*.'

'That is an excellent name,' said my father.

'You like, yes?' She flushed with pleasure and turned to me. 'The stage must be like another room in your house. When you step out there, you smile at your friends, you bow, you enjoy sharing your music. You feel like fish.'

'A fish in water?'

'Of course.'

At nine, I fancied myself a veteran of the stage because of my starring role as Fairy Queen in the Year 3 operetta. My mother had made my first diva frock, with a satin, sequinned bodice and tulle skirt. Armed with a cardboard wand coated in glitter, I had stepped out onto the stage and found myself at home. On the final night, as I delivered a bouquet of flowers to Mrs Vaughan at the piano, a smile seized control of my face and threatened to consume my head.

A Spectrum of Piano Music promised an equal glory. It was to be on 18 September; all other dates in the calendar now existed in relation to this one. In our lessons, we moved through the small preludes and the *Anna Magdalena Notebook* to the inventions and sinfonias. Mrs Sivan took me through each part repeatedly, considering the intention of each note, the attraction that bound it to its neighbours. It was not enough to play each part, to feel it in my hands: I had to sing it in my head, follow its contour, tell its story. Then, when I put the parts together, by a sudden miracle I could hear them all at once. It was as though I had three minds, or three sets of ears, operating in parallel. The first time this happened, I turned to her, astonished. My consciousness had expanded; I could feel air rushing into unused parts of my mind. 'Exactly!' she said. 'Otherwise will be *awful*.'

As the concert drew nearer, my lessons became longer. After one lesson in the school holidays, I went to my best friend Sophia's house for a sleepover.

'What took you so long?' she asked. 'We've been waiting to watch *Thriller*!'

'My first two-hour lesson,' I explained smugly.

In our lessons, Mrs Sivan sat beside me at the piano, seizing my hand and correcting it, forming my fingers into shape, or playing alongside me two octaves above, the intensity of her sounds ringing in my ears: 'Do you know how little is different? But huge, *huge*. This we call science in arts. The more you understand each little thing, the more you understand all.'

As I played, she talked or sang with the music. Sometimes, she asked me to move aside and played for me, but this was rare. 'I don't want you to *copy*, monkey-style.'

She explained the circle of fifths to me, piling fifths one above the other, always brightening, until we arrived back in the key where we had begun. I blinked, amazed: it was improbable as an Escher drawing. Then she unravelled us through perfect fourths, travelling backwards past G-flat major and C-flat major, with their great hoards of flats, returning to the daylight of C major. The mathematics of it delighted me.

'Do you understand?' she asked.

'Yes,' I replied.

She turned to my father, beaming. 'I have never met such an intelligent nine-year-old, who can understand at first telling the circle of fifths.'

At such moments, I walked out of her lessons sky-high, unassailable. At other moments, I felt smaller. When I was tiring, she would stop and address me urgently.

'What is we need is to feed our spirit, constantly. And feeding ourselves with other people's food is not great nutrition for our soul. Must digest. Look sometimes at people growing older, and wisdom coming inside. Start of what I call *digested wisdom*.'

In the early days, these speeches baffled me, and I sat there with eyes averted, trying to make myself as inconsequential as possible. When the great force of her conversation halted at a question mark, I ventured a tentative yes or no, searching her face for the right answer.

'You are too intelligent a girl to guess,' she reprimanded me once. 'What comes after translation? *Interpretation*. First you must translate composer's wishes exactly, and then you're free to do interpretation, otherwise you *automatically* restricted.'

As she offered me this, I snuck a glance at the clock. Soon I would be back in the car with my father, tracing those dark streets back home to Nailsworth, where my mother would be preparing dinner. Then I could settle in to watching *Diff'rent Strokes*, and it would be another six days before my next lesson.

*

The dress rehearsal for *A Spectrum of Piano Music* was held on a sunny spring afternoon, but there was a hushed twilight in the imposing hall, with its dark wood and red plush seats. Mrs Sivan's high-school students were scattered around the auditorium, exuding adolescent cool. I walked in holding my mother's hand, and immediately regretted my lolly-pink overalls.

When it was my turn to play, I climbed up on the stage, grimaced at my mother's enthusiastic applause and began a Bach sinfonia. I had rehearsed the opening many times with Mrs Sivan, until the small bells of its *moto perpetuo* had become second nature and my hearing automatically expanded to accommodate its three voices. But as I progressed to the second line, a worry intruded: *What does the left hand do next? Imagine if I had a memory lapse in front of all these high-school students!* The individual parts lost their focus, and the three dimensions of sound contracted back into one.

'Not hearing!' Mrs Sivan announced from the audience. I stopped and started again.

'Not!' She called out an instruction which I couldn't hear, so I kept playing.

'Never just playing but hearing *inside*!' she exclaimed, but my grandparents had said my sinfonia was excellent when I played it at Sunday lunch, so I continued.

'We will work!' she called out, and climbed up from the audience onto the stage. As she started talking to me again about depths, or about not sitting, or about breathing spaces, or about all the other things I was not doing, I felt overwhelmed and started to cry.

'My darling, what is this?' She wrapped her arm around me. 'Always can be better, always growing. You must not cry, except for good tears, when you are so moved by the music.'

Against my will, my bad tears continued. I was so humiliated to be crying in front of high-school students that I started heaving with sobs. My mother stepped up to the stage.

'I think I might take her outside for some fresh air.'

'Of course,' said Mrs Sivan. 'Enjoy beautiful day, and then we continue.'

My mother took my hand and walked me down the aisle, past the staring high-school students, into the spring day outside.

'I don't understand,' I wailed, my shameful secret now public.

She held me to her and rocked me in her arms. 'Don't be a goofy goat,' she said, as the afternoon sun beat down on us, and my pink overalls dug into my crotch, and the oblivious adult world continued around us.

When we returned to the hall, Mrs Sivan put her arm around me and led me back to the stage and pulled up a chair so that we could work.

'My darling, life in music always learning, always growing. What is the difference between good and great musician?'

I knew the answer by now, even if I did not yet understand it.

'Little bits,' I said.

'Exactly!' she replied, delighted. 'Little bit more hearing, little bit more freedom.'

She had to tell me everything. She had to fit out this alternative universe for me, item by item, word by word, sound by sound. It is never enough to tell a student something once: teaching is constant repetition, constant correction. She repeated her lessons and anecdotes as a musician performs repertoire: each time reinterpreted, and so made new.

On the stage of Elder Hall she again took me through the breathing spaces and conducting lines of this sinfonia. I played with a heavy-handed punctuation, inking every musical sentence with an emphatic full-stop. 'Do not sit,' she reminded me. 'Bach never stops.' In Bach, every ending is also a beginning. Over time I came to understand the quiet that lies at the heart of his *moto perpetuo*.

She held a lot back in those early years, but gave the maximum I could take, and a little more. Gradually, I came to know more of her ideas by heart. By the time I properly understood them, they were absorbed into my body, and I could no longer tell where her ideas began and mine left off.

'This is good,' she said to me later, 'this means this knowledge has come to you. It is *intuition.*' She grinned at this sparkling new word. 'In-tuition. It means tuition that has come *inside.*'

On Friday night at the concert, there were three chairs lined up in the green room. One of Mrs Sivan's adult students, Debra Andreacchio, supervised the performers backstage, ushering us from one chair to the next, each time closer to the stage. Sitting in the third chair, I imagined what it would feel like to be sitting in the first chair, and then I was in it, and now I was onstage, trying to remember to smile at my friends and bow and enjoy sharing my music – and then it was over. It was easier than the rehearsal, and nobody had stopped me. Through the transformative ritual of a performance, Elder Hall had become somewhere warm, somewhere victorious.

At interval, Mrs Sivan gave me a fragrant embrace, and I joined my parents and grandparents in the audience for the second half. As the last performer left the stage, my grandfather leant forward in his chair.

'It would appear that nobody has prepared a speech,' he observed, and strode purposefully down to the front.

'Good evening, ladies and gentlemen. On one of my inspections of the Woodville High Special Music Centre, I was fortunate to hear Mrs Sivan's remarkable teaching, and I drew the conclusion immediately that she was an out-of-the-ordinary teacher of the piano. I feel that after tonight's wonderful treat these initial impressions have been truly vindicated.'

My father winked at my mother; my own triumph burnt quietly inside me. The rhythm of my adult life had begun.

From *Piano Lessons*, 2011

TOURISM

Benjamin Law

My family isn't exactly the outdoors type. Despite being raised right on the coastline, Mum detested the beach (all the sand it brought into the house), while Dad actively disapproved of wearing thongs ('It splits the toes'). We never camped. All those things involved in camping – pitching a tent; cooking on open fires; the insects; shitting in the woods; sleeping on rocks; getting murdered and raped in the middle of nowhere – they never appealed to us. 'We were never camping people,' Mum explains now. 'See, Asians – we're scared of dying. White people, they like to "live life to the full" and "die happy."' She pauses, before adding, 'Asians, we're the opposite.'

We preferred theme parks. For parents raising five children, theme parks made so much sense. They were clean. They were safe. There were clear designated activities, and auditory and visual stimuli that transcended barriers of race, language and age. Also: you could buy heaps of useless shit. This seems to be an exercise in which Asians of all nationalities, ages and socio-economic backgrounds naturally excel: buying shit. Venture into my childhood home, and in amongst the epic piles of suburban debris, you'll still find a plush blue whale wearing a Seaworld cap, T-shirts emblazoned with Kenny and Belinda – the now defunct Dreamworld mascots – and a pox of hideous fridge magnets.

Oh my god, the fridge magnets.

It was family tradition that once a year, our family of seven (eight, including my Ma-Ma) would cram ourselves into my grandmother's 1990 grey five-seat automatic Honda. *Five seats.* We'd travel like this – faces smashed against the glass; no leg room; the two smallest children illegally wedged between various legs – for a good three hours before we reached the Gold Coast. By the time we got to the theme park, our limbs were numb, our nerve endings destroyed. On the ride home, exhausted and drained like dead batteries, we'd fall asleep in extreme angles, our spines contorted and twisted. We'd wake up, our shirts covered with drool we weren't even sure was ours.

On the day of the trip, we'd wake before sunrise to get there by opening time. Despite having endured three hours of vivid pain, we'd feel an overwhelming sense of awe as the Thunderbolt, Dreamworld's fire-branded rollercoaster, emerged from behind the trees that bordered the highway. It would appear so suddenly, like some strange apparition, or a mirage. Our necks would crane back trying to take in the sheer majesty of it all. For a non-religious family like ours, the experience was borderline spiritual.

Once through the gates, we kids would do our best to distinguish ourselves from the actual Asian tourists. We'd make our Australian accents more pronounced. We ended our sentences with 'eh.' Our trousers were pulled further downwards, away from our navels. We refused to wear bumbags, and spoke English very loudly, with proper grammar and syntax. These hoards of Japanese and Chinese tourists would point to the most innocuous objects and proceed to take photographs like idiots. We could only imagine what they were hollering to each other as they ripped through their film. 'Look, a fire hydrant!' 'Over here, a drinking fountain!' 'Wow, there is a toilet: a public, shared facility and receptacle for my waste. Why not take a photo of it?'

Mum would sabotage all our efforts to set ourselves apart. She wore her hair in a Bozo-esque clown perm, and had a strange insistence on wearing her fluorescent Dreamworld T-shirt if we happened to be at Dreamworld (and her killer-whale Seaworld T-shirt if we were visiting Seaworld).

'Mum, come on,' I'd say as she posed us at the entrance of yet another ride. 'Everyone's going to think we're tourists.'

'We *are* tourists, you idiot,' she'd reply. 'Now smile big!'

It would take her about twenty seconds to finally press the shutter, and another five to release it. We'd groan.

*

When my parents split up, I was twelve years old and had just finished primary school. Trips to theme parks became less frequent. Custody was split. Mum hated driving long distances. Dad threw himself into work. The mood became downbeat and glum. The separation also made our family the subject of gossip amongst the local Chinese community, who were mildly scandalised by all the drama. Elderly Chinese women who smelled like mothballs and grease would corner my siblings and me in the shopping centre, literally pulling us to one side, shaking their heads and tutting their tongues, lecturing us in Cantonese.

'*Wah*, what is going on?' They'd raise their tattooed eyebrows. 'You need to tell your parents they must make an effort to get back together! *Ai-ya*, why would any parents split up like this? You're only children! And no marriage is a walk in the park, is it?'

None of these concerned citizens ever visited my mother during this period. Mum was always a tiny woman, but she began to lose weight quickly. Her low blood pressure got worse. She became prone to intense dizziness that would render her immobile for days on end. She almost fainted at my fourteenth birthday party at the tenpin bowling alley and thought she'd need to get me to call an ambulance. We saw Dad less and less.

Mum and Dad instituted a rotating roster of weekend custody. Schooldays were neutral territory; it was the weekend that was considered important family time. Mum and Dad would take turns, Dad taking us for every second weekend. But despite these weekends being technically Dad's, Mum insisted on coming with us, declaring boldly that it was her right as a mother.

Poor Dad. This really put pressure on him to make those four days a month memorable and worthwhile. At the same time, he was working as a chef in a hotel. He couldn't afford the luxury of time, so when it came to his designated weekends, Dad needed quick and convenient options.

He needed theme parks.

*

Let it be known: the Sunshine Coast hinterland is a haven for sad, miserable theme parks. In contrast to the Gold Coast's pleasure domes (Dreamworld, Movieworld, Seaworld), which are show-offy and grand, garish and decadent, theme parks on the Sunshine Coast are poor-cousiny, half-arsed and afterthought-ish. Come to Superbee, where our prime attraction is 'free honey tasting!' Also: you can buy honey! Look, here is a man, dressed as a bee! Here at the Hedge Maze, get lost! In a hedge! We also have scones!

On one of Dad's more disastrous weekends, we travelled to suburban Noosa to visit a deserted tourist attraction called the Big Bottle. It was, as its name implied, a giant bottle. You'd climb the stairs inside, which were made up of hundreds of empty beer bottles. Once you were at the top, a giant metal slippery slide curled around the bottle's exterior, and you'd slide down on a hessian sack. Inside the bottle, it smelled awful – like the piss of a hundred dehydrated men. Because the entire interior was made of beer bottles, you would never know which ones contained the urine. And because the bottles weren't exposed to the sun, the piss would never evaporate. It smelled so bad. We never went there again.

Another time, we visited Forest Glen Deer Sanctuary, a typically neglected drive-in wildlife preserve in Yandina. Despite its catchy television jingle, the place was starting to lose business to the reptile park a few kilometres away, which had recently renamed itself Australia Zoo. We bought bags of feed at the entrance, then slowly drove around the dirt track. The deer came up to the car in packs, and we fed them through the windows. There was also one single emu amongst all the deer and kangaroos. It started walking towards our car, pushing its way past the does and fawns.

'Are we even supposed to feed the emus?' my younger sister Tammy asked. 'Isn't this stuff just for deer?'

'Maybe it's developed a taste for it,' Dad said in Cantonese.

The emu proceeded to eat all the feed from my hand, then moved on to my youngest sister Michelle's open hand. Then, almost out of food, we wanted to move on. But then the emu spotted my paper bag – still full of feed, and reserved for the deer coming up around the bend – sitting next to me. It made a terrible, ungodly noise – an almost carnivorous, honking screech of excitement, not unlike the velociraptors in *Jurassic Park*. Its neck came the whole way in to the Honda as it continued to shriek. We screamed and screamed as feed pellets flew around the car.

'Drive faster, drive faster!' Michelle screamed.

Dad put his foot on the accelerator, and the emu squawked, trying to keep up the pace.

'Wind up the window!' Dad said.

What Dad didn't understand was that because most of the emu's head was in the car already, winding up the window would make the situation worse. But in my stammering panic, I reached out, grabbed the window winder and start winding up. The emu refused to retreat. Its head became stuck, and it croaked and coughed at us, spasming in panic, banging its head against the car ceiling in wild, spastic fits.

'Drive slower!' I said. 'We're going to rip its fucking head off.'

The whole time, Dad was creeping the Honda forwards a little at a time, but the emu was keeping up, walking alongside the car, screeching and honking.

'Stop the car, stop the car!'

We killed the engine and slowly wound down the window. Slowly, slowly. The emu gave the car's ceiling one last bang with its head, before sliding its neck out the window and stumbling away from the car in a daze.

We drove home in silence.

*

A fortnight later, Dad called me at Mum's place.

'So, what's the plan for this weekend?' he asked. 'You got any ideas?'

'I don't know,' I said. 'Haven't we done everything around here already?'

'How about the Ginger Factory? Or Underwater World? You guys like turtles. They're Tammy's favourite, right?'

'We did that last month,' I said, sighing. 'You know, we don't have to go somewhere special every weekend. We could just hang out.'

At that point, I detected a faint click over the telephone line. I coughed loudly – a clear message to Mum that I was aware she was on the other line, tuning in to my conversation with Dad.

'You know, I'm looking to invest in a new restaurant in Pacific Paradise,' Dad said. 'There's a theme park there we should check out. What do you reckon?'

*

Nostalgia Town's motto was 'A Laugh at the Past.' Its main attraction was a family cart-ride, a journey into an era when fibreglass brontosauruses roamed the earth alongside tableaus of Anzac diggers and plastic Aborigines. Slouching, I sat in the back of the cart with Mum, while Dad sat in the front with Tammy and Michelle. In the carts in front of us, mothers and fathers sat alongside each other with their children jammed in the middle. Obese as they were, they even held hands.

I wondered what they thought of our family, and whether they questioned why the Chinese family's parents sat so far away from one another. Maybe it was a cultural thing. I'd continue to watch them, wondering how, and why, their parents got along so well together, and how strange their families must have have been in private.

I'd watch them intently: like an outsider, like a tourist.

*

Nowadays, if you drive through Coomera, towards Dreamworld, you'll see the Thunderbolt has been dismantled. Nostalgia Town has long been torn down, and the deer at Forest Glen have disappeared, presumably having undergone a mysterious transformation into venison. (I don't know what happened to the emu.) That old wildlife sanctuary is now a luxury tourist resort. I can't find a trace of the Big Bottle on the internet, so I can only assume that the piss fumes proved a health hazard, and that it's been torn down too.

Right now, my family is planning to spend New Year's Eve together. (Everyone except Dad. He will be slaving away at a restaurant.) We're throwing around some ideas for what to do, since this will be the last time the family will be in the same place, at the same time, for quite a while.

Someone has suggested we go camping.

THE GAME IS TO HIDE

Rick Morton

In my last year of high school, the town we called home was forced to petition for broadband internet. Residents could have it, they were told, if they proved they would use it, and so for months we were asked to sign paper rolls that would demonstrate our intent to sign up with Telstra. This act of administrative enthusiasm got in the way of my being gay.

Throughout my adolescence, my only window to the gay world was through dial-up internet, though connecting to it stole the telephone line and made a noise so alarming it might have stood in for one of those 'scared straight' programs I'd read about. I didn't know any gay people. My friends didn't know any gay people. There was one character on TV who was gay. Well, I suppose his boyfriend was, too, but he didn't seem very happy with it.

We knew of one gay kid, an older boy who had moved to Brisbane and 'become' gay after high school. He was spoken of only in hushed tones, as if he had gone to prison or died at war. 'Did you hear Paul is gay now?' my friends and I would murmur. Paul had always been gay, of course, but we didn't know that. As near as we could make out, Paul had moved to Brisbane and been involved in a radioactive incident.

When I became that man, the one who suddenly 'turned' gay after moving away – and moving back – a helpful resident of Boonah popped a message in my inbox. It was a fairly meandering morality exercise that ended in the word 'faggot' and a half-decent picture of Jesus Christ on the crucifix. It did not escape my attention, almost a decade later, in 2017, that while getting ready to vote in a petition for my right to marry another man I was receiving junk mail calling people like me an abomination.

Officially, there are more than 46,000 same-sex couples in Australia. There are many more people who are transgender or identify as queer, gender fluid or bisexual. Maybe one in ten Australians fall on this spectrum. Might be more, could be less. Who's counting? I never wanted to be among them and, in some small way, I never felt like I was. How could a man who won't accept himself ever feel included?

Long before I knew what the words meant, my father called every other person he didn't like a faggot or a poofter. He had elaborate ways of figuring out how to spot them, which mostly relied on the presence of a single earring in a man's ear. Paul Reiffel the cricketer was a faggot, Dad told me once when I was five. So was Shane Warne at one stage and some actor on E Street, which was a show I understood less than the word faggot. Mum was nicer, though her world experience was scarcely any broader. She had met a gay man once while working in her youth at David Jones in Brisbane. He had an interest in teapots, she recalled, which became both her red flag and her yardstick for measuring future gays.

Statistically, in those early years on the cattle station, it ought to have been possible that I had met a gay or lesbian person. But if 10 per cent of people are gay, then that presented problems, for it was only my father, mother and older brother Toby who lived permanently on the property. By my reckoning that means 0.3 of one of us was into the same sex.

Mum must have known, though even she mistook her early awareness for causality when I finally came out to her, aged twenty-one. The very first words out of her mouth gave it away:

'Oh darling. Was it the Ken doll I gave you when you were six?' I had already drunk 2 litres of cask wine on a friend's hotel balcony when I made the phone call. The box of Stanley was nestled on my lap as we spoke and I fiddled with the nozzle to top my glass up.

In late primary school, Mum would nudge me in the ribs when *Priscilla, Queen of the Desert* came on the television. I would pretend to be mildly interested while, in my head, planning how I, too, could be draped in 30 metres of space-silver fabric in the middle of the outback.

In high school I conducted a morning audit of the way I moved. I wanted rigid, manly gestures. My gestures had to be mountains, not flowing streams. I practised in front of a mirror. I kept a mental list of the names of girls at school who could be considered attractive so that I could name them should other boys begin the inevitable discussion. I never stared in the change rooms after sport. I found other cover, too.

The telephone company had just introduced a rather complicated feature, three-way calling, which was so new that nobody (me) thought to be wary of it. All I knew was that the thought of being on the phone to one person was tiring enough but three just seemed incalculably obscene. Anyway, the first three-way telephone conversation I ever had was also my last in a personal capacity. It was also how I got my first real girlfriend, which is a shame.

For reasons not entirely clear, a girl in my Year 10 class, Britteny, had become interested in me, and an eager mutual friend, Danielle, decided to do something about it. Danielle phoned me and began asking a series of questions about Britteny. 'Do you like her then?'

Well, of course, I answered. To my mind, the answer was given in the same way I might talk about my fondness for Ace of Base or chicken and mayo sandwiches but it certainly didn't mean I wanted to fuck them. By the time we'd made it to the end of the conversation I was a piece of sandstone worn down by the geological force of teenage sexual intrigue. 'So would you go out with her?' Cornered, and believing it was just myself and Danielle on the line, I said yes. There was a muffled voice on the line. It was Britteny. Danielle announced her to me as my new girlfriend in the style of a gameshow host revealing the grand prize is a new car to a contestant who was born and lives underground. My intricate game of pretend was made entirely more complex.

A week into my new relationship and Danielle was sent to me at the end of one lunch break, an emissary with a message to bear. I wasn't holding Britteny's hand during the breaks and had hugged her only once. This ought to have been a sign but it was construed as playing hard to get. Any confrontation with a teenaged girl could be considered an armed hold-up and so, at gunpoint, I began holding Britteny's hand. This sealed the early fissures in what she thought was a relationship and what I knew to be an elaborate ruse. I was torn entirely between wanting to preserve our friendship and wanting to appear straight, a survival instinct so strong I was living in unbearable stress.

The second big test of this messy dance came when my girlfriend invited me around to her house one Saturday afternoon. 'My parents won't be home,' she said, unzipping a duffel bag filled with hints and scattering them before me. Sometimes, when my brother and I were left home alone, we soaked tampons in petrol and used them as fuses to blow up cans of deodorant. Call it intuition but I suspected that was not what Britteny had in mind.

Her parents owned one of those L-shaped sets of square couches, from which we were to watch a movie. I waited for Britteny to sit on one far end before employing my scant knowledge of mathematics, following the imaginary hypotenuse between the two end points and sitting as far away from her as I possibly could. A glacier of awkward sexual tension, Britteny bum-shuffled closer throughout the movie until she had me pinned against an armrest with no escape route. There were explosions on the screen and, in them, I saw the inevitable destruction of my deceit. We never kissed.

I did all of these things because I was terrified of who I was and how people would react to me. From the age of twelve, I spent every day in witness protection. Every waking hour spent with another person was a gamble.

Boonah is not an especially terrifying place but it is relatively isolated from the rest of the world. It took three years after I moved away to find the courage to come out, but even then it was because I feared what the rumours would say back home.

I didn't belong in my country home town and I didn't belong in my city either. The barbs of my life undercover were still in my skin. I didn't feel happy to be gay; I felt trapped. Whatever life I might have embraced as a proud gay man in the city seemed impossible to square with my internal hatred. I passed in both worlds, but neither of them felt like home. There is something to be said for this listlessness that is hard to understand if one has never been on the outside of anything. Many, though not all, gay people find their home in the queer scene. Perhaps it was my conditioning from a young age, my nature or both, but the 'scene' made me uncomfortable. Everyone was so confident – it was like they'd had two decades to ferret around in their psyches and come up with a way to exist vigorously. It was never that simple but that's how it appeared to this young man, fresh off the drying rack.

Coming out averted an imminent disaster but it wasn't going to hold me together in the long term. It seems hard to believe, even as somebody who has lived it, that these apparently small things can have such a sweeping presence in the lives of Australians in the twenty-first century. As Hobbes says in his piece, 'We bring the closets with us into adulthood.'

I was in Year 5 when Tasmania cut homosexual crimes from its criminal code. I was thirty when same-sex marriage was legalised. If that feels like a burden, what must the lives of those who went before feel like?

To this day, I have never had a relationship with another man. I'd like to, but I don't know how. Most of my twenties zipped by with me having no gay friends at all, something about which I was quite happy. When I first met Shannon, one of my closest friends now, I was afraid he would hate me. So afraid I downed two bottles of sauvignon blanc in quick succession and vomited it all back up while we were sitting smoking on a friend's verandah in Brisbane. 'There, there, get it all out,' he soothed, scruffling my hair in the process.

There is something insidious at work here. Gay people, particularly men, are modelled on an existence that expects rejection. They factor it in at every turn. Some overcompensate with these loud couldn't-care-less attitudes, others just go along with it like I do. The problem is that expectation informs reality. I didn't just think Shannon was going to hate me, I knew it. I have run away from or actively sabotaged at least three potential relationships because I was convinced the men were playing some kind of sick game where they pretended to be interested.

This fear is primed, at first, by family. Mum accepted who I was almost immediately. She had her own questions, as I did, but she loved me and she made it clear nothing would change chat. I never told my father but would come to learn of his reaction nonetheless.

Sometime in 2014 my brother met with Dad for the last time face-to-face and Rodney told him up-front that he 'didn't like' what I was doing with my 'lifestyle'. That's it. There wasn't some great cataclysm. We hadn't even spoken for six years before that point. We had dogs that I knew better and had spent more time with than my father. Nevertheless, the man who had abandoned our family once was leaving me again, this time through words. That was the moment I finally became unseated from a throne of precarious ease with myself.

I had what I now know to be my first anxiety attack when I was twenty-one. Freshly removed from the closet, I was attending the first of my high-school friends' twenty-first birthday parties in Boonah. I hadn't seen any of them in person since the news broke that I was gay. I coped with the violent shaking and cold sweats by drinking myself into a stupor. For the rest of my twenties I kept these attacks mostly in check. They never became severe. Until the day I learned what Dad thought of me.

I now measure my life in two halves: the moment before I heard that news and the almost four years since. Happiness, always so difficult to pin down, seems more distant still.

In his 1989 *New Republic* essay which kickstarted the American debate on gay marriage, Andrew Sullivan makes a conservative case for access to the institution and recognises a fundamental shift in the way queer people interact with society at large. 'Much of the gay leadership clings to notions of gay life as essentially outsider, anti-bourgeois, radical. Marriage, for them, is co-optation into straight society. For the Stonewall generation, it is hard to see how this vision of conflict will ever fundamentally change,' he writes. 'But for many other gays – my guess, a majority – while they don't deny the importance of rebellion 20 years ago and are grateful for what was done, there's now the sense of a new opportunity. A need to rebel has quietly ceded to a desire to belong. To be gay and to be bourgeois no longer seems such an absurd proposition.'

Today in Australia there are some who still reject the notion of joining the team that never picked them. For the most part, however, we are sick of being on the outside. In the internecine, fifteen-year-long public battle for marriage equality, tempers have frayed and I've found myself caught in something of a Venn diagram of not-being-with-everyone-else. A gay man behind enemy lines, so to speak.

In 2011, while still relatively junior at *The Australian*, I was tasked by my editor-in-chief to write a piece about a gay advocate who had appeared on the ABC's *Q&A* program and whom the editor-in-chief believed was a hypocrite for having unsafe sex and talking about the HIV epidemic. But my chief-of-staff refused to ask me to write the story and, having heard about the editor-in-chief's request, I was incensed. The national broadsheet is a broad church but there was no way I would allow my sexuality to be used as cover for a hit-job news story that had no public interest value. When my higher-ups leapfrogged my chief-of-staff and demanded I write the story, I walked out of the office and went home.

The story never ran. That was the last of it. There were no repercussions, no sanctions. Life moved on. But it was this same activist who would later come to attack me and other gay staff members at *The Australian* for being 'complicit' in what he said was an agenda of hate against the queer community. He and others came to the conclusion that we were siding with the enemy by working for the newspaper and demanded we prove what difference we had made by being on the inside. He didn't know about that near-miss.

My mental health had never sunk so low. I felt I was being attacked from all sides for either being me or not being me enough. I was abused on social media by those who are disgusted by homosexuality and targeted by those who thought I was working hand-in-glove with an editorial stance that gave succour to the same anti-queer forces in our community.

For the first time in my life I was earning good money doing a job I loved. It was enough that I could help support myself and my mum and sister when times got tough, as they frequently did. I knew the effect our coverage had on young queer kids. I'd been there myself. But I also knew that leaving wouldn't make it any better. And doing so would cut myself and my family off at the knees after a lifetime spent trying to stand. T hese are the shades of grey in a person's life that always become collateral damage in a culture war. As the last year of my twenties closed out it became entirely clear that I had made little personal progress. I had left the country, where I never felt at home, for a city in which my sheltered upbringing was all too obvious. I was gay, though neither fully embraced by gay culture nor willing to fully embrace it. I was successful but still judged by parts of society as being unequal. Had devotion to my family immobilised my principles or was I just a coward after nil? Culturally, I was a drifter, looking for a place to set down my things but never quite receiving permission, let alone a welcome.

Anyone looking for a reason to explain the rates of suicide and self-harm among queer Australians need only look at the shrapnel wounds of disgust and rejection they've collected over a lifetime. The rates are even worse in regional Australia.

There is much to treasure about being gay. It has opened in me a font of compassion that I'm not sure would otherwise have been there. It has played a role in formulating my ambition to succeed, which has driven me out of my poor teenage-year prospects and beyond the statistics. I hustled because I knew I couldn't stay in the town that had raised me. I worked harder because, well, what else was there to do? Maybe it saved me. Who can say?

Everything has a cost, however, and I've overspent. Those early years spent agonising over whether I would be found out and hung, drawn and quartered in the schoolyard have cast a lasting shadow.

When everyone else was figuring out how to love and be loved, going on dates and breaking hearts, or having their own mashed into the soft earth, I was stuck on this quixotic project of self-preservation. My time would come, I reasoned, because it did for the others I knew. When I turned twenty-one I still told myself my time would come. Again, when I turned twenty-five. My fears burrowed deeper and deeper over time. The anxieties enmeshed with my vital organs. My heart became a tool for the expression only of panic. My time would come, I said yet again. Perhaps when I turned twenty-eight. I spent that year dashing between doctors and psychologists and slowly losing my mind. But the time would come, I said, once this was dealt with. Turning twenty-nine marked a return to the same episodic madness, and thirty represented an uneasy truce. The jangles are still behind my flesh somewhere, vibrating every so often with the accumulated dirt of two decades' reckoning.

As a nation, we have convinced ourselves that all of us have the same standing start, but this is neither true for the working-class whites from broken families nor for those with black or brown skin. It's not true for those without a proper education nor for those who were abused. Researchers call it 'minority stress', of which being queer is just one form. But it is one of the only forms where you go through it alone until the secret breaks open inside of you like a seed. You shoulder it on your own, keep your own counsel, make catastrophes of your own many futures. Then when the time is right you share it around. If you are lucky, the embrace comes swiftly. If not, the bad counsel one kept is made incarnate by the reality of those rejections.

When I was in high school I used to spend my weekends and evenings rushing to hit 'record' on my tape player when a favourite song came on the radio. The dial-up internet made it difficult to download music; you really had to commit to a tune, which seemed an effort. My friends would make these mixtapes for their girlfriends or boyfriends, expressions of childhood love. They got to hand theirs out, secure in the knowledge they gained only via osmosis that this was what teenagers did.

I made them for myself, entire cassettes of the world's worst pop music. When no-one was looking, I danced.

HER MOTHER'S DAUGHTER

Nyadol Nyuon

My daughter's daughter, you have come? She stretched to her toes and reached out to kiss my cheek, but she could only manage to reach my neck – I was too tall, no longer the child she once held in her arms.

It had been more than twenty years since I had seen my grandmother. I was now returning with my mother to see her. I knew she was getting old and I wanted to see her at least one more time before she passed away. She was my only grandparent still alive. The shameless indifference of war means that families become strangers. War reduces the most intimate relationships to meaningless connections. For me, the war not only separated me from my grandmother; I was also separated from my mother and knew little of my father. I grew up with fragments of who they are, the broken links of kinships.

I was too young to even remember the year I was separated from my mother. It was sometime in the early 1990s. It was not until my father was killed in 1996 that I saw her again. On the day we reunited, she was dressed in black. The dark, voluminous hair I remembered was clipped to the skull. She was very thin, her eyes so deeply sunken into the sockets they looked like mere black holes. When she saw me, she dropped to her knees and cried. I stood there stiffly, like a tree trunk. It did not occur to me that tears were appropriate for the occasion.

As for my father, he was killed before I knew much of him.

My father was absent for most of my life. I saw him occasionally when he visited our home in Kenya, and even then, he was busy in meetings. Dad was a freedom fighter: a high-ranking commander in the guerrilla movement waging a war for an independent state – South Sudan. He was so committed to this cause that my only memories of my father are attached to his struggle for liberation. I have no recollection of a shared private moment between us. I have some memories of talking to him, but sometimes I am not sure whether these are the desperate inventions of my mind – a need to hold on to something of a man who should have been a part of my life.

The only real stories I know of my father are those told to me by others. Most of these I have heard because people have stopped me randomly on the streets in Kenya, saying that I look like my father. They tell me he was a brave, intelligent man. They praise his wit, and his courage to have given his life for his country; they tell me I should be proud to be his daughter. I generally leave these interactions with a clear sense of what my father meant to some people and even maybe to his country, but what remains unclear is what he left for his family. In some ways, he had no choice. For my father, my mother, my grandmother and me, war made the choices for us, and made the distance and separation normal.

Growing up without my mother and father left me with few memories of love – what it looked and felt like. The little sense of love I had was a single memory of my grandmother. In those lonely times as a young child, I would imagine nestling into her and then waking up to a warm cup of fresh cow's milk. I still remember the scent – it was like butter on fire.

On the day I met my grandmother again, for a moment, the years and the distance did not seem to matter. She was so happy to see me and my mum return that she began to dance and sing, performing circular movements around her little compound.

She would stop, return to my side and hug me, and then go back to dancing and singing again. The neighbours began to pour into my grandmother's compound, and we were surrounded by a group of curious children.

As we interacted with everyone, it became clear to me that my grandmother was considered the leader of the small town. She had the community telephone in her home, and people consulted her on the progress of a number of things. I was told that she was the first person to have built a house here, nearly two hours' walk from the main town, Gambella, and that all these homes had sprung up around her. Everyone, even the children, knew her name – Man Mary, meaning Mary's mother. I asked her why she had chosen to come and live out here, without running water or much security. I told her we could afford to house her in the town and employ someone to look after her. She tilted her head to look at me and, with a smile, she said, 'People in the towns are lazy, they do not work or farm. Out here, I can work. If I do not work, I will die. Come look at my farm.'

As we walked around, my grandmother pointed out the boundaries of her farm. All over were green plantations of maize. On our way back to her compound, she showed me three partially completed buildings. She said she was building them in case any of her children chose to return – she wanted them to have a home ready. For my grandmother, home was here; all her descendants were to come back to these ancestral lands.

When we got to the compound, it was about time to leave. My grandmother organised for the women who were around to sing some gospel songs. Then we prayed. My grandmother was very religious, and she raised my mother with the same beliefs. I would see that faith comfort my mother when nothing else could. She often told me, 'My God is my husband, my friend and my psychology.' By psychology, she meant her God was her counsellor when she felt overwhelmed.

After the prayers, my grandmother escorted us back to the road. We reached a crossroad, with one of the roads branching off towards Itang, the town where I was born. My grandmother mentioned that she was intending to walk to Itang to ask that one of her cows be brought back. She wanted to sacrifice it, to thank God for my return. We hugged, and she walked off towards Itang, Mum and I waiting at the side of the main road. We flagged down a number of cars and lorries, hoping that one would stop to take us back to Gambella.

Growing up, I had often wondered where some of my characteristics had come from. I could not explain why I did things the way I did or why I felt as I did. I often felt like a stranger to myself. Watching my grandmother on the day we met again, I saw some of who I am in her. I went to bed that night feeling reconciled with part of myself.

In many ways, what I had seen in my grandmother I had seen before in my mother. For a long time I did not want to admit this because of the anger I had towards her. This anger stemmed from trying and failing to forge a life together as a family, as a mother and a daughter, after so many years apart. After so many years without a mother, I just wanted someone to look after me – not someone who came with her own load in life, a load that required understanding, which I was too immature to have, and sometimes too selfish to give.

It would not be until I had a child of my own that I would realise that mothers are not just mothers; they remain their own persons, with their own dreams and aspirations, which do not have to derive from their identity as caregivers. I would realise that my bond with my mother was complicated by culture, and made extraordinarily difficult by war. I would understand that my mother stood as the total sum of what had happened to her – much of which she could not control – and that, in many ways, she had survived with as much dignity as one could wrangle out of such a situation. I would learn that when she spoke to me, she was sometimes speaking to things I could not see, and would never fully comprehend. I would learn all this in Australia, because the chance to live in safety allowed us to spend uninterrupted time together. It allowed us the luxury to not merely survive but to live in the full complexity of being a human being, instead of just a refugee.

Before we returned to Australia, my mother and I travelled through Ethiopia, where my grandmother lived, and to South Sudan. I saw her treated with a level of honour that I had never seen before. She was respected, she was known, and she was relied upon for advice and counsel. She had a voice – a strong voice. It was so strong that her people had once picked her to represent them as a member of parliament.

I could not help but compare that to her life in Melbourne, where she struggled to find work as a cleaner or an aged-care worker. I had watched her struggle with the language, struggle to understand the complex letters sent by Centrelink, insurance companies or banks. It is a blunt contrast to go from having a voice strong and clear enough for the national parliament of South Sudan to struggling on a phone call, nearly in tears, in Australia. It was as if her tongue had been cut out, as if she was socially crippled in this society.

Many people assume that everyone wants to come to Australia. I have wondered whether my mother ever wanted to.

Mum, like many parents, came to this country for her children. She wanted my siblings and me to have a better life, or at least a chance to try to make something of ourselves. No matter how bad her country was, she was industrious enough to have survived – maybe even thrived. I had seen her create magic from little. She ran a small business in the Kakuma refugee camp, in northern Kenya. She negotiated for land to build our home in an area denied to refugees for a long time. We never went a single day without food in Kakuma, when many struggled.

I have always felt that my mother would have stayed in Africa were it not for us. I knew this after our trip to Africa, because she glowed when we were there. She seemed more alive. That light appears to diminish each day she stays in Australia. In coming to Australia, my mother made a sacrifice necessitated by war, and by love – a love for her children.

I cannot escape the fact that I was a big reason for that sacrifice: as her own light grew weak, mine was made brighter by immigrating to Australia.

We came to Australia from a refugee camp that had no running water or electricity and barely met our basic needs for survival. My family depended on food rations distributed fortnightly by the United Nations.

At the time, I attended Kakuma Secondary College, one of three secondary schools servicing the refugee camp of nearly 90,000 people. In choking heat, I sat in a class of about sixty to eighty students. On each bench, around four students sat together on desks that stretched less than an arm's length. I was approaching the end of my secondary schooling and was desperate to leave the camp. There was no university in Kakuma, and my mother could not afford to pay for further education outside the camp.

It had been a couple of years since we had submitted our application for resettlement to Australia. We had heard nothing. My mother would sing gospel songs and pray each night, pleading with God that our application be approved. Sometimes I sang along with her, but most of the time I listened silently, waiting for my turn to persuade God on the 'wisdom' of letting my family and me resettle in Australia.

When Mum stopped singing, I would take over. I waited until my mother had finished singing and praying because I thought God would be in a better mood. When all was quiet, so quiet that I could clearly hear my thoughts, I would begin negotiating with God. I pleaded and promised that if my family made it to Australia, and I got a university education, I would be a good Christian; I would always be grateful, never complain and always, always listen to my mother.

The day our approval for resettlement arrived was the most joyous of my life. On the night before our travel to Australia, I tried to memorise the numbers on our tickets – all ten of them.

I was afraid they would get lost and we would not be allowed on the plane. I was not taking any chances. On the day of our departure I remember being very angry at my mother: she was taking too long to say goodbye, and I was afraid we would miss the plane and our chance for a better life.

We arrived in Melbourne on the night of 15 March 2005. As the plane descended towards Melbourne, I thought the world has been literally turned upside down. It was dark above, but below was a magnificent display of lights that twinkled like a million stars. I could not contain my excitement. For my mother, this journey across oceans to the unknown might have been a sacrifice. For me it was a chance of a new home.

Little did I know then that soon enough doubts would creep in: Could someone who looked like me call this home? Was home something you embraced, or did it also have to embrace you back? Would I always be seen as a conditional citizen, to whom citizenship was not a right, but a gift that could only be kept by an impeccable character? Would any mistakes – even mistakes made or wrongs committed by people who looked like me – mean that my stay in this new home became no longer acceptable? Would any complaint, any sign of ungratefulness, be deemed a lack of appreciation of the opportunities presented to me? Should I consider a backup plan – go back where I came from? Where was home?

I was born in Ethiopia, to parents of South Sudanese background, and I grew up in Kenya. When I moved to Australia, I had never been to South Sudan; in fact, South Sudan did not exist as a state at the time. Where is home? I have never really felt like I belong in any of those countries.

However, even in my confusion, I felt I was better placed than my siblings. Arriving here even younger than me, several have known only this life, but many will see only their blackness – a marker that they do not belong here. I wonder what it would feel like to feel Australian but happen to be black, to wake up one day into the knowledge of your blackness and what that means to some people. How do you hold on to a sense of belonging when it is so often assaulted by racism?

All of these questions were yet to occur to me, on 15 March, when I stepped into the bright lights of Tullamarine airport, and walked into a new life.

EASTER, 1969

Katie Bryan

The day before my fourth birthday my mother made a magnificent cake. She had found the design in one of her magazines – the witch's cottage from *Hansel and Gretel*. I watched, entranced, as she carved the vanilla pound cake into sections. A fat square for the base, and two triangles wedged above it for the roof. The layers were glued together with thick butter icing; not ideal for engineering, as by the time my party came around one-half of the roof was listing badly in the Brisbane humidity. The entire production was on the verge of collapse, and a hasty fix with toothpicks would be needed to prevent it from toppling, minutes before our guests arrived. Family and friends might be impaled by the lurking infrastructure, but the star feature of her party table had been saved.

But that was later. For now, a brown paper grocery bag of sweets sat just out of my reach on the kitchen bench, ready to decorate the cake after the fiddly procedure of icing it. My mother had three bottles of food dye to tint the butter cream – red, green and yellow. I longed to add the drops, but being heavy-handed and partial to primary colours, the end result would gleam like the Rastafarian flag. And in this instance, my mother stood firm.

'No, Kate. If you add too much colour, people won't like it.'

The same rule, it transpired, applied to her guest list. So when I said to her, 'Can we invite Dad's cousins? The nice ones, from the beach?' she hedged, and we began to argue.

My birthday follows Easter and, a few months earlier, my family had motored out to the bayside suburb of Scarborough for some respite from the late summer heat. My mother packed our rusting metal esky with a picnic. Ham sandwiches, cake, biscuits, oranges, a flask of fruit-cup cordial. It was an hour's drive, but it was at least five degrees cooler on the bay than in our home in the western suburbs.

Dad parked his prized green FB Holden Special on the sandy verge, and my mother spread our navy tartan picnic blanket on the grass overlooking the sepia arc of Queen's Beach. My sisters, moody teens, grumbled that they'd rather be at Surfers Paradise. Scarborough has always been a safe haven for children who are too small to be confident in the open waves, but in those days there were no shops, no cafes, no pirate park and no junk food. In short, there was nothing to tempt a restless teen. Just the beach, the pub, and a fish and chip shop, and perhaps a Mr Whippy van, if you got lucky. So while the prospect of a trip to Scarborough was enough to fill a child under five with delight, it was guaranteed to produce a state of resentful ennui in her siblings over twelve.

But the Norfolk pines at Scarborough offered shade, which Main Beach did not, and this was the clincher. My sisters had smooth olive skin a few shades lighter than Dad's; they could stay out all day in the sun and would simply tan to gold. My skin was like my mother's: fair, flecked with freckles and moles. Too much time in the sun would turn us both lobster red, and any exposed flesh would burn and peel cruelly in the following days. My father hated when I burnt, and so my sisters' hopes for a more glamorous destination were dashed. It was simply one of those times when having a baby sister was a drag. They resigned themselves to a day of sullen moping, far from boys, shops and psychedelic 1960s fashions, relegated to building sandcastles in 'the swamp' for the chubby-legged source of their tribulation, and muttering scornfully that Scarborough was 'square' and 'uncool'. The best they could hope for was that their friends would never hear of it.

It was here, beneath the pines, that I first realised my father had secrets. My mother, alarmed that my face was now redder than my bonnet, had reeled me in off the beach and had set me to playing in the shade. Following my own interpretation of what constituted 'shade', I scuttled off to join some children who were sliding down the steep grassy embankment on flattened cardboard boxes. These had been cadged from the pub. Kids these days may have Xboxes; but back then we had Four-X boxes. And they were ripping good fun. But the hill was steep and my legs were short, and my sisters grew weary of pig-a-backing me up the incline. So when I spied a family group rounding the headland, and their father called out a fond greeting to mine, I trudged back to our picnic to see what it was about.

A man with smooth dark skin and a look of my father stared down at me. For a moment it seemed to me that he was suffused with light. As if the spirit that lit his amber-hazel eyes was at once a beacon, a magnet and the warmth of a homecoming camp fire. Years later I would describe it to an elder. He would rock back in his chair and stare at me intently before he spoke: 'Ah. That's kinship recognition. That's how you know your mob.'

The scowl on my mother's face told me that she could see no elfland glow. She looked out at the world through eyes that saw calloused hands and bare feet and muddy streaks on lithe brown limbs, and frayed clothes that had weathered years of hard toil and had been ruthlessly boiled clean in an old copper. Her eyes were at first disapproving, and then suspicious.

But the man paid no mind to her; he was looking at me.

'Is this your little one, Tom? Jeez, look at those eyes. She'll be a heartbreaker when she grows up. Doesn't she look like Ruby!'

'She looks like her mother,' my father growled, a warning look in his eyes.

'Who's Ruby?' I had never heard the name before. 'Ruby? Why, Ruby's your grandmother. Your dad's mum.'

I had never met my paternal grandmother. She was a patient, loving voice that chuckled at my stories on the far end of our phone line.

'Oh, you mean Marnie. But she lives in Perth. How do you know her?'

'Well, me and your dad grew up together. We're cousins.' 'But Dad is an only child. And so's Marnie. We don't have any cousins.'

'Well, maybe so, but there's all kinds of cousins. My mother and your dad's grandmother were sisters. So me and your grandma Ruby are first cousins. And that means me and your dad are first cousins once removed. So I'm your cousin too. And this lot.'

He gestured at his children, and launched into a long and involved explanation of our degrees of separation. It was too much; I was still struggling to comprehend how my grandmother could have a cousin who was younger than my father. The man looked at me kindly and ruffled my bonnet.

'Never mind, love. You'll understand when you're older. Hey! Is that Kaye? And Dodi? My god, you've grown. You'll remember my girls, surely.'

From the uncertain look in my sisters' eyes, I wasn't sure that they did. But girls their own age were an improvement on my company, so they nodded and went along with it. There was a tall boy with the man too. Perhaps four or five years older than me. The boy was staring at me, gobsmacked, and understandably so. We looked alike enough that a stranger passing by might have taken us for brother and sister.

My newfound cousin rested his hand on his son's shoulder, looking at him with affection and pride.

'This is my youngest, Dan. Listen, love, your dad and I are just off to the pub for a drink. We served in the war together, you know. And it's been a while. We've got a lot to catch up on. Dan, you take your little cousin back to her friends to play, and mind you look out for her.'

Ever my father's shadow, and confident there'd be pink lemonade to be had from it, I elected to follow him and this intriguing new development in extended family into the pub across the road. In the 1960s, you didn't have a lot of choice when it came to fizzy drinks in a bar. Pink lemonade was exotic; it was produced from combining plain lemonade with a sweet red syrup and, if a long trip with a garrulous child was in the offing, a good strong nip of cherry brandy. And possibly it was this that prompted my father to drop his guard. He forgot the age-old wisdom that little pitchers have big ears, regardless how charged up they may be on Dutch liquor.

My father cut to the chase. 'Olly, you can't go telling people we're Aboriginal. Especially not my wife. It isn't safe.'

'But there's nothing wrong with it!'

'That's not what they think. My wife's father – he's a doctor. He thinks that anyone with Aboriginal blood has something wrong with them. He thinks Aboriginal people are primitive. Another species. He wouldn't want to think his daughter married one. He'd think there'd be something wrong with our kids.'

'But that's rubbish!'

'It doesn't matter. It's what they think, and if something goes wrong, they'll take your kids away. It happened to me, with Kaye and Dodi, when their mother died. I couldn't look after them, and I had to put them in a home for a while. One of those church orphanages. Somehow they found out, and they turned on me. I nearly lost them forever. I was lucky that I found Katie's mother. I wouldn't have those girls now, if I hadn't married Barb.'

A long and involved discussion ensued that went right over my head. I think it shifted between politics and eugenics. What was clear to me was the fear the two men felt. I saw it in their eyes. That, and something that might have been disappointment, and a sense of hurt and betrayal. They had given up the best years of their lives to fight Nazis and they hadn't reckoned on coming home and marrying into families that espoused similar views.

'You can never tell anyone. Not even your kids ... they can let things slip. And definitely not your wife. If things go wrong ... ' I felt my father's fear, and I climbed up on his lap to cuddle into him. 'I love you, Daddy. I don't want the bad people to take me away.'

He held me close. 'I'll never let that happen, Katie darling. Whatever I have to do, I'll do it. I'll never let them take you away.' Dad's cousin was pensive. 'It's alright for you: you're blond, you're blue-eyed, you're a generation further away from it than me. How the hell am I meant to explain this?' He made a sweeping gesture that drew in the totality of all that he was.

Dad shrugged. 'Tell them you're black Irish. Or Spanish. Anything. They're idiots. So long as you stick to your story and cover your tracks, they'll never know.'

'What's a Black Irish, Daddy?'

'The real thing. Unlike your mother's father: he's Orange Irish.'

'What's that?'

'English. And someone who pretends to be something they're not. Ha! Perhaps I've got more in common with your grandfather than I thought.'

Peals of laughter rang out. The bar was full of gnarled wiry men with rich tans and broad noses and ears, and deep heavy lines around their eyes and their brows. They smelt of sweat and strong tobacco and almost all of them wore dark navy singlets – a shift must have just finished, down at the docks. My father and his cousin grinned. They were safe here – they were amongst their own. Looking more at ease, they ordered another round.

My father spoke the language of the docks, but my mother never knew it. Like other Aboriginal children in the 1920s, he was obliged to leave school at the age of twelve and went out to work as a labourer, loading fish. He had been raised by his mother and his grandmother with the support of his great-aunts and-uncles in a multicultural area of north Perth. Weekends of his youth were spent camping with his mates at the beach. They volunteered as lifesavers at their local surf club. When the war came and the army recruited SLSC boys for their courage and their discipline, his opportunity to rise up in the world came along.

The ADF did IQ tests and my father scored in the top five per cent. Acknowledging his genius for mathematics, they sent him off for training with the RAAF. He became a navigator with Bomber Command and spent five years in the UK, flying missions over France and Germany. His experiences would haunt him till the end of his days but, by the same token, the war provided an opportunity for upward social mobility that would not have been possible otherwise.

My father was charismatic and mercurial, a born entertainer. In another life he would have been a natural on the stage. He was a quick study and a talented mimic, and by the time the war was over he had used his ear for music to develop a resonant, cultured speaking voice. It was enough to fool my mother into thinking the dashing RAAF officer with his two pretty little motherless girls was a part of her world. They had married in 1961, and they had a good life together until I came along. My sisters had drawn my parents together; I drew them into the cultural chasm that would tear us all apart.

Back in the pub, those two cousins had the double bond of kinship and their war service, and they did indeed have a lot to catch up on. They lingered over their beer long enough for my mother to be annoyed. She'd been left to make small talk with our cousin's wife and when we returned it was plain from the look on both their faces that the discourse had agreed with neither of them.

The shadows had grown long and it was time to pack up. My mother shook the crumbs off our picnic blanket and folded it away. Our cousins waved and walked off, picking their way over the rocky foreshore like long-legged seabirds. Cousin Olly called back over his shoulder that we should stop in for a cuppa on our way home.

I was looking forward to this stopover, so when we drove past the turnoff and headed for the toll bridge, I threw a monster tantrum, jumping up and down on the back seat of the station wagon. There were no such things as seatbelts back then; children were restrained by their mothers reaching over into the back seat and administering a stinging slap to the back of your thighs. The last thing I remember from that trip is my sisters drawing away from me to stare out the windows, after giving me 'the look'. As in: *one day you'll learn not to argue with her, you can't win, you know*. They grimaced at me as I screamed and drummed my feet on the bench seat until, finally, the cherry brandy kicked in and, to everyone's relief, I dozed off.

My father began to sneak out to the bayside to see his cousin. They'd meet up in the Seabrae Hotel at Redcliffe or the bar near the Sandgate War Memorial while my mother was working, my sisters were at school and I was riding shotgun in my father's taxi. My father was a different man when he was with Cousin Olly. He seemed comfortable inside his own skin. For a while he would shed his cloak of artifice and guarded vigilance. It made him short-tempered and ill at ease when he took it up again as we returned home. The easy banter and laughter that flowed between the cousins was in stark contrast to the grim wall of silence that grew between my parents, brick by brick, with each deception, every lie.

I loved these sleepy afternoon sessions in the bars, and not for worlds would I have ratted them out. But four-year-olds are not reliable secret-keepers, and it was only a matter of time until I slipped up. The timing was unfortunate. One of my mother's friends, Hilary, had invited us to a garden party, and while my father and my sisters had found pressing reasons to be elsewhere, I was looking forward to it almost as much as my mother. All her old private-school chums would be there, along with her colleagues from university. Forays into her old life must have been bittersweet. Motherhood had brought home the reality that in marrying my father, she had taken a step down in the world, and it was beginning to dawn on her that she lived with a complex man who she barely knew. Moreover, I had the unhappy knack of embarrassing her in front of her important friends, so she extracted a promise from me that I would be on my very best behaviour.

The motivation to follow through on my oath was high. I liked Hilary; she was what my mother called 'a good stick'. She lived in a grand colonial plantation house set on acreage out past Moggill. Every room was a treasure trove of books and fine art and antiques. The twin living rooms had pressed metal ceilings and a chandelier and an ornate tiled fireplace. The verandah was encircled by iron-lace fretwork, and from there landscaped gardens sloped down towards the tennis court and the narrow brown bend of the river. Peacocks trailed languorously over manicured lawns by a shimmering fountain and – glory of glories – there were ponies in the paddock adjacent. It was the life my mother must have imagined for herself, and the life that her own mother had been born to. It was undoubtedly the life that her parents had anticipated she would attain by an advantageous marriage. Their collective disappointment in my father was always palpable.

The day of Hilary's party arrived. Matching linen frocks in a delicate pastel pink hung on a hook in my parents' bedroom, safely out of my reach while my mother busied herself with her toilette. She had left me to play with my scrapbook and colouring pencils, having confiscated my felt-tip pens due to my past indiscretions. She would not have me appear (again) before her friends in a frieze of rainbow-coloured stripes and dots that invariably seeped into my skin while I was preoccupied with my artwork.

I sat at my play table in my vest and knickers, my hair pinned up in rollers, and pondered what to draw. Resenting the loss of my treasured felt-tips – and certain that my subject would sympathise with my plight, I selected the most colourful character I knew. I began with a large ship, crossing a staccato line of waves. Aged fifteen, so he told me, Cousin Olly had run away from an unhappy home life and had gone off to sea. The anchor tattooed on his arm symbolised his service in the navy and the swallows that flew around it tallied the number of times he had crossed the globe. Given my mother's moods of late, running away seemed an enviable life goal, and I gave myself over to memorialising it in art. My mission achieved, I tilted my head to survey my handiwork, trying to recall how many swallows Cousin Olly had.

At least two, or was it three? Mine thus far numbered fifteen.

Perhaps I'd rather overdone it with the swallows.

My mother agreed. Rounding the doorway in her starched linen frock and pearls, she spied the ballpoint pen reserved for her shopping list in my hand and she shrieked, aghast. In my quest to be like Cousin Olly, I had inked a fair likeness of his anchor onto the length of my forearm, and in anticipation of how far and how often I planned to run away, an entire flock of swallows soared in flight from wrist to shoulder.

My mother was livid. Naval tattoos, it seemed, and the accompanying language that I turned on her when she tried in vain to scour mine off, were not a part of the image she had hoped to present to her society friends. Tattoos, I was given to understand, were the insignia of the working class; not only were they vulgar, they were *common*.

An unpleasant scene erupted later that evening, when she held up my wrist to display the lingering ink to my father. It was undeniable evidence of our guilt and, disturbed that Cousin Olly was getting under my skin, she decreed that all contact with him must stop. He was unsuitable company for a child. Henceforth, the men of her family would guide the development of my character. They were of unimpeachable moral virtue and could be trusted to check my natural inclination towards deviance. It was the end of our happy visits to the peninsula and, to ensure it, my mother enrolled me in crèche. If my father kept the visits up, I didn't know.

So there was no hope that my mother would relent and allow Dad's cousins to attend my birthday. Her parents would be there, and to have them under the same roof with Cousin Olly would be untenable. My maternal grandmother and her sisters still spoke with unyielding English accents, despite it being over a century since their family had arrived with the first fleets of free settlers. They upheld a rigid devotion to God and Empire and a social system based on wealth, class, caste and colour. Cousin Olly had the same rough voice and silty skin tone as the gardener who tended my grandfather's roses and the domestic who came each morning to clean my grandmother's house. He was beneath them. If they'd joined us, my mother would never have heard the end of it. Only the 'right sort of people' could come to my birthday, and every other one to follow. My mother would see to that.

WEI-LEI AND ME

Aditi Gouvernel

Barry West was a rude little boy with a pug nose. He had the red stained face of Australian summers.

'Don't touch me!' he screamed.

All the kids were playing tag and I was 'it.' I was running through the playground, my ponytail slapping my back as my feet hit the ground. My heartbeat pulsed in my head. I grazed Barry's left shoulder with the palm of my hand. He stopped, turned around and faced me.

Anger stretched across his face and he screamed, 'I'll have to wash this shirt now – you wipe your butt with your hands.'

'No I don't,' I screamed back, startled and confused.

'Yes you do … You're Indian and I've got your Indian shit on me.' He ripped off his shirt and threw it on the ground. The other kids gathered around us, watching and listening.

*

I was six. It was the early eighties and my parents had moved our family from the aristocratic world of Delhi, a city filled with palaces, temples, gardens and tombs. They moved me from my playground under the tower of the Qutab Minar to Canberra. The only thing the two places had in common was they were both national capitals. Our new suburb, Melba, spread its backside up Mount Rogers, a lofty title for what was really a hill. Each night my father and I would climb the hill and watch the sunset turn Lake Ginninderra a bright pink. 'This is our chance,' he would say, as Belconnen became a small cluster of lights. 'This is a place we can make ours.'

Delhi, with its eons of history, was not a place that could be 'added to.' Australia, on the other hand, large, spacious and full of gaps, would be a place where we could create a new identity.

We became Australian in 1982. I recall very little of this ceremony, which took place in a small room in the cinder-block building of the Department of Immigration. My parents held up their palms while a man read an oath from a piece of paper. People clapped, some whistled and small flags were waved. The citizenship papers given to my parents were locked in a bank vault with my mother's jewellery.

My parents met Australia when they started work and I met Australia in the school playground.

*

The playground consisted of a large expanse of grass, at the centre of which stood a dark wooden structure rising out of a pit of tanbark. Some days it would be a fort, and we would defend ourselves from an imaginary attack. Other days it would be a ship, and we would be pirates and sailors. The days our child fantasy minds were tired it would just be the playground and we would hang from the monkey bars, or jump off the platforms. It was fun until the day Barry told the world I wiped my butt with my hands.

That lunchtime as I climbed the fort, Barry screamed, 'She's infected. Don't touch the fort! You'll get her germs.' I watched as the kids around me jumped off it like a crew abandoning a sinking ship.

Over the next couple of days the kids stopped talking to me, as though my words, like my body, carried an infection their immune systems couldn't fight. On the rare occasions they did pay attention to me they would combine their hatred in a human circle around me.

'She even looks like shit,' said Amy Pulawski.

'That's so gross,' added Cris Kovacic.

'No I don't,' I screamed again and again at them. Once I was forced to pull my top up and bare my chest to prove I had nipples when Barry had the idea Indian girls 'have no tits.'

On these days, I would go home with tears in my eyes and wonder why we couldn't move back to Delhi. I would beg my mother not to send me back to school. 'You have to face the world,' she would say. If this was the world, I wanted nothing to do with it. I pretended to have various illnesses – flu, malaria. Once I claimed I had gout. My mother ignored all my attempts to miss school. Each day she would send me out the door with a brown paper bag and a piece of fruit and each day I hoped things would change. They did, the day Wei-Li arrived.

*

It was a cold autumn day. I ran into the classroom and warmed my hands against the metal gas heater bordering the walls. My teacher walked in, a halo of curly red hair, her arm attached to a honeycoloured boy with a smile of excitement on his face.

She wrote his name on the blackboard, 'WEI-LI,' in white chalk. The boy stood in front of the class and in a sing-song voice introduced himself.

'My name is Wee Lee.' He smiled.

Titters ran through the classroom. It took the class exactly thirty seconds to shorten his name to Wee. By morning recess he was called Piss. He lost his smile at lunchtime when, to my relief, he became the object of their attention. The kids mauled Wei-Li the way a cat would maul a toy. They pawed and prodded him and the circles that used to form around me formed around him. He was hit, spanked and kicked. He was spat on and forced to pull down his pants and show his penis when Barry had the idea Chinese boys 'have no dicks.'

Wei-Li's shoulders started to stoop and after a week he would walk outside and avoid talking to anyone.

*

I watched everything from an aluminium bench. It was far enough away from the kids to avoid their attention but close enough to watch their activities.

Today the bench was freezing. I was folding my legs underneath myself in a sort of lotus position when Wei-Li walked into the playground. I saw Barry walk straight towards him, his arm held behind him and his hand in a fist. As Wei-Li faced the playground, Barry made a full arc with his arm and punched Wei-Li in the head. Wei-Li fell to the ground. Barry jumped on Wei-Li, his butt on his chest and both his hands pulling at Wei-Li's school tie. Wei-Li's face turned red and a strange sound escaped his mouth.

'Think you can tell on me?' Barry threatened.

Wei-Li shook his head.

Anger rose inside me. I wanted to help him. When the abuse had been directed at me, I had always wanted one of the other kids to hit Barry. I wanted someone to make it all stop, and for the first time I realised the 'someone' could be me.

To the left of the bench was a rock the size of my foot. I picked it up and walked up behind Barry, the rock firmly in my hands. I could see Wei-Li's tongue poking out between his lips. I threw my arms over my head and brought the rock down as hard as I could. It made a loud crack when it connected with Barry's head. He fell forward, lying on top of Wei-Li, who had regained his breath and was wiggling out from under him. When Barry started moving, Wei-Li and I ran in opposite directions. I could hear Barry screaming, 'You're both dead.'

The afternoon passed like a death sentence. Barry stared menacingly at me from his desk. As soon as the bell rang I leapt out of my seat and ran out of the class. I started running up Le Gallienne Street and as I was about to reach the first cross street, I saw Wei-Li standing there. He grabbed my hand. 'C'mon,' he said. I followed him up the narrow side street and onto a footpath. On one side was a row of houses and on the other side a nature reserve. 'Lets go this way. It's longer – but we'll be alone,' he said.

*

In Tamil, my father's native tongue, there is a word, *jalrah*, that means shadow. From that day on, Wei-Li became my jalrah.

That Saturday, Wei-Li stood on my doorstep and rang the bell twice. My mother was cooking and the house smelt of mixed spices. Cumin, chilli powder and garam masala floated through the air like a scented rainbow. My mother opened the door and called out my name with a smile on her face. I saw Wei-Li standing there. A second later, as he entered my house, I saw everything Indian come to the foreground as if lit by a spotlight: the wooden statue of Ganesh, the fabric birds hanging on a string, my father lounging around in a dhoti. Everything Wei-Li saw could be used as evidence for my difference. But Wei-Li didn't notice anything, or if he did he never mentioned it.

From that day on we spent every possible second together. We would ride our bikes or secretly rifle through our mothers' purses, pilfering loose change that we would then pool and buy a Mars Bar. All sugared up, we would re-enact our favourite TV show, *Monkey Magic*. Wei-Li would be Monkey and I would be Tripitaka. We would find large sticks and pretend they were swords and staffs and fight imaginary foes who looked like Barry.

*

Hiding from Barry had become an art. At lunchtimes, Wei-Li and I would sit in the library, or jump on the Olympic-size trampoline in the gym. If there was no adult supervision we would be sent to the playground no matter how much we pleaded. On those days we would sit on our aluminium bench and share our lunches. Wei-Li would eat my samosas and I would eat his sandwiches, filled with pork balls and grated carrot. When we were together, we felt safe.

But one day, there would be no lunchtime. We were going on an excursion to Parliament House. The day was divided into two sections. In the morning, half of the class would play cricket on the lawns while the other half took a guided tour. When the first tour was finished the groups would swap. I was excited until I realised the teachers were filing us alphabetically onto the bus. My last name was Vishwanathan and I was told to sit directly in front of Barry West. For the first time since the incident with the rock, I was alone. The bus ride lasted thirty minutes. Thirty minutes of Barry kicking the back of my seat. I didn't say anything. I just stared straight ahead.

The bus stopped and the kids pointed at the white building with its small steps. I couldn't enjoy it; I was angry. It was a gut-wrenching anger that was growing each second in its volatility. Barry left his seat and walked towards mine. When he reached mine, he leant close to me and spat straight in my face. He walked off laughing, leaving me to wipe my face with my sleeve. Tears gathered in my eyes, but this time I felt I could do something – the rock had taught me that.

I walked off the bus, and as the bus driver opened the cargo hold, I waited. As the bus driver brought out the sports bags, I calculated. Wei-Li walked up to me. 'What's going on?'

'Nothing,' I said, my arms folded and a look of determination on my face. I waited until the bags were opened and the teachers had started organising the activities. When I was confident the teachers were distracted, I walked over to a sports bag and grabbed one of the bright yellow cricket bats. I ran over to Barry and bashed it against the back of his neck. He fell and again I held up the cricket bat; this time I bashed it against his face. I couldn't hit him anymore because the teachers had grabbed the bat and were pulling me off him.

Barry was as fine as he could be with a bloody nose, tissues and tears. While the other kids walked through the House of Representatives and the Senate, I sat on a seat, guarded by a teacher who phoned my parents.

My mother arrived, apologetic and angry. She bustled me into our red Subaru and said repeatedly, 'What's gotten into you? You can't behave like this.' I was silent until she said, 'You must apologise to that boy.'

'Never,' I said.

My parents had a meeting with the school principal and Barry's parents. I wasn't punished and neither was Barry. The next day I discovered why.

*

It was Friday and our teacher stood in front of the class and said, 'Barry has an announcement. Come up here and tell the class your news.'

Barry walked to the front of the class and stood there for a second.

'I'm moving to Jakarta. I'm leaving next week,' he said.

That lunchtime Wei-Li asked, 'Do you think it's because of the cricket bat?'

'Nah,' I said, shaking my head.

Wei-Li and I counted the days, crossing them off an imaginary calendar in our minds. Barry's departure was marked with cupcakes and wide smiles.

On our first day of freedom, Wei-Li and I went home. We walked up Le Gallienne Street, now claiming it for ourselves. Wei-Li's grandmother opened the door to two beaming kids.

'Why you so happy?' she asked suspiciously.

'Barry's moving to Jakarta,' Wei-Li said.
She smiled and hugged her grandson.

*

Things changed rapidly after that. We grew up and as our faces changed, so did Canberra. An Indian restaurant, *Jehangir*, opened on Swinger Hill. Canberra's Chinatown became so busy you couldn't find parking. When I was sixteen I went to a private high school on the other side of town where people described me as 'pretty.'

Wei-Li and I gained a group of friends who we would meet at the chess-pit in the centre of the city. We would sip lattes under the gas heaters at Gus's Café and dream about a better life after uni. At night we would sit on scrappy vinyl-covered chairs in a bar called The Phoenix and, after a couple of beers, rant about how we hated homogeneity and longed for difference. We had become what we thought we could never be: Australian.

RED DUST, JET STREAMS AND CHANEL NO. 5

Gayle Kennedy

Among my earliest memories is one of standing on a table, surrounded by smiles as I sang the old country song 'I Want a Pardon for Daddy'. The faces are beaming, encouraging. The faces are black. My next memory is being trapped inside an iron lung; this segues into a leafy garden and a boy called Brian. Both of us are victims of polio. We cannot walk.

At the rehab hospital, we have created our own little world, Brian and me. We call each other 'Mummy' and 'Daddy' and have tea parties with teddy bears and dolls. The nurses indulge us with cups, saucers, cake and a teapot filled with chocolate milk. We ask for extra cake or biscuits for our toys. We hide those extras for secret picnics. It makes us giggle to think we have fooled them.

Each day we swim in a hydrotherapy pool filled with soothing emollients, along with a little girl who has been burnt from head to toe. The girl is allowed into our imaginative domain during those sessions. We are three children who have no idea there are others in the world who are strong and able, with smooth, undamaged skin and limbs that obey commands.

When we emerge from the pool, we are spoilt and cosseted by the nurses, the orderlies and the cook, Linda. The hospital is our castle, and we, its rulers, are already unknowingly acquiring the mental skills we will need to survive what life has in store for us, the different, the damaged. We pay no heed to how others see us. All that matters is how we view ourselves.

I see no other black faces during the three years I am in the rehab hospital. Everyone is white. There are no mirrors; I am reflected solely in the faces of those around me. I never take the time to observe the colour of my skin. It is of no consequence in my world. I am, for all intents and purposes, the same colour as everyone else in the hospital.

I sleep very little in the ward. My overactive imagination turns the shadows into monsters, and the children's breathing around me is loud and threatening. I always end up whimpering and being gathered into the arms of a nurse who dries my tears and carries me to the nurses' station. I am fed buttered arrowroot biscuits and cold milk and entertain them with childish stories and remembered songs. I feel loved and safe.

After countless hours of physiotherapy, hydrotherapy and encouragement, Brian and I gradually learn to walk, and are fitted with our callipers together. Little do we realise that this means we will soon be separated, never to see each other again.

The day my life changed is etched in my memory. I was up early as usual: breakfast and bath. But there was something different. There were tears in the nurses' eyes as they collected me for my bath. Afterwards, I was dressed in special new clothes: a little fawn-coloured pinafore, a pretty little blue jumper, new socks, a ribbon for my hair. My callipers were polished. I was excited by the clothes, but also suspicious. Why new clothes? Why the crying? Why was Linda fussing over me at this hour? I didn't usually see her until later in the day. She grabbed me and held me as tight as she could. Her tears wet my face. I started to become alarmed.

The head sister told me I was to meet my mummy and daddy. Mummy and daddy? What did they mean by that? Me and Brian were Mummy and Daddy, and I told her so in no uncertain terms. But she insisted that my real mummy and daddy were coming, and they would take me on a long journey. I was going home, she said.

'But I'm already home.'

'This is a hospital. You came here when you got sick. Your mummy and daddy are taking you back to your real home, the home you came from before you got sick,' she responded.

Eventually, confused and scared, I was taken into a room where there stood two people who seemed as though from another planet. They were introduced to me as my parents. I remember recoiling in horror as they handed me to the strange dark lady.

'This is your real mummy,' the nurse said in her most soothing voice.

I would have none of it. 'She's not my mummy! He's not my daddy! They're black!'

I remember tears streaming down their faces. How my words must have hurt.

I know now that it was not their fault they couldn't visit me in hospital. They were two people without money, living in a society where Aboriginal people needed permits to work and to travel. There was no independence for my parents back then. You had to have permission from the powers that be to do anything at all, really. The circumstances of the time meant there were no gentle introductions, no reorientation programs. There was no scope for us to get to know each other. I was thrust into the arms of strangers with no warning and they, in turn, had no idea what to do with this screaming child who looked at them as though they were monsters.

I was allowed to say goodbye to Brian, who wept and screamed as much as I did when they finally managed to prise us apart. To this day, I still think about Brian and Linda the cook and the little girl with the badly burnt body and wonder what became of them. The strange couple carried me, still screaming, into crowded Central Railway Station, trying desperately to ignore the suspicious stares of strangers. All their comforting and stroking was to no avail. I continued to weep as we boarded the train. Eventually, with a shudder, it pulled out. We passed through suburbs with poky backyards and thin children who raised their hands to wave and grey washing flapping on clotheslines that stood like drab sentinels of late 1950s Sydney.

Then we were in the countryside, and my childish interest was piqued. Cows, sheep and horses grazed in green paddocks. I had only seen these animals in books until now. I stopped crying long enough to ask if they were real. The two strangers grasped the chance to connect with me at last. Each animal was pointed out, named. I calmed and started to relax into the warmth of the dark-skinned lady, who seemed soft now that I was not struggling against her. Her eyes were big and brown and tear-filled. She stroked my hair and whispered, 'We're going home now, baby girl.'

'Back to the ward?' I asked.

'No, baby girl, home to your real home. You have a brother and a sister. They're called Buddy and Lulla. You have a grandma, a grandpa and cousins. There are horses and dogs. You'll see. We'll take good care of you.'

The journey seemed to last forever, but the kind, gentle lady held me throughout. I became sleepy and nestled my head into her breast. Her blouse was damp from our intermingled tears. I finally slept.

*

The next morning, the train pulled up at a small railway station in the middle of nowhere. There were a few ramshackle houses and what looked like vast expanses of red dirt. There were no trees, just scrub. Connie Francis's 'Lipstick on Your Collar' was blaring from the stationmaster's radio. We stepped off the train, the only passengers. The stationmaster greeted Mum and Dad like long-lost friends. He smiled at me and welcomed me home. We walked into the searing heat, with only the echo of the station radio breaking the eerie silence.

I began to think that these people might be aliens. They had taken me to some far-off planet. I whimpered in fear. The man who I now know is my father, seeing my distress, hoisted me onto his shoulders and we continued across the red earth, bare except for strange little trees every so often.

We seemed to walk for miles. It was so hot. An emu darted past us, and lying in the shade of the saltbush was a goanna.

Then the sound of laughter and children's voices floated over on the wind. I could hear someone playing a guitar and singing 'Mona Lisa' as we walked into a clearing where there were huts made from scrap, tents and a caravan. Dogs and kids were running about, and all the children and adults were the same colour as the people who had brought me here. And, as I soon realised, the same colour as me. People surrounded me. An old man with silver hair and twinkling blue eyes took me from my mother's arms and held me tightly as he whispered, 'My little Topsy is home at last.'

I was passed to a woman named as my grandmother, Edie, and then to uncles, aunts, cousins. Finally I was introduced to the little people: my brother, Buddy, and sister, Lulla.

My new home was a far cry from the quiet, sterile hospital I was used to. A caravan had been bought especially for my homecoming. The toilet was a deep pit over which a wide wooden seat had been built, and it was enclosed in a tin shed with a wooden door. Dad knew it would be impossible for me to use, so he built me my own little toilet He painted it blue and adorned it with pink cabbage roses cut from a magazine.

Somewhere between the hospital and my new home, something had shifted in me. I lapped up the love that was showered on me like rainfall.

*

Soon I forgot about the convalescence home. I came to love my family. We moved to a bigger town with a river and paved streets.

Dad bought a block of land and got a job with the Department of Main Roads, New South Wales (now known as Roads and Maritime Services). I settled into my new life, but little did I realise that this was not the end of my tumult and upheaval. In a way, it had only just begun. For the next decade, I was taken twice a year, kicking and screaming, from my mother's arms for the seventeen-hour train journey to Sydney, to a place called the Drummond Far West Children's Home, for more treatment. The Far West Home in those days was a cold and forbidding place. The playground was all green concrete and high fences. No trees, no flowers, no grass, just a solitary merry-go-round, or 'hurdy gurdy' as we called it. Particularly galling was that it was directly across the road from Manly Beach. The inmates and I could smell the sea, fairy floss, toffee apples. We could watch beachgoers laughing and having fun. We soon learnt that if we pressed our noses against the wire, these people would sometimes take pity on us and slip us bags of lollies.

To break the monotony, there were occasional outings to the beach and to the marina and fun fair at Manly Wharf. Sometimes television, movie and music stars of the day would visit. We were treated to concerts by Jimmy Little and Col Joye and the Joy Boys, taken to meet people such as Donna Douglas, who played Elly May on The Beverly Hillbillies, or to meet visiting royalty. One friend met Princess Anne and I got to meet Princess Soraya while in Camperdown Children's Hospital, but mostly it was the same dreary routine. I think that's why I have such a hatred of routine, and why I've never really fitted into a conventional workforce, with its rules and its nine-to-five mentality. It was so different from home, with all the chaos of a big family. At home there was life, animals, a river, grass, trees – and when it rained, the unbelievably beautiful smell of water on dry earth. At home I was black and went barefoot, except to school and on outings. At Far West I was unsure just what colour I was, and I wore those hated callipers from six in the morning until seven at night.

My family didn't have the money to come and see me, and in

a way I was grateful for that, because while there I could adjust to my life as it was without the distraction and longing that seeing them would have brought. Instead I developed a rich and wonderful gift: the ability to be in the moment. Where I was, was where I was.

I formed a rich inner life. I learnt to treasure solitude because when alone I could be anyone I wanted; I could be anywhere I wanted. My legs may have been encased in callipers, but in my mind's eye they were strong and muscular. On my feet I wore delicate silken butter-soft slippers and danced like the ballerinas I had seen in films and on the stage. Or I was barefoot and ran like a streak across vast expanses of beach and desert. I wasn't tethered to the earth. Oh no! I leapt onto strong stallions and rode bareback beside princes and warriors. I flew like a bird and rode on magic carpets and cast pity at the people below as they scurried across the earth, harried and worried and unable to see me smiling down on them.

I never saw myself as disabled. I was unaware of my pronounced limp. I was always so surprised when a child or a cruel adult at Far West pointed it out. I would look around to see who they were talking about. The realisation may have momentarily hurt, but never for long. There were too many adventures and romances – there was too much magic – to conjure.

Lying on the ground watching clouds, tracing the streams the jets left as they streaked across the deep blue sky, I would imagine the people in those planes, wonder at the places they'd been or where they were going. I was sure I would be in one of those planes one day. I could not countenance a life where this was not possible.

*

Others did not share my confidence in this future.

When I was twelve, my mother took me to see the local doctor for my dreadful migraines. He said to my mother that they should start looking into getting me on a disability pension before I finished school. I went into a fury: 'I don't need a pension. I have a brain!' My mother knew then that I would be alright in life.

She and Dad did everything they could to ensure I had the best possible education, because they knew that would help me achieve any dreams I had.

A scholarship to a prestigious girls' high school in Sydney gave me entrée to a society with people who understood me. I made lifelong friends there and, on leaving, found work easily.

As an adult, it came as a fabulous surprise that I too could have boyfriends and know the loving embrace of men, that I could give and receive sexual pleasure. Men loved me, and it didn't seem to matter to them that I limped. They always looked surprised when I mentioned it, and were often puzzled as to why I brought it up. They saw the inner me. I lived a gloriously happy life for many years, full of music, laughter, food and friends.

A decision to move back home would change me. At first, it was wonderful to be with my family and in my country. I met a man I thought was the answer to my dreams, and we got married. But I had married an illusion, for no sooner was the ring slipped on my finger than he turned into a drunken, violent monster.

Eventually I was able to gather enough resources and leave him, returning to Sydney, but I was flat, emotionally stripped. People said I'd lost my glow. I kept up a front for a while, and suppresed my deep hurt and anger as I dealt with the onset of post-polio syndrome, which resulted in the loss of mobility that resulted in me living in a wheelchair.*

---

* Post-polio syndrome (PPS) is a condition that affects polio survivors years after recovery from the initial acute attack of poliomyelitis. The most common symptoms are slowly progressing muscle weakness, fatigue and gradual muscle atrophy. Pain from joint degeneration and increasing skeletal deformities such as scoliosis are also common.

It's hard to pinpoint when my mojo went walkabout. But it was probably when I stopped wearing lipstick and started going out in trackie daks and t-shirts. I gave up my beloved Chanel No. 5, lost interest in flirting and couldn't pick up on the signals from men. Eventually I took to sleeping incredibly long hours, and sometimes felt so weighed down by life that the simple act of rolling over in bed became a chore. I would lay there with my ear hurting but lacking the will to simply turn onto my other side. My mind, with its seemingly infinite capacity for imagination and pleasure, was failing me, clouded in a miasmic fog that I couldn't think my way out of. For the first time I could remember, I was tethered to the earth and merely physical. It was a scary place to be. I sought help but could not relate to the white psychology. The drugs I was prescribed didn't make a difference, and drinking only exacerbated my blue feelings.

I knew I had to find my way back. The alternative was too devastating to contemplate. I needed to look deep inside and reclaim my wild and free self, with its capacity to discover joy. I needed my silken, butter-soft dancing shoes again. They were still there, I was sure. I just had to dig through the mental wreckage to recover them.

I started by sifting through all the anger and hatred I felt towards my husband. Although my thoughts were dark and murderous and filled with rage, I revelled in these extreme feelings because they made me feel alive again. I then began to let them go, one by one. Each day I became lighter as I discarded the emotional detritus. Those feelings of wrath turned to pity, and soon thoughts of him became feather-light, desiccated husks that I simply sent away upon the softest of breezes. He could no longer hurt me.

Next I had to deal with my feelings about my loss of mobility and come to terms with using a wheelchair. I could no longer sustain a full-time job. I had to find new ways of making a living and of living in general. I decided to become a writer, and told my friends about my plan so I would not be able to back out.

I entered competitions, pitting myself against other would-be writers, and to my amazement I started winning. I submitted articles to various newspapers and journals, and they published them. I wrote a book, and this took me all over Australia to talk to readers.

I have since written five children's books, as well as many articles and short stories. I speak at conferences, I run writing workshops and I teach children. My life is organised to suit my needs now and not the needs of others. I have a five-second commute from bed to desk. I can wear my nightie to work if I so choose, and my natural nocturnal ways rule. My friends say I keep rock-star hours and know never to call before noon.

I have my dancing shoes back. I am no longer anchored to the earth by the past; I can go anywhere I want. I have my lipstick, Chanel No. 5 and pretty dresses back. I have my blokes back. I have my life back. I have my mojo back.

I knew the return to myself was complete when I travelled to Europe and visited all the places I'd dreamt of as a child. Flying home after a wild and wonderful trip, a mere hour away from Sydney, the plane tracked over my home town. I looked out the window through the mid-morning light and smiled. I was finally in a plane leaving jet streams in the sky. I was the one returning from faraway lands. As I looked down at the disappearing speck of my childhood home, I wondered if there was another little girl gazing up and dreaming of one day travelling on a plane that briefly left an ethereal signature in the sky. I hoped so.

LAND'S EDGE

Tim Winton

A still summer night a world away in a house that smells of cactus and dust and musty kapok. I am six years old and almost asleep in the hollow of the clapped-out mattress. Outside in the Tuesday dark a high tide cracks against the bar at the river-mouth. My skin is pleasantly tight with sunburn and smelling of vinegar. A stubbed toe throbs under the lightness of the sheet. The fridge kicks in and whirrs across the sleeping sounds of my mother, my father, my sister and brother. I am drifting, rising and falling in the early current of sleep when suddenly, above me, there is a snap and a scream that lasts less than a second. Somewhere in the dark a terrible struggle. I lie there transfixed, totally awake now, and something warm dabs onto my forehead.

I hear my mother murmur sleepily and my father scrabbling for his torch. The beam comes on and strays drunkenly around the long room of iron bedsteads and cast-off furniture before finding the shuddering pendulum above me. My mother gasps but does not scream. Snug in its trap, a great dying rat swings from a few metres of cord tied to the rafters, and as it passes in its horrible arc with its hairy whip of a tail a few centimetres above my face, the creature offers up another glob of blood that hits the sheet with the tiniest sound imaginable.

*

For a few summers my family had Christmas holidays in a shack at the mouth of the Greenough River, just south of Geraldton. A strange house in retrospect, to a child it was the most remarkable place to have year after year, and I sometimes think that it was this house that caused me to become a writer. It was certainly the prime cause of my obsession with the coastal life.

Fronting the tea-coloured Greenough and overwhelmed by vast paddocks of hay stubble behind, it was a simple, peculiar shack in a lake of doublegees. The front yard was a dead stretch of buffalo grass upon which stood the most hideous concrete statues of birds and animals, all with marbles for eyes. I gave them a wide berth and often found myself shooting glances at them across my shoulder as I scooted along the big wind-blown veranda.

Out the back was a watertank, high on a rough jarrah stand, and sheds that contained the generator and the bucket shower I came to dread. Further along was the thunderbox dunny, a place of mystery and fascination, and a sort of half-open greenhouse crammed with cactus.

From the front windows you could see out beyond the eyelid of the veranda to the bright limestone road and the rivermouth. Out there, the sand was packed hard and cars could be driven across between river and sea. The surf hammered night and day, never calm, never quiet, blue all the way to Africa.

The house itself consisted mainly of one huge L-shaped room lined with beds, remnants of other houses and times and places. They were a wild assortment and a kid could jump from one end of the place to the other without touching the bare concrete floor that was always adrift with balls of dust and streaks of beach sand. Under our beds we had boxes of comics – *Archie*, *Donald Duck*, *The Phantom*, *Casper the Friendly Ghost*, *Richie Rich*, *Little Lotta* – and there were boys' and girls' annuals from England, books of adventure, scuffed blue-spined novels that smelled of antiquity and fried bacon.

Above us were the rat traps on the bare rafters, and in every corner, under every battered cupboard and gutless armchair, were neat little saucers of Ratsak. In the mornings my father would clear the traps and bury the rats out in the paddock where he emptied the thunderbox, out in the evil field of doublegees where no thong was thick enough to protect you. Dugites and bobtails rustled out there, and in the evenings, bronzed by the sun as it dunked into the sea, whole mobs of kangaroos lined the ridge until they became silhouettes and childish cutouts of themselves in the last of the light.

There was so much mystery in that house. The kitchen was a fairly basic affair – sink, kitchenette, fridge. It smelt of gas and kero, spent matches and rusty cans. The sink emptied into a bucket in the cupboard below and around the bucket were piles of strange little tins that kept all of us gasping as we read the labels. There were sugared ants, Italian anchovies, pâté from England, olives from Spain, and squarish tins of frogs' legs that we hardly dared to handle. The whole cache was shocking and hilarious. Now and then, on a dare, my father would hack a can open and bravely squelch some-thing down, his cheeks red with valour, and he'd murmur with great satisfaction and offer it around. We scattered like gulls.

I never ate anything out of that cupboard, but I went back to it regularly to work through the contents and wonder at the cities on the labels. These were things from the outside world, some-how potent and terribly exotic. Somewhere there were people who ate this kind of stuff!

There were two other rooms in the shack. One I can only dimly remember as a sort of parlour with a rat-chewed chaise longue and glass cases full of whisky miniatures, ash trays and knick-knacks of the pub trade. The other room, the room that really interested me, was the library. The shack at Greenough was the first house I ever knew to have its own library.

The owners of our beach place were my mother's relatives from Geraldton, Clem and Connie Penniment, former publicans and substantial figures in the port town. As a freckle-faced kid of six I thought they were my uncle and aunt, though I later discovered that they were in fact my great uncle and aunt. Large and imperious, they were also old and rather eccentric. The concrete animals should have told me something. The poor moulting black crow in the cage behind their newsagency might have offered a hint. The rooms of *stuff* above the shop, the fistfuls of brightly coloured tablets they took like so many mixed lollies, the way Uncle Clem looked down at his skiff-like brogues and muttered to me, 'Hm, what d'ye think?' before striding off grandly – and then saying exactly the same thing to me next year. Really, these things should have let me know they were quite unlike the people I knew in my raw little suburb of plainness at home.

What finally sent the message was the library. It was no bigger than a bedroom but it was four walls of books, a world unto itself. There were regiments of books, whole blocks and processions of uniform editions; Somerset Maugham, Dickens, George Eliot, Balzac, Melville, Twain, Mrs Gaskell, Virgil, Homer, Edmund Burke, Galsworthy, J. B. Priestley, Poe. There was a fruity, illustrated edition of *The Decameron* in two volumes, and an early edition of *Mein Kampf*, whose author sounded familiar. Leather spines, dustjackets from the twenties, thirties and forties, pocket editions, bookclub editions, rat-punctured art books, Gilbert and Sullivan librettos, tomes on medicine and the human body. All this finally told me that the tall people who slipped me the odd *Archie* comic on our weekly bread and milk trip were not ordinary people. Ordinary people had a Bible, a set of cheap encyclopaedias, stacks of *As You Were* and *Reader's Digest*; a yarn by Ion Idriess, perhaps, but not all this. This was outrageous, and it was probably just the overflow they couldn't squeeze in at home.

I spent a lot of time in that library. It was there that I discovered Robert Louis Stevenson and then *Robinson Crusoe* and *The Swiss Family Robinson*, the books that snatched me from the world of the *Archie* comic and never quite let me go back. Physical and compelling, these stories were the world of the desert island, the lonely beach, the still lagoon. I read *The Coral Island*, about chaps making do on whatever was to hand, and though I knew for sure that I'd never end up a chap and say 'Grand!' a lot, there was the chance that I could make do quite nicely on crayfish and rabbits and sleep nights in the warm sand. These were the first books that offered me some of the real world I knew, then carried me off completely to somewhere that didn't exist at all. Since then I've lived with a weakness for old-fashioned books from that library on my own shelves today. In many ways I'm still that open-mouthed boy, turning the pages, wanting to know what happens next; who pored, perved, flicked and sniffed his way from wall to wall every afternoon all those years ago.

For the library was an afternoon place. On the west coast in summer the morning is for the beach and the afternoon is a time to find shelter. The western summer is ruled by wind. Here the wind is a despot. It rushes off the land before dawn, ploughing out into the sea, full of wheat dust and pollen, crashing at the curtains and rattling every loose sheet of tin, warm and unrelenting. It heats up with the coming of day, an allergenic blast that scorches flat everything in its path. Wild oats and Paterson's Curse lie down before it. Out of the mysterious interior it barrels to tear the tops from breaking waves and hollow their troughs into glittering cylinders. On a summer's morning the sea smells of the land and the dunes become airborne. Sand falls far out beyond the smoke of bushfires to become a haze in the water, a puzzlement to fish.

It's morning when people are about, when the sea is bullied flat by the wind and the air is hot and dry. Just before noon the easterly mellows and becomes benign and before long it gives out altogether. The ocean glasses off, cicadas and birds find full voice in the sudden quiet, the coastline briefly becomes Mediterranean. This mild interlude might last five minutes or an hour, but it is never more than a lull, an imitation of gentle weather.

Before long the horizon begins to go wobbly. It stacks up mirages of boats, islands, capes, and the milky sea is streaked with lines of gooseflesh. You can see the Doctor coming in the distance, a ruffling line, an advancing front that curves in from the sou'west. When it arrives, there is a sense of relief, a cool rush of air and a softening of the sea. Then a light chop appears and confuses the surf. People begin to open up their houses. On the beach they shake out their towels and, out at sea, anglers haul anchor because, within a few minutes, beach umbrellas will be uprooted and sand flying as the sea loses its colour and gathers a nasty chop. Great plumes grow from the backs of the dunes and the heathland rattles with the afternoon gale. The sky goes white with sand and the trees on the coastal plain kiss the ground they grow on. The afternoons are the time to be inside on a bed with a book.

Just after dawn on those holiday mornings my father would shake me awake quietly and slip out to make himself a cup of tea. I'd find him in the kitchen scratching his whiskers in the blue glow of the Primus.

Out in the morning breeze he carried a hessian bag of shucked abalone and ham hocks for cray bait. Together we walked down along the mud-smelling river and crossed the crisp white of the bar to head up the bush track behind the dunes. We never said much, just listened to the close sound of our feet in the sand.

Down on the reef at low tide the rock pools and solution holes were brimming pits in the great exposed shelf. Octopus clambered about from hole to hole and startled sweep blurred away as we passed. Out at the edge of the reef where the surf clapped up against its face, the bag was handed to me and my father pulled the jarrah-slat pots up onto the limestone shelf. We snatched out the creaking, twitching crayfish, baited up again, and he heaved the traps back into the deep. Now and then a big swell hit the reef edge and reared up to come charging across the platform at us as a wall of boiling foam. I stood wide-legged and side-on to it as I was taught, holding the waistband of his shorts, feeling the crays kick and butt the bag against my legs. The force of the water was immense and terrible. Sometimes I was blasted completely off my feet, only to feel my father's grip anchoring me to the earth.

Back at the shack, where the rest of the family were stirring, we tipped the crays out onto the concrete floor to let them crawl around in their backward, sleepy manner. The little kids shrieked with delight.

Some mornings I slept in and walked down alone to the reef to meet my father. It felt very grown-up to walk so far on my own. The bush was strangely quiet, the sea a murmur on the reefs. The saltbush was pungent and the light was orange. Rabbits, and once a fox, crossed my path. One morning, when my father had taken the Holden instead of walking, he came hammering up the track flat-out to keep from sinking in the powdery sand and fishtailed around a bend to find me standing in the middle of the track. He swerved, I dived, and we had a few solemn minutes of digging and shunting to get the FC out of the scrub. I trembled all the way to breakfast.

Summer days were long at Greenough. We swam in the river and surfed on the beach when the rips weren't too treacherous. We rowed around the estuary and fished for bream and stood out on the jagged limestone point and baitcast for tailor. Every day my little brother went down to the caravan that served as a shop to try to buy lollies with bits of glass and bottle tops. He had more success some days than others, but at the end of the holidays Mum had to go down and settle his account.

There were horses in a paddock behind the dunes and some mornings my brother and I walked over to watch them. He had a strange fascination with them, a compulsion really. When he was eight or nine he got sick of watching and took to slipping through the fence and mounting them bareback. I watched in a sweat, terrified that he'd be found out and I'd be the one to have my bum kicked, but he only thought of the moment as he road around with his hands in the scruffy mane like the natural he was.

He was the same in the river. At the edge of the sandbar, where the bank fell away to deep water the colour of tea, he strode out repeatedly, convinced he could swim. My mother dragged him out by the hair and went on with the lesson. That's where we learnt to swim, there in the river, within tantalizing sight of the sea that crashed on the other side of the bar. Swimming is a great mystery, like riding a bike, like reading. Suddenly, after days and weeks of trying and failing, one morning you can do it.

Some mornings when the tide was right out we went onto the reef with screwdrivers to prise off abalone, which we called muttonfish. Dad shucked them and bashed them with a mallet under the tankstand and fried them in butter. We ate tailor, whiting, bream, crayfish and they made up for the frozen bread and milk, the cans of camp pie and baked beans, the dreaded tinned beetroot.

In the afternoons while the seawind brawled in across the rivermouth we lay on our bunks and read. Our noses were peeling, our feet scabby, our hair bleached, our lips chapped. The afternoons were quiet, exhausted, contemplative. Dad read Zane Grey and I remember Mum reading Errol Flynn's *My Wicked, Wicked Ways*. The house was full of the smells of fried fish, vinegar and Coppertone. One year I lay there for three weeks, in the midst of broken Christmas presents and Scrabble tiles, and read Jules Verne's *Journey to the Centre of the Earth*. It smelt of the library, another world. The print was so small it made me giddy.

When I went to browse in that library someone would have to throw a beach towel over the stuffed eagle in the corner. That bird's eyes were brown and glassy and they followed me round the room. Its upraised wings and fierce beak were threats I recognised in many a library and classroom later on. A kid can't always have a towel handy, but those afternoons I was safe and the world of books opened up to me like a dim shaft into the centre of the earth.

Those summers were both active and contemplative, the weather always fair but never gentle. Morning and afternoon I learned the pattern of my life, of hunting and gathering and picking over flotsam in the outdoor world – fishing, diving, swimming, surfing, lighting fires, rowing boats, feeling the landscape rush in from all sides – and of retiring indoors to wonder and write and read where only the breeze could reach me, in there where my dreams were. I would never be content with only one world or the other. At the time it felt like the ideal life, that coastal summer idyll, and maybe I've lived all my years a hostage to a six-year-old's fantasy.

HIPPOTHERAPY

Alistair Baldwin

Whenever I meet someone else who grew up disabled in Australia, there's only one key thing I want to know about them. I go through the small-talk motions, I feign interest in how their day went, I wait a respectful amount of time before I derail the conversation with the question I've been dying to ask.

'Hey, did you have to ride horses too?'

It is one of life's great tragedies that 'hippotherapy' has nothing to do with hippos. Had I, at age eight, received hippo-riding lessons, I think I would have grown up to become a very different man. More confident. More self-assured. Khaki would probably feature more prominently in my wardrobe.

The boring reality is that hippos have to do with horses (*hippopotamus* derives from the Ancient Greek word for 'river horse'), and it's horses that have to do with hippotherapy.

When it comes to treatment options for a young boy with a congenital muscle disease, one's mind doesn't instinctively jump to horses. Yet therapeutic horse-riding, or hippotherapy, got an emphatic tick of approval from my neurologist, my physio and my occupational therapist.

Such is its popularity that in every state and territory of Australia you can find Riding for the Disabled Association (RDA) centres – made moderately affordable to non-aristocratic disableds through government subsidies. Owing to both ubiquity and these subsidies, I've found that Australian adults with a disability are nearly as likely to have grown up horse-riding as Australian adults who were child actors on *The Saddle Club*. Which is to say, quite likely.

My local centre in Perth was called RDA Capricorn. Its stables and paddock were located next to Perry Lakes Stadium, the multipurpose sports complex specially built for the 1962 Commonwealth Games. It was a somewhat ironic neighbour. Perry Lakes was where my able-bodied classmates played basketball, where inter-school athletics carnivals I couldn't compete in were held. I doubt many people knew that within limping distance, hidden among eucalyptus trees and down a discreet dirt road, was a bunch of adolescent cripples on horses.

I would go to the centre once a week, wearing knock-off R.M. Williams on my tiny, flat feet. I'd head inside, to where they kept the helmets, and try to find one that fit well. Then I'd go through to the back, my boots digging into wood mulch, where there was a series of ramps leading to platforms of different heights.

The platform you used depended on which horse you were riding that day. Rather than attempt hoisting themselves onto a horse with strength they didn't have, each child would walk or roll their wheelchair up to a platform approximately matching the height of their assigned horse. You'd get into the saddle with the help of a volunteer, who would almost invariably be a horse-obsessed teenage girl whose time and generosity were rewarded with the opportunity to ride for free after all the disabled kids went home.

In my first year or so, I always rode Albert. He was an old pony, relatively low to the ground, white with mottled grey specks. Later, as I gained confidence and skill, I rode Apollo – a proper horse, much taller and more muscular, with a chestnut coat.

In each session we would ride around the rectangular paddock a couple times, then crisscross from corner to corner, weave in and out of traffic cones and jump over small obstacles.

There was something exhilarating about turning your steed with the slightest pull of the reins, nailing a jump, shifting gears into a fast trot. What I enjoyed most was the sheer novelty of it. I was, finally, in control of an able body.

The jury's out, though, on just how much riding a horse can really help disabled people.

One of the first recorded people to posit the health benefits of horse-riding was Hippocrates (also nothing to do with hippos), circa 400 BC, who called it a 'natural exercise' that benefited the body, mind and spirit. However, in a separate scroll, Hippocrates wrote that for those with a passion for riding, 'the constant jolting on their horses unfits them for intercourse'. As someone who once landed wrong on the downbeat of a trot, I can say (in a slightly high-pitched voice) this assessment has some basis in reality. If I were a conspiracy theorist, I'd say that's why the government pays for it – it's all part of a long game to stop us invalids infecting the gene pool with our subpar DNA.

A cursory google search tells me another key horse-therapy believer was Lis Hartel, a Danish dressage champion who contracted polio in 1944 at the age of twenty-three. Paralysed below the knees, she continued competitive dressage against medical advice, becoming the first woman to win a silver medal in an Olympics event open to men and women. She credited horse-riding with improving her polio symptoms, and began advocating for hippo-therapy for disabled people after she retired from sport.

The official RDA website states that hippotherapy helps develop 'postural control, equilibrium reactions, balance, coordination and spatial orientation'. A 2015 medical article tells me that it has been used to treat 'autism, cerebral palsy, arthritis, multiple sclerosis, head injury, stroke, spinal cord injury, behavioural disorders and psychiatric disorders', although 'the effectiveness of hippotherapy for many of these indications is unclear'.

What do I think? The truth is, I don't know if it helped me. In theory, it probably improved my core strength, in the same way that sitting on a yoga ball improves core strength – the shifting stability awakening deep, moth-eaten muscles in my abdomen. But I certainly didn't notice this at the time. It's hard to assess progress or decline from inside a disability, especially as a child. It's near impossible to compare yourself to how you were six months ago, because all you want to do is compare yourself to your friends and your bullies – and that's all they want to do right back.

My mum did declare countless times that horse-riding had helped my posture, that I began sitting on couches as though I were a vigilant security guard. To this day she still brings it up. She was a fan of the whole thing because I'd finally found a physical activity I was okay at. My older brother was a sporty kid, playing both footy and basketball, and he received ribbons, trophies and Most Valuable Plater certificates semi-regularly, placing them on a shelf above his bed. As part of her tireless efforts to ensure I never felt I was living a diluted version of childhood, Mum went to a shop to custom-order horse-shaped trophies for me (marked 'achievement' of a nondescript variety), and she would award these biannually. The shelf above my bed soon looked as shiny as my brother's, until I got to the age where showing off my mum-ordered, store-bought trophies for 'achievement' in a prescribed therapy became supremely embarrassing. Then I took them all down and put them in a box.

When I decided to stop horse-riding for good, I think Mum was more upset than I was. But she respected my autonomy, and she agreed that the freak event that drove the final nail into the coffin of my horse-riding career – an event as traumatic as it was bizarre – was a good enough reason to call it quits.

Western Australia does not have daylight saving. The matter has been the subject of four state referendums – in 1975, 1984, 1992 and 2009 – and was rejected by Western Australians all four times. I remember it being, inexplicably, the defining debate of my youth. It provided local talkback radio with countless hours of content, as a divided population went into bat for either saving time or experiencing it as nature intended.

It's the 2009 referendum I want to talk about – or, specifically, the years leading up to it. In 2006, a three-year trial of daylight savings began, so that people could try it on for size before buying it for good. The event that led me to quit horseriding happened a week after we all, sceptically, put our clocks one hour back.

I had my afternoon session as usual. Everyone got the memo and arrived on time. It was a nice, peaceful day. Then, halfway through, we all heard it.

Click. Hissss …

The Perry Lakes Stadium grounds that the paddock bordered relied on an automatic sprinkler system – those powerful, pressurised ones that always seem to pop out of the ground just as you've laid down your picnic blanket. The system was scheduled to come on at 5.30 p.m., partly so the sun didn't instantly evaporate the water as it sprayed out, and partly because Perry Lakes had been informed that these powerful jets of water spooked the RDA horses, so it was best they didn't go off during a hippotherapy session. But unfortunately, Perry Lakes had not recived the daylight savings memo.

Time slowed down. In the millisecond after the *click-hiss*, Apollo got sucker-punched in the face with water. Before I realised what was happening, I was halfway across the paddock.

Riding horses have four main gaits, ascending in speed like gears in a car. At RDA we only used two: 'walk' and 'trot'. 'Canter', graceful and smooth as it is, was above our abilities. When the sprinklers went off that day, every single horse instinctively shifted into their fourth gear: 'gallop', a gait you may recognise from watching a horse race. In an instant, a dozen tiny, disabled children were flung into the atmosphere.

Apollo's speed suddenly threw me back into the saddle, my spine slamming onto his rump. One leg began waving in the wind like a flag as he charged from one end of the paddock to the other. The other foot remained in the stirrup, and my hands somehow kept hold of the reins.

Apollo was making a dash for the paddock gate, which was shut during sessions, and it was his graceful, speedy jump over it that finally dislodged me from the saddle and sent me down into the mulch with a thud. I fractured two ribs, and couldn't attend the school excursion to the movies the next day.

It's easier to get back on the horse when it's not literally a horse. It's easier when it's pilates, or a daily sudoku, or any other activity with an almost non-existent risk of injury.

I knew you shouldn't let one setback stop you pursuing something you enjoy. I recovered pretty quickly, as did my fellow horse-riders; we were all roughed up a little, but the incident didn't make any of us more disabled than we already were. But I was scared it would happen again, or something else would, something worse. The odd confluence in my injury of daylight savings and sprinkler systems made me fear even the most banal things, like how it's impossible to look at a stapler or a rake the same way after watching the *Final Destination* movies. As a little disabled kid, in and out of hospitals, in a body that's constantly discussed in terms of its weakness and frailty, it's easy for your mind to jump to death as a consequence for almost anything, even when your specific condition isn't immediately terminal.

I asked my parents if I could study Italian, and going to a weekend class soon became my extracurricular activity. Then, a year or so later, RDA Capricorn moved its facilities from Perry Lakes to Pinjar, a much longer car trip away, so even if I had decided to return to riding it would have been inconvenient.

My dad had been on the volunteer board at the centre in his spare time, and continued to do so even after I stopped riding. He would occasionally update me about their new programs or sleepover camps. He eventually left too. The last thing I remember hearing about the centre was that Albert, the first horse I regularly rode, had died.

Despite their unfortunate and abrupt end, I look back on my horse-riding days with fondness.

Even now, I feel a strange affinity for horses. Partly because of the afternoons I spent with them as a child, and partly because, as with humans, a horse's value to society is inextricably, albeit unfortunately, linked to its abledness. It doesn't take much more than a vague grasp of history and a little imagination to see that, if they could, abled people would melt the lame down into glue.

Beyond that, I'm just glad I was lucky enough to grow up doing something, anything, surrounded by other disabled kids. 'Sail-ability' was a popular kid's maritime activity recommended by my occupational therapists, as was Surfing for the Disabled. In another life, I'd be writing a charming short story about how daylight savings set off a sequence of events that nearly led to me drowning at sea.

At school, all my friends were abled (as were my enemies). I put so much effort into trying to hide the gap between our abilities. In horse-riding, I never had to disguise the odd way my shoulders rounded, my strange gait, the weird way my hands grasped things. It's exhausting to fight the way you naturally exist. The spaces and moments in which you can relax into how your body truly is are sacred. And that's what horse-riding gave me.

That's why I like asking other disabled people if they did horse-riding too. In a world where you can feel impossibly different to everyone around you, there's comfort in finding people you share a perspective, an identity, a diagnosis or an experience with.

BOOBS, RAGS AND JUDY BLUME

Phoebe Hart

'When will I get my boobs?'

I was eleven years old, and ever since I'd finished Judy Blume's seminal work, *Are You There God? It's Me, Margaret*, I was in our kitchen moaning to Mum on a daily basis about my glaring lack of mammary glands (Ms Blume has a lot to answer for).

Mum made no comment, just shifted her weight slightly on her feet and continued standing at the sink with her back to me. I sighed and resolved to return to my bedroom to do some more breastenhancing exercises. 'I must, I must, I must increase my bust ... '

I'm not sure how this technique was supposed to work, but I hoped it would – and soon! My gaggle of girls (I had dubbed us 'The Gang' so we sounded tougher than we actually were) was due to arrive in a few hours for a weekend get-together at my place and I was still as disappointingly flat as the proverbial surfboard. There were seven of us, and I'd worked hard to make these friends after swapping schools a year earlier, in Grade 6. I watched with envy as they all got their 'marbles', which gradually developed into well-formed little breasts. I only had fleabites where two nice little mounds should be.

I would try to fool my mates by popping down the front of my top some dried up balls of 'Slime in a Bucket', horrid kids' gunk sourced from a showbag I got at the local agricultural show in Townsville in Far North Queensland. That got old when my snot-green goo boobs slipped out of place, or worse, fell out and onto the floor.

'Phoebe's got fakies!' screeched the other girls, as I burned with shame.

Cute as my struggles seem in retrospect, my overdue puberty eventually became beyond a joke.

One by one, members of The Gang came to school with a certain look in their eyes – an unholy mixture of pride and horror – and announced they had got their 'rags'. Each time I felt a choking jealousy that made my head fuzzy. It was like the sensation of sand being sucked out from under your feet as waves break on the beach. My ears blocked up. I barely heard my friends as they gushed through the gory details of the arrival of their monthlies.

'It's raining down south!' one would say.

'Nosebleed in Tasmania,' another would reply.

'Clean up in aisle one,' piped in a third.

Resounding giggles. I moved so I could sit on my hands.

'How about that new Madonna video clip?' I would offer weakly, desperate to appear somewhat mature and cool. 'What do you think she's on about when she says, "Papa don't preach"?'

The girls would stop to eye me before going back to listing their top ten euphemisms for menstruation. For my part, I would resist the urge to flick their trainer bra straps until their backs bled in tandem with their vaginas.

But now was not the time for revenge. Rather, I was making a blue-chip investment in my popularity stock, which would soar to an all-time high when I held a rockin' pre-teen sleepover. This would be our chance to gossip about hot boys and choreograph some new routines to the synth-styles of '80s pop music like 'Girls Just Want to Have Fun' by Cyndi Lauper or, if we were feeling a tad more artistic, something like 'One Night in Bangkok' by Murray Head. It was going to be a bonding time for us all, and I sure as heck didn't want to be on the outer for that.

I spent a lot of time making sure it would all go perfectly. My bedroom was looking just right: plastered with teen idol posters of the boys from Pseudo Echo and Wa Wa Nee and the permanent paint murals Mum had allowed us to splatter the walls with as she was 'going to wallpaper over them as soon as we moved out when we turned seventeen' anyway. The fridge was cram-packed with drinks and snacks – mini pizzas, party pies and fizzy drinks – and my little sister Bonnie had been banished to one of her own friends' houses for the afternoon. Everything was set to go.

Only Mum seemed out of sorts.

I'm not sure of the precise moment when my mother's attitude began to change. It might have been when I refused to wear white t-shirts out of the house unless I had a singlet on underneath. Or it might have been the hours I had begun to spend gazing at my own reflection at all angles in the full-length mirror. Maybe it was when I started bringing up awkward subjects such as pregnancy, abortion and birth control. Mum became a little jumpy around me. I couldn't quite diagnose it, but I could sense her unsettled energy and decided the best course of action would be to steer clear.

Finally, the first cars arrived to drop off my friends. Parents waved farewell to their youngsters behind a plume of Winfield Blue smoke and ash as they sped away down the street, leaving my friends to trudge up our steep driveway. Before long, my bedroom had reached a fever pitch of squeals, shrieking laughter and the other assorted sounds of pubescent lounging and lolligagging.

When one gal pal chucked an unused tampon in another's lap, resulting in an extra shrill scream, Mum poked her head in long enough for me to see her disapproving expression. I pretended not to notice, and she stalked off in a huff.

'Oh my god, Phoebe, I think your mum doesn't like us!' one friend whispered theatrically.

'Don't worry about her,' I said. 'She's probably about to get a visit from Aunty Flo.'

Wild hilarity. Pitch and timing perfect. Put them off the hot topic of my own deficit with some on-topic humour. Excellent decoy.

'So …' ventured another friend, 'has George come to visit *you* yet, Phoebe?'

Damn!

'Er, no, not yet.'

Loaded pause. The girls looked at one another. One broke the silence.

'You're nearly twelve, Phoebe. Maybe something's … wrong?' 'Yeah, maybe you should ask your mother about it?' someone added.

A general mumble of agreement.

'You think?' I said, looking up from my lap at all six faces through my fringe. I'd been avoiding the subject with my mother. 'Sure. That's what we'd do.'

All nodded earnestly, wide doe-eyes. I straightened my back and injected some bravado into my voice.

'Alright then, I'll ask her *right now*.'

A sudden burst of energy and everyone got up as a chattering whole to leave the room together.

'Maybe you guys should stay here.'

My suggestion was met with poutiness and smirks. I turned away from the tittering tits and went searching for Mum. I discovered her in the backyard, watering the plants.

She saw me sidling towards her and angled slightly away, aiming her nozzle at a despondent soursop sapling.

'Um, Mum,' I said sheepishly. 'Can I ask you a question?'

Mum flicked her eyes at me. Muffled laughter came from the back window and I turned to see The Gang all peering through to eavesdrop on the exchange. Mum looked up and saw them too. She rolled her eyes and pivoted, yanking the hose towards a remote corner of the yard.

I shooed the girls and waited until they'd reluctantly moved away. Hearing them retreat back to the bedroom, I approached Mum again with trepidation. A few metres from where she was standing, facing the garden, I stopped and waited for her to acknowledge me.

'What is it, Phoebe?' she said exasperatedly. I swallowed and went for it.

'Umm. Everyone's been asking me, and I was wondering … when will I get my periods?'

Mum stiffened and half-turned towards me.

I'm not sure why I phrased my question in this particular way. I expected her perhaps to simply say 'Soon' or 'Be patient, it will happen in time', and that would be the end of the conversation. Funny things, expectations.

Mum sighed. 'Phoebe, you'll never get your periods.'

I stood blinking in the afternoon light, stunned. My lips formed a basic monosyllabic response.

'Why?'

Mum's mouth tightened. 'Because … you don't have a uterus. So you can't have periods, and you can't have a baby.'

My head began eddying with thick, dark thoughts. The inner part of me was screaming *Whaaaaatt!?!* but the outer part was completely blank, speechless.

'You can adopt, though, if you like,' Mum added. A beat.

'Really? Are you … sure?' I said eventually. 'No periods?' Mum nodded.

'Okay then … at least I've got something I can tell the others. They've all been asking why I haven't got my period yet—'

For the first time, Mum whipped around and faced me, eye to eye.

'Don't you tell them anything!'

My eyes must have popped out of my head. Mum calmed herself a little before proceeding.

'It's not a good idea to tell anyone about this. Your father and I haven't told anyone else, not even Grandma and Granddad.

So let's keep this a secret. Our secret. Okay?'

Her words snapped me out of fogginess into a clear, tangible focus and I sensed blood pounding in my temples. I had a secret. A really, *REALLY* big secret. I couldn't believe even my beloved grandma wasn't allowed to know.

'Is that everything?' Mum was looking at me. I got the feeling she didn't want me to ask another question.

I stood there for a moment longer, before turning around quietly and re-entering the house. My memory of what happened next or what I said is murky. I suspect that, in a trance-like state, I nodded, left Mum to her garden and stumbled back to the bedroom with its air of breathless anticipation. I imagine that The Gang was dying to know what had happened – something, anything! – but I can't remember what I told them. Most likely, 'It's nothing.' But it was *something*.

In the end, my breasts did start to emerge, little by little. But by then I had assigned myself apart from the girls and their feminine ways. There was nothing in any Judy Blume book that could explain this to me, and no one to ask 'why'? It would be ages before I understood the reason – many years before I learnt that I am intersex and that my sex chromosomes and organs are male.

All I knew was I was different. Very, very different. It was a profound feeling that shaped my adolescence and my life for a long time to come.

Looking back, I have mixed emotions about this time. It was the start of my journey towards understanding my body and myself more, although it was rough and things didn't get much better any time soon. I still struggle sometimes to accept I'll never be normal, whatever the hell 'normal' means. In these times, I feel confused and lonely, much like the eleven-year-old me. But as my knowledge of human experience has expanded, I've come to realise I'm not alone in feeling this complicated mélange of shame, loss, discovery and, finally, pride. And now I know I am accepted for exactly who I am.

NOBODY PUTS BABY SPICE IN A CORNER

Miranda Tapsell

There have been many moments in my life when I've had to take control of my own identity. I think in many ways, some more subconscious than not, I've always wanted it to be left up to me.

When I was about four, I really wanted to be a ballerina and I would dance along to Tchaikovsky's *The Dance of the Sugar Plum Fairy* whenever my dad played it. One morning I came into the dining room for breakfast, and he greeted me affectionately with, 'Good morning, Sugar Plum.' Forgetting I had previously pirouetted to Tchaikovsky, I turned to him in disgust and said, 'Not Sugar Plum! Am I a fruit?' This four-year-old told him what was what. Women aren't objects, dammit. Another morning I came in for breakfast and he tried to greet me with, 'Good morning, Golden Girl.' I looked at him in confusion and said, 'I'm not a Golden Girl, I'm a Black Girl.' Poor Dad couldn't catch a break.

So as you can see, I've been an intersectional feminist since the age of four. I knew exactly who I wanted to be. And I'm sure you've already noticed, it was something that my parents never censored. I did most of my schooling at Jabiru, which is 200 kilometres from Darwin in the Northern Territory. 'Jabbers', as the locals affectionately call it, is in the middle of Kakadu

National Park. We moved there from Darwin when I was five years old.

My dad was the town clerk of Jabiru Town Council, and my mum was the Aboriginal education officer at Jabiru Area School. I got to know most of the Indigenous students through Mum. Because of the gap in education between the Aboriginal and non-Indigenous students, it was Mum's job to support the black kids through an intimidating Western education system that often left a lot of them behind. During her time there, she ran the breakfast program, which ensured the Indigenous students didn't skip the most important meal of the day before class started. She got the school to donate uniforms so that they had fresh clothes after they showered. She'd check up on them when they hadn't been to school, take them to the clinic when they were sick. She also made it mandatory for me to attend the homework centre, which was an initiative to assist the Aboriginal students who might not have had the space or the assistance at home to get their homework done. At the time I hated it and couldn't understand why I couldn't just do mine at home. In hindsight, I now know that because she only got to Year 11 – and really struggled with schoolwork herself – she didn't have the confidence to help me. She wanted me to take the opportunities given to me in my education that weren't given to her.

Mum didn't have the answers to closing the gap in health or education. When the media ask me about it now, I don't know either. But I grew up without judging anyone who had lived experiences outside of my own. Every individual, every family, every community needs different things. But my mum had – and still has – the biggest heart of anyone I know and was there for these students whenever they needed her.

Jabiru Area School was that tiny I ended up being friends with most of the kids in the school. Even though I got on with the Aboriginal students, I still felt like an outsider in the group. While there was an unspoken solidarity between us, I didn't have a lot in common with them. First case in point: I loved the Spice Girls and Hanson; most of them listened to either Tupac or Biggie. A lot of the mob lived and breathed AFL; I had no idea what was happening during the games. I was loud and shameless most of the time; the rest of the Aboriginal kids just played it cool.

It also wasn't my country: my people, the Larrakia, come from the Darwin region, and the traditional owners of Jabiru and its surroundings were the Mirrar people. A lot of non-Indigenous people think that because I grew up in Jabiru, I must have come from there. But there were a lot of blackfellas who had come from other places and most know it's like living in Spain if you are Portuguese. I was a weird in-betweener. The one who got on really well with lots of non-Indigenous people, but also the Aboriginal mob.

And because most of them lived outside of town, I ended up making friends with the mining kids who lived in town with me. Now, at this point I should tell you that I was the only black girl in my group of friends. So I think lots of my non-Indigenous friends chose not to see colour. I was just like them. But when they were reminded of my Larrakia heritage, it made them uncomfortable.

The first time I really became aware of this was when I was eight years old. My class were colouring in the same picture of a family in front of a Christmas tree. It a was great time because we were nearing the end of term and there was less homework. Now, normally when I drew or coloured in, I would colour in all the people as blond-haired and blue-eyed. I guess that's what happens when that's all you see in your books, TV shows and movies. Also, I was sitting next to my non-Indigenous friend, Iggy*, who was colouring in the people in the picture with blond and red hair like her family. So, naturally, I was copying my friend.

But then I saw another Aboriginal girl in the class, Jacinta*, colour in her family all brown. That's when it occurred to me that I was whitewashing my own pictures. I thought to myself, 'Why on earth am I copying Iggy?' That wasn't what I looked like. It's not what my mum looked like. So I coloured in my family the same as Jacinta.

In my picture, the mum and kids were brown. I kept the dad white, just like mine. That essentially meant leaving him the colour of the paper. I liked this picture. Sure, colouring the people brown took more time, but something about it made me feel validated. Proud.

Suddenly there were so many brown people in my pictures that it seemed to start bothering Iggy.

'Why do you do that all the time?' she asked me. 'Do what?'

'Colour in all your people brown?'

I was so caught off-guard when Iggy asked me this. All of a sudden I felt really bad. Was I being divisive making people in my pictures brown? I didn't think I was – I thought I was just reflecting the kind of people I interacted with on a daily basis in my artwork.

In hindsight, I should have asked Iggy, 'Why do you colour your people blond-haired and blue-eyed all the time?' Instead I shrugged and said, 'I dunno, I just like it.'

But from then on, whenever we did art, I would draw brown people. I should add here that we did do maths and English at school – it wasn't all just colouring in and drawing. It used to bug Iggy a lot, and she would feel the need to comment on it. It seemed to me that whenever my friends were reminded of my Aboriginality, they wouldn't know how to navigate it. Their uncertainty would turn to anguish, and it would be my fault that I was making them sad or angry.

As I entered my pre-teen years, my friends began to see my colour, and things would still get awkward when they didn't need to be. When I was eleven, my mum and a few others working at Jabiru Area School organised a Blue Light Disco, and it was fancy dress. At the time, my friends and I were still very much obsessed with the Spice Girls. If you were to ask how obsessed I was with the Spice Girls, I would say to you: does having the Posh Spice doll, the pencil case, their posters plastered all over my walls, every single lyric to all the songs memorised off by heart mean being obsessed? Absolutely not. That's called being committed.

I loved them so much because their songs were about how awesome girls were. Listening to their albums made me feel great to be one. Sure, the songs were heteronormative, but I liked that their songs demanded respect from their male lovers. For those of you who didn't grow up in the 1990s like me, you seriously missed out and need to listen to the lyrics of their hit song 'Wannabe'.

Essentially they were telling eleven-year-old Miranda that if my future boyfriend was not going to treat me like his equal, then I needed to say goodbye. A relationship not built on trust and respect was not worth my time. I had to prioritise my friendships with other girls first and foremost.

My friends and I had decided that we would dress up as them for the disco. So who would be who? I was really into Ginger, but I didn't know how I felt about her Union Jack dress. I mean, slightly problematic for me, don't you think? Everyone in my group was all about Ginger, Posh and Baby.

One of my friends, Corrine*, said I needed to be Scary Spice. Really? I didn't get why I *needed* to be. I didn't *need* to wear that much leopard print. I didn't *need* to stick my tongue out like a frilled neck lizard. When I asked why I needed to be Scary, my friend told me, 'Because no one else is brown!'

Looking back, I wonder if Corrine felt uncomfortable about dressing up as a brown celebrity. I mean, it was the 1990s, and white people still struggled with dressing up as black or brown artists without the added melanin. Let's be real, not melanin – boot polish.

I didn't know what blackface was at that point in my life, but I definitely knew that colour didn't make the costume. Those five female singers had such iconic styles that most people my age would instantly recognise the Spice Girl you were dressed as. With *wigs*. And *clothing*. While I was very proud of the heritage that my mother had passed onto me, I didn't want to dress up as Scary just because I had brown skin like her.

So I started to realise that even though I didn't have much in common with the Aboriginal kids in Kakadu, it seemed I didn't have much in common with the non-Indigenous kids either. I think Spice Girls, Hanson and *Smash Hits* was about all we had.

Thank goodness for Heather*. She was my closest friend in the non-Indigenous group, and is still my best friend to this day. As five-year-olds, Heather and I started school on the same day and have been inseparable ever since. Because the group didn't consider Heather conventionally girly they thought she should be Sporty. Now, Heather was not sporty at all. In PE she would always point out the ball for someone else to get, even if she was closest to it. It was like the opening of the MTV animated series *Daria*. In fact, everyone began calling her Daria. They only cast her as Sporty because she never wore dresses and wore sneakers a lot of the time. I could tell that Heather wasn't that keen on being Sporty, but she was so shy and would rather go along with it than confront anyone. She was less fussy than I was.

Now, I don't have anything against Scary or Sporty, but I couldn't help but feel that they were the two Spice Girls that our group were indifferent towards. I couldn't shake the feeling that Heather and I were given the less favoured choices.

When I got home, my mum asked me who I was going to dress up as. I told her about Corrine, and how much she lost her mind over my objection to being Scary Spice at the Blue Light Disco.

'You don't have to dress up as Scary Spice,' Mum assured me. 'You have a pink floral dress that looks like something Baby would wear.'

I was hesitant about wearing the dress, because I was still worried about what Corrine would think. I didn't want to be hated; I just wanted to have a good night without having to deal with her saying something hurtful. She made me feel awful about wanting to be someone different from whom she wanted me to be.

I began to annoy my mother with this. Don't get me wrong, she is the fairy godmother of this story. But my fairy godmother was strict, and she had overcome many limitations placed upon her just to make a good life for herself. If society hasn't allowed you the freedom to express your feelings as an Aboriginal woman, then god help you when you're granted a daughter who expresses every feeling she has in every single moment of her life!

'Why do you care what she thinks?' Mum asked me, exasperated. 'You can be whoever you want to be.' That's right, fairy godmother just wanted Cinderella to get on with things and go to the goddamn ball.

On the night of the disco, I put on the pink flowery dress, and Mum put my hair up in two high buns like Baby Spice. I even used glitter hairspray in my hair! I really need glitter hairspray back in my life.

Mum was a supervisor at the disco, so I rocked up with her. As I had predicted, my friend saw me and got really upset.

'I told you, I'm Baby Spice!' Corrine yelled at me.

'Why can't I be Baby Spice too?' I asked her.

She moved away from me and spent the whole night sulking. Eleven-year-old me felt sad that my friend didn't want to hang with me. I wasn't dressed the same as her solely to upset her. I think that's how she saw it.

But my mum had taught me something valuable that night – even though I'd continue to care what my friends thought of me. I didn't take anything away from Corrine, and I shouldn't be made to feel bad because I wanted to be Baby Spice.

Sissy, an Aboriginal girl, came up to me and asked, 'Are you Scary Spice?'

Was she serious?

'No, I'm Baby Spice,' I told her.

I could not believe this! At what point did Scary wear pink

or *flowers* for that matter? Did Sissy not collect the posters out of *Smash Hits*?

'Oh, why weren't you Scary?' she asked me.

Poor Sissy, she was conditioned like all of us to believe brown people could only be Scary.

As for Heather, she just rocked up as Sporty Spice in clothes I'd often seen her wear at school. I loved that about Heather. For her it was more about being there and having a good time.

So I went through puberty learning that, unfortunately, there would be a lot of people like Corrine; non-Indigenous Australians who would be disappointed and angry at the fact you wouldn't conform to how they saw you. If it's not having a problem with you being Baby Spice instead of Scary, it's you being Aboriginal instead of being Australian.

As I look back at my childhood, I realise that I wanted to become an artist because then I could take back the control of who I wanted to be. I was tired of the limitations people were putting on me. But growing up I learnt that people aren't always going to agree with how you define yourself. And while my identity is now something that I have some control over, I had to learn to deal with the idea that saying you're Aboriginal is a political act. To paraphrase the Spice Girls' song 'Move Over', I decided to take some heat and go with the flow. Okay, look, out of context it might not make sense, but the sentiment is there. Just have a listen to the song on Spotify.

Thank you, Spice Girls, for giving eleven-year-old Miranda a bit of Girl Power. No one puts Baby Spice in a corner.

* *Names have been changed.*

THE WALL OF SHAME

Natalie Macken

On the bus home at 3.30 pm, it's still hot. Every time a girl gets up to get off, her thighs make a sound like they've been velcroed to her seat. At my stop – me, some other kid, and three boys who shoot Girl Guides with cap guns get off.

I have to walk home with the other kid, who's having a piano lesson with Mum. It's the longest eleven minutes of my life. After two blocks of silence, my neck and throat are smarting with awkwardness, so I do what I can.

'Do you reckon some people can see their eyebrows?' I ask. He looks at me like I've just licked a street sign. 'No,' he says.

I wait for more, but that's it.

Whatever comes next has to last two streets, so I go mainstream. 'Are you doing three-unit music next year?' I say.

'Probably not,' he replies, mercilessly.

Like a demigod, my neighbour, Mrs Lalor, appears in her driveway and waves to me. She's wearing three different types of denim. I walk through our front door and head straight up to my room, bypassing the kitchen and an unsupervised Milo-straight-from-the-tin opportunity.

I have drum lessons on Wednesdays while Mum's students play melodies that make the piano sound like it has dementia. I'm debuting my new padded drum-kit stool, hiding behind my hair, nailing a paradiddle rudiment on the snare. A cheap and desperate pine-scented deodorant overrides the smell of limp lettuce coming from my schoolbag. My almost-a-man drum teacher seems impressed with my progress, and I prepare myself for a compliment. Instead, he asks, 'What's wrong with you?'

'Why?' I ask.

He's staring at the far wall of my bedroom. 'All other girls your age have posters of boys on their wall,' he says.

I feel my whole body fill with white-hot shame. I barely blink, swallow my bile, slow my breathing and, with the nerve of a sniper, say, 'I took them down when we painted the walls.'

After he leaves my room, I wait for him and his pine-accented armpits to get paid for being only a bit better than me at drums. I stay still and hold my breath until the don't-get-found-out snake has slithered over my feet and back into its box. Then I open my bedroom door and come out into the space the rest of me takes up. I close the door on my boy-bare wall.

With beats on repeat in my head, I decide to walk up the road to buy a copy of *Smash Hits* magazine. Mostly because that's where Heather Brewer got her folder cover of Christian Slater.

'Yeah, it's hard to look at all day – NOT,' she'd said. I think he permanently looks like he's mildly surprised while squinting into direct sunlight. I don't get it but … whatever.

With my shoes keeping a solid four-four, I lock into the tempo until I pass Eddie's petrol station with its huge new 'Shell' sign out the front. I press play on my Discman and Tracy Chapman's 'Fast Car' comes on. I keep walking the four.

Deep in the rhythm – that's when I know it's not going anywhere, the gay.

I know it's not what other people are, so I decide to paint my puberty by numbers, copying the moves Heather Brewer makes because she makes the right ones. That's when Tracy got in her Fast Car, and I went along for the ride.

Jeff at the newsagency has an unspoken ten-minute rule for flipping through magazines. After that, he'll say, 'Better buy it to see what happens next.' I always let him get that one out, but I try to pay before he plays the 'I'm not a library' card. I make a detour around *Cosmo* and *Dolly*, and pick up a copy of *Smash Hits*. But, instead of reading it, I open it on a random page to play 'Six Degrees of Kevin Bacon'. Who knew that only six or less steps along a *Footloose* path were what separated the whole world?

Julia Roberts. Too easy. She was in *Flatliners* with Kevin Bacon. Her Bacon number is one.

I don't really want *Smash Hits*. It's very Corey-heavy. There's also a healthy side of Vanilla Ice, Jason Priestley, Emilio Estevez, Charlie Sheen and Rick Astley. In between all the testosterone, there's Julia Roberts, like some weird uber-smiling mistake. The thing is, everyone's got it wrong: I don't want to be her, I want to be *with* her. And I know there's a difference, on a cellular level, on the level where it's about your skin and your blood and not just about your mind.

'I'm not a library, you know,' says Jeff.

I buy the shitty magazine, and Jeff counts out my change on the counter, including two two-cent coins and one one-cent coin.

'Don't exist anymore,' he says, holding up one of the copper coins.

Yes I do, I think, but out loud I say, 'Yeah, they're supposed to start disappearing.'

*

That night, I wait for the lull after *Home and Away* and dinner, when everyone's doing their own thing. My brother's annoyed with me because I got the same stereo as his, and I'm annoyed with him because he eats too slowly. He's playing the Chili Peppers in his room while I pull out posters of shiny, improbable-looking boys from a centrefold of teenage sexuality. It feels alien and abrasive. I feel like I'm betraying myself.

I Blu Tack a panorama of perky-pecced boys onto my wall so I can use them as human shields; my hunky disguise, my boyband safeguard. All I can hear is gay static. There are no discernable gay sounds anywhere on my radar. No gay people in my orbit, no gay news, no gay dogs even.

It's dark, and everything and everyone has shut up except for the Wonga pigeon that's taken over my four-four. All the Coreys have combined, and they're pushing down on my chest. I can't sleep because I feel like my wall is too loud.

*

In the morning, before I get up, I decide I want Julia up there too. I reason that twenty-two boys cancel out one woman. I put her on the second-last row from the bottom, using the same logic you'd use to answer a multiple-choice test without knowing the answers.

THE LITTLE TOWN ON THE RAILWAY TRACK

Kerry Reed-Gilbert

After many years of travelling from town to town and living in tents, paddock shacks and rented houses, we were finally going to get a home of our own – one that was stable, one we could call home. Our house in Condo had burnt down many years ago, and since then we had been travelling from one paddock to another, one place to another.

When Mummy was looking for a house, she had to think about its location, as we needed a good spot because we had to travel to pick fruit when various fruits were in season. So we were very lucky finding this little house in Koora, because we had tomatoes and asparagus in one direction and cherries in the other. And our fruit-picking paddocks didn't stop there. We could go and do the prunes at Greenthorpe and the tomatoes at Goolagong as well. We felt very lucky because we'd have paddocks surrounding us in three directions.

The big day comes and we're moving: we've got the new house and it even has some acres to go with it. Mummy's so proud that it's ours, and so are we – and the best thing is, we don't have to travel all the time and live in strange places.

The most important thing, though, is the welfare can't get us: we'll have our own house and they can't say anything. When our house got burnt down all those years ago in Condo, Mummy and our family built a shack with a bus for us to live in, and the welfare didn't like it so much and came and told Mummy she had to get us a house or they'd take us to the homes. So we packed our bags and headed for the paddocks.

You see, us four younger kids, we were state wards: two boys and two girls; we came in twos – Paddy and Lynnie, Kevin and me. I'm the youngest and I'm twelve years old when we move to Koora. We have bigger brothers and sisters in our family, but they are all grown up and don't live with us. For us kids, moving to this little town meant that we had a place to call home.

Our house is a bit run-down, but we're happy and I'm in heaven: we have a bath tub but it's got a copper in it – that means we have to light a fire so we can have hot water. I won't mind chopping wood for this fire at all. I run into the kitchen telling Mummy I 'bags' first bath. She turns around laughing at me, saying 'yes' and that she'd even get the boys to light it for me today as a special treat.

Our Uncle Raymond (Mummy's brother) came down from Sydney to help us move; him and Paddy do all the heavy lifting. Mummy helps as much as she can – we all do. My older sister Maureen is here too helping us, but she's big and pregnant; her belly sticks out, making it hard for her to do much.

All the furniture's inside the house, and finally we're done. All we have left to do is pack away our clothes. After all the work is done, Uncle Raymond asks Mummy if Paddy can go up to the pub to have a drink with him, as he's just turned eighteen. She lets him go; it's his first time – he's never been to a pub before. We don't have alcohol at our house, and no one is allowed to bring any home.

Time passes and us kids are playing outside on the road – the dust is flying all around us as we play tag – and all of a sudden we hear noises and lots of screaming coming from up the main street. Kevin runs inside the house, yelling about all the noise. Mummy and Maureen rush out as they know straight away the men are in trouble – they didn't need to be told. Mummy tells us kids to stay put and not to follow them.

We stay and wait but they don't come back. Kevin jumps on his bike and rides to the park so he can see what's going on. When he comes back, he says, 'The pub, the whole pub, are fighting with them.' Kevin, Lynnie and me run to help, and we're halfway there when we meet them coming home. Blood's dripping from a gash on Paddy's face, and Uncle Raymond has blood on him too but he's trying to laugh it off. I think he's trying to stop people worrying too much. The men are smashed up a little bit, but they reckon the other blokes look worse than them. Mummy just wants to get them home.

They tell their story about how some blokes in the pub started making comments about blacks, saying they don't want any blacks living in their town and they don't want blacks in their pub either. Mummy's running around tearing up an old sheet to make a bandage for Paddy's hand – he doesn't know how he hurt it but it has a big cut on it. The kettle is on, and Lynnie and me are making a pot of tea while we listen.

Uncle Raymond tells us how all of them at once jumped him and Paddy. Uncle Raymond laughs and says, 'Don't worry, they got more than they bargained for. Serves 'em right.' A few more swear words come out of his mouth and then he gets even angrier as he calls them 'gutless' because, when Mummy and Maureen arrived, they even wanted to fight them. Uncle Raymond's a returned war hero so he is really furious. He reckons they wouldn't have lasted in the army for a day.

Us kids talk about it later and start laughing. Serves them right – we hope Uncle and Paddy flogged them real good. That'll teach them for messing with the blacks. I hope they got hurt real bad. Mummy tells us to be careful: we are not to go anywhere alone at all; and we aren't even allowed to play out the front in case any of them decide to come down for another round.

Paddy comes and sits with us younger ones outside under my favourite tree; we all talk about what happened and we get pretty fired up about the people in the town. We all agree we can fight with each other and that's alright, but no one else can fight with us. We hate this town already; we've only been here a little while, not even a day, just moved in and already they're causing us heartache. Tears form in my eyes as I realise this town isn't going to be our little slice of heaven after all.

But even after all that, our spirits couldn't be squashed, because it was still wonderful to have our very own house. Days go by and soon it's time for me to be enrolled in the primary school here. Lynnie and Kevin head to Young High School: they catch the bus every day; it's a long way for them to travel back and forth.

Mummy's still worried about what happened at the pub so she walks me to and from the school each day; I tell her I'll be alright but she doesn't listen. She may be able to protect me outside the school, but she can't once I'm inside. I get teased and taunted every day.

Some of the kids write my name in the dirt and write things about me there. They make sure the teacher's not around, and when I walk out of class there's a message calling me a *gin* and saying other things too. I fight with them. I have punch-ups with the boys when they say things to me. I ain't scared of no one.

After a few punch-ups, though, they leave me alone because I can beat most of them at fighting. I have a best friend named Heather, and she's white and pretty cool. I hate school but I don't tell Mummy what's happening there.

The grown-ups in the town are real mean – they hate us blacks. Even the policeman, Constable Saunders, is as bad as the rest of the town. He ran over our dogs for no reason, and they were only little ones. And people did terrible things to the rest of our animals: we had some pigs and one day while we were away somebody came and shot pellets into them, even into their teats. I wonder how can people do mean things like that?

They even shot at Mummy one time. We have a cow called Mini Moo – she's named after Lynnie – and she had a baby, and one day Mummy went to feed them and the lady across the way shot at her. The bullet went through Mummy's hair. Mummy goes to see Constable Saunders and he says he'll talk to our neighbour. He comes back and says to Mummy that the woman thought Mummy was trespassing on her land and he does nothing more. She knew it was our land; that's just an excuse. I hate this town.

Mummy wants her charged. 'She could've killed me!' Constable Saunders still doesn't want to charge her. Angry and determined, Mummy drives the seventeen miles to the police station in Cowra and gets her charged. They go to court and the woman gets about two hundred hours of weekend detention. They should make her rot in jail for months as far as I am concerned. Mummy feels sorry for her because she's a little bit *gwarnnee* (gone in the head) and she has a new baby. I don't feel sorry for her. I hate her for trying to hurt my mother.

The people in this town persecute us. They stalk our house at night-time; we can hear them outside, laughing and talking, trying to scare us into leaving town. Mummy walks outside, sings out to them, calling them cowards and telling them they had better watch out if she catches them. She tells them she has a gun, but she doesn't really.

None of us kids are allowed to go anywhere outside after dark by ourselves. We can't even go out to the toilet at night: we gotta go in twos, and Mummy stands at the door and watches. She has a big *bundi* ready in case there's any trouble. But if it gets too late and we gotta go to the toilet, we've got a bucket inside to use if we need it. Terror is outside our door, and we can't do anything about it.

Constable Saunders is more racist than the whole town put together. He harasses us kids, even when we go to the shop or the disco that they have at the town hall. He comes along and lets the tyres down on Kevin's and my pushbikes. We start arguing with him, telling him 'he has no right to do that. What about the other kids' bikes? They're standing right beside ours.

Is he gonna let them down too?' He never touches anyone else's, only ours.

After he leaves, we swear about him and call him names. We've gotta walk our bikes home now. When we get home we tell Mummy. She goes after him – she won't let anyone harass us, even if it is a policeman. He tells her he's the law and he can do whatever he wants and she can't stop him from harassing us all the time.

She's had enough of him and one day she decides to write to his boss and put in a complaint. She tells him about being shot at, about Constable Saunders not charging our neighbour – how she had to go to Cowra to have the woman charged. How he deliberately ran over our dogs, killing them. How the townspeople were shooting our animals and stalking our house at night and how he picks on us kids whenever he sees us up the street without her.

Constable Saunders is in big trouble and he doesn't like it. He comes to Mummy and asks her to withdraw the complaint and he will change his ways, but Mummy says, 'No.' She has a favourite saying – 'a leopard doesn't change its spots' – and I think that suits him down to a tee. He's never going to change.

Constable Saunders is sent elsewhere and we're happy to see the back of him and hope there's no blackfellas in the town he's going to 'cause we know they are gonna cop it real bad. Soon our life settles down, and the majority of the townspeople start to accept the blacks living in their town. The kids become our friends, but my special schoolgirl friendship with Heather will always be the guiding light of what true friendship is about, as she too took on the town when she decided that she would be my best friend.

Looking back, Koora was a hard town to live in, especially when you knew that most of the people in that town hated you not because of you as a person but because of who you represented. I often think of my mother trying to keep the welfare from our door, a roof over our heads, clothes on our back and food in our mouths. We grew up trying to stay out of white people's sight, but our Aboriginality made us the target for every man and his dog who wanted to hate us on the basis of race.

When people say to me 'you mob live in the past', I say to them, 'No, the past lives in us, because if I can stand in front of you and talk about the segregation and apartheid that I've experienced in my own country, it can't be the past because I am very much living.'

SAM

Faustina Agolley

Mum always finds it hard to talk about him.

One day, around age five, I come home from school and ask her why I don't have a father. She isn't prepared to answer at the time, yet she's been expecting this question for a while. The next day at work, she calls a friend in tears, trying to find ways to broach the subject with me.

As I get older, I talk about him factually.

My father passed away from a car accident in London when I was a child. Never 'my dad'. It seemed too casual. *Father*.

People ask more. I tell them other stray facts I've learnt from hearing Mum speak of him in public. Facts that make no sense to me.

How old were you?

Seven weeks old.

Oh my god, you weren't a child, you were a baby.

How old was he?

In his thirties.

That's so terrible. Your poor mother. And her?

Thirty.

The only other facts I know until I'm a teenager are that his name was Samuel and that he was from Ghana. I learn to say that Ghana is in West Africa, for people who don't know where

Ghana is, or think Africa is a country. I also explain this to make a point to those confused by the sight of a Chinese woman with a black child. *Yes, this beautiful Chinese woman is my birth mother.* Heads turn when my brother and I walk into a Chinese restaurant with our family for yum cha on weekends.

I grow up knowing his absence, instead of his stories. Random consequences follow his passing. I am pulled out of class to sit with an apparent counsellor, who asks me to talk and draw about my feelings. Mum has to juggle three jobs. My brother gets into fights at school. He runs away from our house in Clayton to my grandparents' home nearby. The second time he runs away, Mum makes the decision to move us all under their roof. It is all because of my father. My father, who passed away when I was a baby.

And your mum never remarried? No.

She's so strong.

If I ask Mum a question about my father, she usually says that she can't remember the answer. If I am persistent, her voice quivers, a long silence follows and her soft brown eyes turn to anguish. Tears roll down her gentle face. In these moments I know I've gone too far. Asking questions, being curious, wanting to know anything beyond the violent, bleak facts of my father's death causes unattended trauma to the only parent I know and love. So I learn not to ask.

And yet, the trauma still looms between the three of us: trauma is conflated with a man who had a full life. A life I want to know about. But asking about it stuns Mum into a bereaved silence, the news of his death makes strangers horrified. I am lost.

Television

I spend a great deal of the early years of high school faking being sick so I can stay at home and watch *The Oprah Winfrey Show*.

I know the usual rhythm of the morning and the exact time to hijack it. Our rooster trumpets to punctuate the arrival of dawn and, although I always expect it, the sound makes me chuckle every time. I hear the familial tones of Kung Kung and Mama saying their twice-daily rosary, the smell of rice cooking, Mum quietly slipping out for another shift in the oncology ward at Moorabbin Hospital, and my brother leaving for a day of lectures and lab study at Monash University. Then, alas! My imagined sickness strikes, and I helplessly remain in bed.

Kung Kung observes me as he walks past my room. Then my grandmother, Mama, comes in.

'Ah-Mei, Ah-Mei, school now.' 'Mama, I'm sick.'

I cover my face with my doona. The sheets shield any evidence of me breaking character.

I hear Kung Kung, in his dulcet tones, inform Sacred Heart's secretary that I won't be in school that day. Once the phone hits the receiver, I feel free. There's a quiet celebration beneath my sheets, before I settle quickly back into the mysterious illness that has supposedly befallen my long-limbed, now-fragile body. The sickness conveniently remains until the day shifts closer and closer to Oprah's time on screen. Moments before Oprah's show begins, I am miraculously healed.

Besides my brother and the South African Perez family down the road, television is the portal to my black collective experience. My people are Will Smith and the Banks family who live in a town called Bel-Air. The sisters I party with are Lauryn Hill, Missy Elliott, TLC, Alicia Keys and Destiny's Child, who show up reliably every weekend, on *Video Hits*.

They all make me feel special and part of something bigger. But there's something else about Oprah. Oprah is our matriarch.

She radiates on screen. A full hour with Oprah is worth trading a day of school for. In a world of trashy, once-a-dog-always-a-dog television talk shows, she teaches me how to be a better woman in the world. Her audience screams with joy at the sight of her, and I feel their exhalation all the way from Chicago to Clayton. 'I'm going to work for you one day,' I say to Oprah, on the television screen. The words fall out of my mouth and I don't know why. All I know is that the pull is strong.

Boxes

Springvale is different from most suburbs in Melbourne. It's a home away from home for people from Malaysia, Vietnam, China, Indonesia and many other places. The main streets are lined with storefronts signed with bold fire-engine red and gold Asian writing. Roast duck and crispy pork hang in restaurant windows.

Most weekends of my teenage years are spent following Mum to stock up on groceries we can't buy elsewhere. We collect a lotto ticket from the newsagent adorned with Maneki Neko cats waving their motorised paws for good luck, and then I get to eat my favourite food: steamed and baked *charsiew baos*, a *banh mi* loaded with extra shredded pickled carrot, and coconut-filled *kweh*. If Aunty Rose is in town from Malaysia, we visit her too.

Mum and Aunty speak in part Fouzhou and part English over tea and treats. I zone out of the conversations and walk around Aunty's backyard. One weekend I look inside her garage. It is full of boxes. I notice a pile with my surname on them. *AGOLLEY* in large print gives me permission to open them at once. I break the seal on the box closest to me and release a burst of mildew. I look inside; I pull out vinyl records. The Supremes, The Beatles, Dionne Warwick. On closer inspection, handwritten on each of these records, in blue or black ballpoint pen, is the name *SAMMY*. The ends of the S's curl more elaborately than most handwriting I've seen, and the A's, the double M's and the Y's look like they were written with striking speed: their strokes sharp and confident.

The hairs on my arms stand tall. I pick up the box, race inside Aunty's home and interrupt their conversation. My discovery is more important.

I show Mum the records. A shock of recognition dawns upon her face. She professes forgetting that she brought any of his belongings to Australia. Unlike a lot of the times she has told me she can't remember, I believe her.

Aunty Rose isn't surprised, and says they've sat in her garage the whole time. A whole thirteen years.

Huh.

We all head back to the garage to inspect the other boxes. There are photographs. I lay my eyes on my father for the first time. He's tall and handsome, with a 1000-watt incandescent smile. No wonder Mum fell in love with him. Almost every photo seems to capture an intangible quality. He's the life of the party: he brings a presence, a magnetism. He looks like he *knows* it.

There are photos of them from when they were dating. Young love. His arms around Mum by their Mini Cooper. In another photo he's smartly dressed in a brown suit, dancing among England's snow. In the summer months, he wears flared denim jeans, and yellow t-shirts that hug his strong, lean physique.

A flood of memories come to Mum. She begins to tell me stories. She refers to him endearingly as 'Sam' or 'your dad'. I've never heard Mum speak like this before. They met when Mum was studying to be a nurse. My father was already a nurse, and specialised in psychiatry. Mum tells me about one of their first dates. He took her to see the Temptations. He was Mum's first and only partner.

I find a diploma in social studies. He wanted to work for the World Health Organization. They had a beautiful wedding, with twenty friends at best, because neither set of parents could afford the tickets to fly to London. And they had dreams to move to Australia, my mother and father, I'm told.

I find precisely ten photos taken at my birth. A lot of them are taken by my brother, who was seven years old at the time, and have been shot inaccurately. You can see the tops of our parents' heads and a lot of wall and ceiling. Despite these shoddy attempts, there's a photo of my father and me. He's holding me and, unlike in the many other photos I see of him, he looks exhausted. I'm at the bottom of the photo, which is mouldy from water damage. There is just the one photo of us together, and it's disfigured by nature, which gives me the chills. But it will do.

Sound

The boxes moved to Mum's townhouse the day we left Aunty's.

I ask Mum to buy a record player. I wipe the mould off the vinyl discs. I feel that the first record I play is important, like ushering in my father's soul to dance with me. Diana Ross and the Supremes seems appropriate. I place the needle on the vinyl, and the machine picks up speed and plays 'Stop In the Name of Love'. I've heard this song many times before, but the vinyl makes the song sound warmer, like I've returned home to its original precious form. It's an awakening. Although the song is familiar to me, the sound is astonishingly new. It's as if my father, posthumously and in spirit, is revealing something different about our shared love of music. Unlike previous times, I hear every instrument, every intention, and the orchestration is perfectly mixed. It's clear that all the times I heard this song before were counterfeits. I thank Mum for keeping the records. His once-forgotten possessions are ours again, and this man feels even more real to me.

I try to call him 'Dad'. It sounds weird coming out of my mouth, but I keep trying now and again.

After some months, Mum and I make time to tend to the boxes again. She excitedly breaks the seal of one of them in her living room. A smaller box is inside. Mum is intrigued and opens it. There's an envelope that reveals a macabre discovery. Someone took photos at Dad's funeral. His dark coffin is closed, but there's a window that reveals his face. Markings from the car accident. He's scratched and wounded. He's there but he isn't: as if his essence left his body a long time ago.

I look for Mum's reaction. She's breathless. There's the usual silence, but then, this time, Mum bellows out a guttural, harrowing cry. I've never heard Mum cry like this before. It rams into my body and the trauma fills every part of me, and I cry at her distress and mine. But I feel guilty for my tears.

In another photo are the solemn faces of men and women on the church steps. My mum stands outside; her eyes are vacant. My brother's hands are on the hearse's window. He peers in to see the coffin … Dad … before the hearse pulls away.

Alizata Mahama

The phone rings at Kung Kung and Mama's house. It's for Mum. On the other end of the line is Dad's sister, Aunty Alima. She tells Mum she travelled from Ghana to London, and arrived at our doorstep to find out from our neighbour that we moved to Australia over a decade ago.

I don't know what else is exchanged on the phone call, but it's enough for Mum to take money off the mortgage for our first overseas trip.

'It's important you know your dad's side,' she says to my brother and me.

We land in Ghana at night. When the plane door opens, I'm almost bowled over by the hot tropical air. We walk out of the airport, and it's so different from a crowd in Melbourne: all the faces we see are black as midnight. Alima's husband, Adam, emerges from the crowd. He's our host for the two-week trip, as Alima is still in London.

Adam takes us to see our grandmother for the first time. Mum hasn't even met her before. Her name is Alizata Mahama. She's a lot taller than my Chinese grandmother, and there's a peaceful reverence about her. Language is a barrier between us all: she speaks in Ga, and Adam needs to translate.

She blesses Allah for this moment, and then gently directs her attention to my brother and me. Adam translates: 'She says you look just like your father.'

We already knew this in some way, but with him being gone for so long it feels ephemeral. Her words ground us in a sense of home: in our dad, in her and in Ghana.

We're all moved by this moment, and by all the circumstances over the years that finally culminated in us being together.

Grandma makes fufu for us for our first night in Accra. I sit over the two bowls. One looks like spicy curry; the other, the *fufu* itself, looks like raw dough. It smells sour. I'm told it's cassava and plantain. We're taught to pick the dough with our fingers and dip it into the soup. I pick the dough, and it's soft and sticky. I dip it in the curry and place it in my mouth. It's the spiciest soup I've ever tasted, and the fermented smell of the *fufu* singes my nose. I've been hungry for a couple of hours now, but I can't stomach this. I feel awful for not liking Grandma's dish. Word gets back to Grandma that the dish is too spicy for me. The next day, Grandma arrives from the market holding a live chicken and makes a milder stew. It's custom to slay a live animal for the arrival of family. These gestures, the cooking, all imbued with love, are akin to my life in Australia with my Kung Kung and Mama. I couldn't be prouder of my dual roots.

Throughout our trip everyone we encounter wants to know our name, and once they hear we are Agolley there's a recognition. 'Ah, you are from the north!'

We're of the Bawku people, and our tribe is Kusasi. Hearing that I am from a lineage of an actual tribe makes me feel like the coolest kid on the planet. Bawku runs close to the border of Burkina Faso and Togo. We consider going there, but we're told it's much hotter than Accra, and the fact that I've fainted a couple of times already quickly makes that decision.

Slave ports still sit on Ghana's coastline. I stand on the history that binds us all globally, the violent colonialism. I see shackles, and cannons that point out to a turbulent sea. There's a sign above a door that says *POINT OF NO RETURN*. I stand under the sign and touch the door frame. I ruminate over the thousands of lives that were forced through there, a shared global black history, and a past that cannot be undone.

I find out that my dad had a brother named Peter Agolley. One day, at age sixteen, Peter went missing walking home from school. He never returned home. He was likely taken for modern slavery, which was common at the time, and still common today. Throughout my grandmother's life she would ask, 'Will I see my son before I die?'

My time in Ghana puts a fire in me. I come back to Australia a changed young woman. Knowing that I have learning difficulties, I read every prescribed textbook and novel in the summer. Then Year 10 commences, and I sit in the front of all my classes, ready to make the most of what I've got.

Video Hits

The discovery of my father's records; skipping school to watch Oprah Winfrey; my love of black music; my newfound confidence and work ethic – all of these memories collide when, years later, while studying at two universities, I land my dream job hosting *Video Hits* at Channel 10.

My work doesn't feel like work at all. Most of it is self-directed research in an office, in front of a computer with access to a vast archive of music videos. The payoff is the privilege of sitting opposite artists that have soundtracked the lives of millions of people – from emerging artists of the time, like Florence Welch and Calvin Harris, to living legends such as Ice Cube, Big Boi, Jack White and Green Day, to idols in the making, like Bruno Mars, Rihanna and Adele. I sneak my dog, Bo, into the fancy hotel room with Rihanna. I host Adele's first Australian television interview from a beautiful hotel in Soho, London. Adele picks up my guitar and plays 'Crazy for You'. Then she names my guitar Bruce. I get to meet some of my sisters from watching *Video Hits* in my high-school days. I dance with Kelly Rowland in downtown Los Angeles; I interview Alicia Keys backstage at Homebush Stadium. 'You … I like you,' Keys says. 'You did a great job!'

I'm sure all of this would've made Dad proud. I'm sure he would've been pinching himself with me: life in Australia, a place he wanted to live, and a daughter with an education, the opportunity to travel and living her full life.

I am his legacy, and I hope to do him proud.

PERFECT CHINESE CHILDREN

Vanessa Woods

If there was ever anyone I wanted to stab in the heart with a chopstick, it was my cousin David.

'What happened to the four per cent?' my mother says, looking at my maths exam.

'I got ninety-six. What else do you want?'

'Don't talk back,' my mother snaps. 'Ninety-six isn't 100. If you want to do well you have to try harder. David just got 99.9 on his HSC.'

I dig my nails into my chair and wait for the punchline.

'He asked me to ring up the school board and contest the score. Ha! Imagine that. The lady on the phone laughed.'

My mother shakes her head in wonder, as though David is the god of a new religion she's following.

'It really was 100,' she says confidentially. 'They had to scale it down for the school.'

Usually Chinese parents don't have bragging rights over other people's children, but my mother tutored David through high school, so his HSC score is her crowning victory.

My maths exam, with the scrawled red '96' that I was so proud of, begins to look ratty. Untidy figures rush across the page as if they're about to make a run for it. David's handwriting is famous for looking like it came out of a typewriter.

'He's going to medical school,' she sighs. 'He's going to be a heart surgeon, just like Victor Chang.'

The reason my mother harps on about David so much is probably that her own two children don't warrant much praising over the mahjong table. My sister Bronnie has been expelled from piano lessons twice, and me, well, I am trouble on all fronts. I'm the child who talks back and gives viperous looks to her elders. In all my life I've only learnt two Cantonese phrases: *Kung Hei Fat Choi*, Happy New Year (saying this at the right time earned you *lycee*, red envelopes stuffed with cash), and *gno sat neyko say yun tow*, a phrase I hear often from my Aunty Yee Mah that roughly translates to 'I will chop off your dead man's head.'

'Jasmine just bought her mother a $600,000 apartment in Hong Kong,' mother says wistfully before going for the touchdown. '*In cash*.'

Jasmine is David's perfect sibling. She is a stockbroker in New York, married to an investment banker. The photographer at her Sydney wedding cost $12,000.

'Jasmine only got 80 per cent on her HSC.' My mother looks hopeful, as though retards like me might have a chance after all. Then she shakes herself out of it. 'But no one paid any attention to her until she started making money.'

My mother looks around our tiny two-bedroom apartment. The kitchen is fine if you're a troll and enjoy dim, cramped spaces. The carpet is grey and curling around the edges. The furnishings are the type you pick up by the side of the road. There are occasional glimpses of the life we had before. A Ming vase. A black lacquered screen with flourishes of gold. But the priceless antiques give the apartment the ambience of a refugee camp, as though we managed to save a few precious things before catastrophe threw us into squalor.

When I visit my cousins in their two-storey palaces, their kitchens as big as our apartment and their lucky trees with life-sized peaches of jade in the foyer, my secret pleasure is to creep upstairs and press my face into the pale, plush carpet.

*

We are poor because my mother's financial history has been overshadowed by unlucky four – *sie*, which sounds uncomfortably close to *sei*, death. She was the fourth child born in the fourth decade of the century. Her father gave all his money to Chiang Kai-shek, the Chinese leader of the Nationalist Party who lost China to the Communists in 1949. My mother's brothers and sister were also left destitute, but they all married suitable Chinese spouses who helped them earn back the family fortune.

My mother, with her silken black hair and face like a doll, could have done better than anyone. But instead, she married my father, a *gweilo*, a ghost person, a white man. In our world, inter-racial marriages are unheard of. We don't know any other Chinese who married Australians.

'Barbarians,' Yee Mah would say. 'Chinese were using chopsticks while *gweilos* were eating with their hands.'

My father was a charming but troubled Vietnam vet, prone to occasional psychotic episodes and heavy drinking. When he brought my mother home to meet his family, my grandfather's first words to her were, 'Jesus Christ – a chongalewy-chow Sheila!'

My mother did everything required of a dutiful Chinese wife. She spent three hours baking *dun tahts*, the pastry as flaky around the warm egg custard as those served for the Kangxi Emperor at the Manchu imperial feast. She did the ritualistic two-day preparation for Peking duck and gave herself RSI from rolling perfectly circular Mandarin pancakes. She served orgasmic banquets to my father's friends and unwittingly to his mistresses.

It wasn't a surprise to anyone except my mother when my father divorced her and left her for a white barbarian when I was five and my sister was two.

My mother almost slit her wrists in shame. We didn't know

anyone who was divorced. Chinese spouses had affairs, slept in separate rooms and barely spoke to each other, but no one divorced. It was a matter of saving face.

Her own life in shreds and two dollars in her pocket, we became her only hope. We would be brilliant at school, earn accolades and awards until the day when we were educated, rich and could lavish her with the money and attention she deserved.

Unfortunately, it isn't quite working out that way. As a result of the impure blood of my father, my sister and I don't even look Chinese. We both have Chinese hair, dead straight and completely resistant to the crimping tools crucial to the '80s, but my sister's hair is blonde and mine is the colour of burnt toast.

As time goes by, it becomes clear to her that we are going the way of *Australian* children. The ones who don't work as hard, are loud and uncouth and, worst of all, talk back to their parents and hold chopsticks near the pointed ends, like peasants.

Until the divorce, we had barely seen my Chinese relatives. Suddenly, from our big, comfortable house in Turramurra, we were living in a troll cave in Kingsford near Vietnamese boat people. Instead of a mother who stayed home all day cooking delicious and exotic meals, I had a mother who worked as a secretary for fourteen hours a day. And every day after school, my sister and I get dumped with my Aunty Yee Mah and my three cousins.

It is well known among all my new relatives under the age of sixteen that you do not fuck with Yee Mah. Yee Mah isn't fat but there is a heaviness to her. The back of her hand feels like a ton of bricks. She once broke a bed just by sitting on it. Besides the famous 'I will chop off your dead man's head,' she sometimes pulls out a box of matches, holds one out close to our mouths and hisses, 'If you are lying to me I will burn out your tongue.' In a way that convinces you she absolutely is not joking.

Her daughter Erica is seventeen and the high-achieving darling. Robert is number one son and therefore immune to any criticism or punishment. However, her other son, Patrick, my sister Bronnie and I, we are all under ten and therefore under her complete jurisdiction.

So every day after school, Bronnie, Patrick and I get up to mischief and then try to stop Yee Mah finding out. On the weekends there are more cousins, aunties and uncles to visit, most of whom aren't even related to us. The hope is that some of their Chineseness will rub off on us and Bronnie and I will become bright, smart vessels and alleviate some of my mother's disgrace.

Bronnie and I never quite blend in, but our new playmates are always too polite to mention it until one day, Erica storms out of the playground.

'Australians are retarded,' she says churlishly. Erica is seven years older than me and I worship her. She is everything a good girl should be: smart, respectful, and her boyfriends buy her large stuffed animals that I secretly covet.

There's a rhyme going around the playground. The kids pull up the corners of their eyes, then pull them down, chanting: 'Chinese, Japanese, hope your kids turn Pickanese.' On 'Pickanese,' they lift one eye up and one eye down, giving the clear impression of mental retardation. Like all bad jokes that come into fashion, this one is going around like wildfire, and Erica has apparently been socked with it 150 times during lunch.

As we wait outside school for Yee Mah, I catch Erica giving me a sideways look, as though she is seeing me for the first time, realising that I look more like one of *them* than like her.

'Yeah,' I quickly say. 'Australians are dog shit. Their babies will all eat dog shit and die.'

I have to be liberal with the faeces because the week before, my cousin Victor was bashed at the 7Eleven in Maroubra. A local gang was targeting Asians, and a couple of them beat up Victor and stole his bike. I saw him staggering down the road, bleeding from his nose with scrapes along his arms. The cheekbone beneath his eye was swollen and red, like a ripe fruit about to burst.

There is also a rumour going around that Asian-haters have been stabbing Asians with syringes full of AIDS blood in the cinemas on George Street. As a result, we don't go to the cinema for at least a year.

Yee Mah's car pulls up and we all climb in. Erica doesn't speak to me for the rest of the day. Without knowing why, I am ashamed.

*

Every Saturday, about twenty of our 'inner circle' go to yum cha. The children are fed *cha siu bao* pork buns to fill us up so we don't eat any of the expensive stuff, while the grown-ups brag about themselves by bragging about their children.

'Patrick just passed his Grade Seven piano exam,' says Yee Mah. 'And Erica is top of her class. Again.'

Aunty Helen talks about Jasmine's new office in the World Trade Centre and David's internship.

And my poor mother sits with nothing to say. No awards we have won. No praise from our teachers. No marks high enough for medical or law school. It is the ultimate aspiration for any Chinese mother to have a child who is a lawyer or a doctor. The best-case scenario would be a lawyer who defends doctors in court.

'You would make such a good barrister,' my mother sometimes tells me. 'You and that slippery tongue of yours.'

Such two-faced compliments are the staple of my existence. '*Ho liang*,' my relatives say. 'How pretty.' But I always sense another implication: at least I am pretty, because there isn't much else going for me.

Even worse, Bronnie wants to be an actress and I want to be a writer. My mother can't think of anything less likely to lead to one of us buying her an apartment.

'You'll end up penniless in an attic,' she tells my sister. As for me, she clips out cuttings from the newspaper to prove that most writers end up dead of starvation in the gutter.

*

To twist the chopstick even deeper, I am developing an aversion to school. In class, I am miserable, churlish and awkward. I don't have any friends, and a boy called Owen throws rocks at me after class. There is another charming game going around the playground in which you pinch someone and say, 'Tip, you've got the germs.'

I am always the original source of the germs.

Finally, to escape being the human turd, I lock myself in the school toilets for three hours. When a teacher comes to find me, I tell her I've been vomiting. Half an hour later my mother pulls up outside school and drives me back to our apartment. She cooks me chicken soup with noodles and wraps the bed sheets around me so tight I feel like I am in an envelope, about to be posted somewhere exotic. I love the garlic and chilli smell of her hands. She takes my temperature and smoothes my forehead and continually asks if I am all right.

I suffer another week through the germ game until I lock myself in the toilet again. This time, Yee Mah picks me up from school.

'What's wrong with you?' she demands.

'I threw up in the toilet.'

'You don't smell like vomit,' she says suspiciously.

'It was only a little bit.'

She looks at me slyly from the corner of her eye. 'Do you know why your mother is poor?'

I shake my head.

'Because of you. She has to pay your school feels, very expensive. You see how tired she is? You must pay her back with good marks. Otherwise you will make her shamed.'

The emotional terrorism continues until we get to her house. There is no chicken soup or tucking into bed. I have to sit on the couch with Bobo, her mother-in-law, for six hours, watching daytime television until my sister and Patrick come home.

*

'Mum,' I tug on my mother's arm during Saturday yum cha as she chews on a prawn dumpling, part of yet another meal she can't pay for. She looks down at me absentmindedly. 'Mum!'

'Yes, sweetheart?'

'Can you buy me that fish?'

'What?'

There are over fifty brim stuffed in the tank of the yum cha restaurant. They are squashed so tight together they can hardly move. In the middle there is a beautiful golden one, with scales that shimmer in the light of the crystal chandeliers. I want my mother to buy it so I can take it to Bondi Beach in a plastic bag and set it free in the ocean.

'Don't be stupid,' my mother says. 'They are for eating.'

The eating habits of my sister and I are yet another source of embarrassment. We are very wasteful. We don't eat chicken's feet. We don't suck the jelly out of fish eyeballs and we refuse to eat the creamy filling inside prawn heads.

'Just that one. *Pleeeeeeease*.'

'No.'

'Why?'

'We can't afford it,' she hisses.

I let go of her hand and catch up with my sister and Patrick, who are playing in the elevators. We like to go into the elevators and push all the buttons. Go all the way up. Go all the way down. Occasionally, we get out on a floor we aren't supposed to be on and run up and down the corridors.

It doesn't bother me that we are poor. I've found a way to combat it – I steal from other children. When I get kicked out of class for misbehaving, which is often, I rifle through the school bags of all the other kids and steal their lunch money, as well as anything else I like.

When I finally get caught, I'm terrified Yee Mah will burn off my tongue like she's always threatening. Instead, my mother sits me down at the dining-room table. She is very quiet. She puts her hand on my hand and says, 'What do other children have that you don't?'

If I were smarter, I would hear her heart breaking.

'Erasers with Snow White on them,' I say without hesitating.

'All right,' says my mother. 'Go to your room.'

As I leave, I see her bow her head, as if she's carrying a great burden. It's shame. And she's not ashamed of me, she's ashamed of herself. For failing to teach me the difference between right and wrong. For failing to make me feel like I am warm and safe and don't need to steal from other kids to make up for everything I don't have.

The next day, the Snow White erasers are on the dining-room table. I don't even want them.

*

When I finally ring my mother to tell her my HSC score, she sounds delighted.

'You got 88.8? Very lucky number. You will be rich for sure.' There is an odd note in her voice, one of momentary regret. That this isn't the moment when I exceed all her expectations.

'Very rich,' she says again, as if to comfort herself with an ancient Confucian wisdom: *Just think how it could have been worse*.

As for me, I've given up hoping she will tell me she is proud. I no longer begrudge my friends their mothers who overflow with constant affirmation and nurturing encouragement. When she criticises me with all the sensitivity of a Japanese scientist harpooning a whale, and I feel the slow-burning resentment building to rage, I bite my slippery tongue.

Instead, I fossick through my memory for one of my earliest recollections.

My mother is in the kitchen. Steam rises from the wok and oil spatters over her hands. There is a delicious smell of soy sauce, garlic and chicken. She tips the contents of the wok into a dish, then spoons out chicken wings onto beds of rice. Chicken wings are the cheapest part of a chicken. She has bought all her salary can afford.

On my sister's plate there are two. On mine there are two. On hers, there is only one.

And in her sacrifice, I see love.

BE GOOD, LITTLE MIGRANTS

Uyen Loewald

Be good, little migrants
We've saved you from starvation
war, landlessness, oppression
Just display your gratitude
but don't be heard, don't be seen

Be good, little migrants
Give us your faithful service
sweep factories, clean mansions
prepare cheap exotic food
pay taxes, feed the mainstream

Be good, little migrants
Use leisure with prudence
sew costumes, paint murals
write music, and dance to our tune
Our culture must not be dull

Be good, little migrants
We've given you opportunity
for family reunion

equality, and status, though
your colour could be wrong

Be good, little migrants
Learn English to distinguish
ESL from RSL
avoid unions, and teach children
respect for institutions

Be good, little migrants
You may fight one another, but
attend Sunday School, learn manners
keep violence within your culture
save industry from criminals

Be good, little migrants
Intelligence means obedience
just follow ASIO, CIA
spy on your fellow countrymen
hunt commies for Americans

Be good, little migrants
Museums are built for your low arts
for your multiculturalism
in time, you'll reach excellence
Just waste a few generations.

QUESTION MARKS AND A THEORY OF VISION

Andy Jackson

I didn't grow up disabled. My body and its place in the world seemed normal to me. Why wouldn't it?

I grew up in Bendigo, a goldfields city in central Victoria, a city small enough to safely ride around on a bicycle unsupervised, but large enough to have a shopping mall and the first Myer in Australia. We lived in a relatively new suburb, with clusters of mid-century quarter-acre homes surrounded by former quarries that had become vacant lots. In the imaginations of the children who lived there, they were far from vacant. As soon as I could ride a bike, I was out there on those hillocks and dunes, daydreaming places where I could escape myself and belong at the same time.

My father was a salesman, tall and unusually shaped, with a prosthetic leg. I only learnt this latter detail later on. Mum was stoic and uninterested in focusing on the negatives. In photographs from the time, Dad wore white business shirts and had slicked-down hair. My brother and I clambered around him, his posture suggesting love, albeit undemonstrative, and mild disinterest. To remember him, I only have these photos, because when I was two, before my brain had the chance to develop the capacity for long-term memory, he had some kind of cardiac event, was rushed to hospital and died.

We lived halfway between the showgrounds and the hospital, and that now seems fitting. As it would turn out, I spent quite a bit of time being examined by medical specialists, on show.

*

My mother tells a story – I don't remember this, so you'll have to take her word for it – that on my first day of school she wasn't sure how I'd handle it socially. I was quiet, sensitive, bookish. So she told the teacher to keep half an eye on me. At some point, I disappeared from the playground. Soon enough, the teacher found me in the library, in a corner, reading to a small circle of other kids. Mum tells this story, as parents do, to show just how unusual, how precocious I was. But somewhere at the centre of that reading circle is someone preparing to put themselves on show – like being a poet, where the focus is both me and not me.

*

I didn't grow up disabled. Disabled was other people. People different from me. Pale-blue Spastic Society buses that drove haltingly through our neighbourhood, picking up and dropping off kids whom I had nothing to do with. They went to a special school. The air between us was charged and strange. There was so much I didn't understand about bodies, so many things that could go awry.

In late primary school, my best friend and I decided that we should start a private detective agency. We'd read lots of books, especially adventures and mysteries that could be solved with the right combination of confidence and intelligence. For some reason we thought Bendigo must have an abundance of unsolved riddles and problems that prepubescent boys could unravel. We placed a hand-drawn advertisement on the noticeboard of our classroom, which no one responded to. There was nothing special about us.

*

Around the age of twelve, I entered a growth spurt, and suddenly this blond-haired, pale-skinned, slightly gawky child began looking deformed. My spine bent and curved under the pressure. It pressed outwards and tilted me to the side. Unbeknown to me, my mother had been watching for years, wondering, quietly worried that I might have inherited something that would catapult me towards – what, exactly? A stareable body? Disability? My father? My spine was a kind of question mark.

Mum took me to an orthopaedic specialist in Melbourne, who said confidently, 'Yes, we really must operate soon.' Severe spinal curvature, especially if left unchecked, can cause great pressure on the internal organs. I needed to be stabilised, corrected. I thought 'soon' meant that very afternoon, that I'd be whisked into the Royal Children's Hospital nearby, home of the annual Good Friday Appeal, tragedy and sympathy, and within hours I'd be under anaesthetic, being fixed. In fact, the surgery would occur about two months later.

*

On my first night in hospital, after I was admitted, I watched Mum leave the ward with my older brother, who was fourteen at the time, walking beside her. She seemed quieter than usual, less upright, more uncertain. Unusually for him, he placed his arm around her, as they disappeared out of view. I know now he was telling her everything would be okay.

Later, Mum would tell me how fascinating it was that the sickest kids in the hospital, shadowed by cancer or aflame with burns, tended to be the least complaining, while the kids with minor ailments were endlessly pressing the button to summon the nurse, for painkillers, for attention. By implication, I wasn't one of *those* kids.

Another memory: standing exposed in a windowless room somewhere in the hospital, my clothes in a neat pile on a shelf. The click-flash of the camera, me in my underwear, an expression on my face that might be called blank but is more awkward, ambiguous. I might be hiding my embarrassment, or just hoping it will be over soon because it's cold there. I am standing as upright as I can, but this skeleton's version of normal is cursive.

*

The operations were, as is often the case, not entirely successful. The curvature was slightly corrected but continued with a vengeance as I grew. I have the same genetic condition my father had, Marfan syndrome, a heritable disorder of connective tissue. This means, apart from my visible difference, the valves of my heart will always be at risk of fraying and tearing. So far it's fine, thanks to medication and annual check-ups. When I was first diagnosed, the medical consensus was that a lifespan of over forty years was unlikely. I'm now forty-eight, almost the age my dad was when he died. These days, most people with Marfan – in Western countries anyway – will live until old age. Although mortality is always there, a companion, it doesn't loom quite so menacingly.

There's no doubt it's reassuring to have a name for your difference. And medicine can make life more manageable, can even save your life. But you always have to leave the hospital or the clinic, face the world and its hostility to question marks.

*

In my teenage years, was I disabled? I was Hunchback. Quasimodo. Someone to stare at, or shout things at as you drove past. Someone to pick on, or pity. A classmate with a Yorkshire accent as thick as his glasses, sitting in the bus seat in front of me on a school excursion, taunted me the entire two-hour trip. A young apprentice in overalls sped past me on his bike, asking, 'What's under your shirt, hunchy?' As I walked from English to Chemistry, I overheard one of the cool girls joking to her friend that I was someone she wanted as a boyfriend. Laughter isn't always contagious. And being stared at is a strange kind of fame. I absorbed it all, quietly, not knowing what to do with it. Well, I wrote some things in exercise books, but I didn't show anyone.

*

Plato had a theory of vision that now seems scientifically absurd but makes a lot of sense to some deep part of me. Instead of light coming into the eye, which is then interpreted by the brain, the idea was that the eye sent out a kind of 'fire' that then brought back information about what it encountered. A fire within each of us, lighting our way. This was the dominant theory until only a few centuries ago. Stories – especially ones that rely on their being a source of light inside us – are hard to shift. In fact, recent research suggested that around 50 per cent of adults believe in some version of the theory, even now.

We have all felt that uncanny sensation that someone is watching us. We can't see them, but we feel something over our shoulder, their intense gaze. It's as if their eyes are sending out tiny, tangible sparks of light, which tickle or singe our skin. To be physically different is to be continually assailed by these missiles of looking. Those of us who are stareable absorb these sparks into our bodies. We carry burn marks and develop scar tissue. We are tense, bracing ourselves for unwanted attention. We doubt ourselves, our beauty. These fires disable. They can even spread out beyond the hearth to burn others. At the same time, harnessed, they can warm and sustain.

*

One more memory: an open-mic poetry session in the back room of a Brunswick pub, early 2000s. A small circle of writers and those who hoped they could be. I'm around thirty years old. Grown up, but still green. I've been reading my poems in public for a few years now but haven't yet really written – or spoken – directly about my bodily difference. The MC says my name and I walk to the stage, a slight tremor of nerves fanning the embers in my chest.

I begin: 'I have a hunch / that curvature / can be aperture / given that light, like water, / does not travel in a straight line …'

A stunned, warm silence fills the room. When I finish the poem and the applause fades, I rush to the men's bathroom to cry in relief. I then pull myself together and emerge into a slightly different world.

For me, poetry is a way of affirming that bodily difference is a source of insight. It asks questions. It is an opening. It suggests another way of being together.

The same is true of saying *I am disabled*, as I do now.

WHEN WORLDS COLLIDE, WORDS FAIL

Thinesh Thillainadarajah
திநேஷ் தில்லைநடராஜா

On a September morning three years ago, Appa called me, crying on the phone.

Two weeks earlier, I had dropped off a letter at the mailbox around the corner, unsure of when it would reach Appa's tender hands on the other side of the world. Hands that swiped the metro card at four in the morning, wading through Canadian avalanches to make ends meet. Hands that had hung a canvas print of Mufasa and Simba on the wall above the bed he and I used to share, symbolic of just a morsel of the love that only children of immigrant parents know. The same hands that used to hold me on Saturday mornings as I split open chocolate eggs to reveal the plastic magic contained inside, magic that Appa revelled in as much as I.

When I saw 'Appa calling' on the screen of my phone, my heart sank, anticipating the disappointment of my parents, the breaking of a chain that stretched across the globe, holding them and me together. My white boyfriend, our relationship just shy of three years, stood in the doorway to our bedroom speaking to his own parents, as he had for years, in a kind honesty and openness I had never known.

Appa sobbed. He asked why I was choosing this. Through his wails, he asked why I had not told him earlier, said that he would have had another child to be my keeper. I wanted to comfort him, but in that moment I failed to do so, unable to articulate my thoughts the way my letter had, the way six months of writing and rewriting had allowed me to do. I never hated myself more – for speaking Tamil, if you can even call it that, with a childish cadence and a Western intonation, unable to bridge a canyon's worth of vocabulary between us. I wanted Appa to hear past my inarticulate sentences. I wanted my words to convey precision and conviction. I was desperately grasping at all the Tamil I could, but I could only muster up '*alavendaam*' ('do not cry'), removed from the poetic world of Surya and Jyothika – reminiscent of a lilt you'd hear in children's programming.

I choked on the silence and pain, unsure of where to take the conversation. No amount of YouTube videos and queer think pieces prepared me for this moment. But I was not naive enough to think they would. It does not get better. It just gets lost in communication.

Amma interjected. She said that someone she knew had got married – and had separated shortly after. In coded language, she insinuated that she was familiar with my secrets. She asked if I was okay – I was. She asked if I needed to speak to someone – I did not. She thanked me for sharing this part of myself and said I needn't worry. She dismissed Appa's sobs and wails, and said that he would get over it.

I felt a sense of calm take over. As I looked out the window of my apartment, the Australian sun's morning rays seemed to shine brighter with the glimmer of a salvageable relationship. Of course Amma, level-headed Amma, would know how to handle this. Amma, who would run to catch the bus in her $20 wedges to get to her factory job miles away, would again know what to do so we could make it through.

'Do not tell anyone about this,' Amma then said. And just like that, my heart sank to the floor.

There was silence, and in that silence it became clear that private tolerance – even private acceptance – was still public shame.

Amma and Appa now knew my deepest truths, and we were at the brink of a relationship we had never had before that morning. But the fear of stigmatisation, exclusion and gossip fodder would follow Amma and Appa, snapping at their heels like a pack of hungry wolves. That fear would drive them to keep up appearances for *Sithappa* and *Sithi* overseas, *Oor* gatherings, and *Kōyil* folks, enabling them to continue living their lives in relative peace. I was stupid to think that my parents' love could not withstand who I loved. It was not them not loving me or accepting me that would keep my love for him a secret. Rather, it was their fear of sharp tongues spitting venom and spreading lies about them, isolating them from their community and shredding their souls, and consequently shredding mine.

My queer identity took me away from not only my family, but also my Tamilness. I had split open the Red Sea, and torn myself away from the world that my parents had built for me stone by stone, and moved to Australia – a land that rejects my Tamilness – trading it in desperation to feed my queer soul. In the blood-orange desert, my queer identity was a battle I could fight alone, wrestling with myself in isolation, saving Amma and Appa from an unnecessary struggle with Tamil society. They'd spent their entire lives fighting for everything else that they had. Who was I to deprive them of the only community they connect with? The only space they have allowed themselves to have so I could grow up free from trauma and with the privilege of choosing to leave?

Now, as I sit in chrome birds suspended in the night sky, memorising the layouts of yellow flickering cities below me, I think about how the person I loved made the same journey across the world to understand where I came from, knowing it was unlikely he would be welcomed with open arms. I think about how he stayed in my old room, felt the *manjal* between his fingertips, dunked the *vadai* into the *sambar* at my best friend's wedding in a *Kurtha* – as just my 'friend'.

I wanted him to experience a fraction of Tamilness the way

I had and get to the fulcrum of my straddling identities, to sit through problematic *Rajinikanth* films with Appa, fall in love with the melodic richness of *Anjali*, eat *roast paan* and *sambal* on my family's cloth-covered couch with Amma, with the Tamil radio humming in the kitchen and Sun TV simultaneously blaring from the TV.

But even then I could see the wolves nipping at my parents' door.

When the wheels hit the tarmac, I wonder whether my queer existence will ever be reconciled with the duties of being an only child in the Tamil community. I want to care for my parents into old age, ensuring they feel a sense of belonging, despite having embraced their queer son. How much longer will I betray myself into small silences? Will I ever be able to rejoin Tamil society, having fleshed out my queerness on my own terms, while raising a queer family of my own? Or will I be ground into dust, waiting for someone else to speak?

I dream of creating space and having a queer presence within the Tamil community. I am tired of waiting to be represented. There are queer Tamil activists doing amazing and much-needed work in white spaces. However, I want to weave together my Tamil life and my queer one, because there are undoubtedly many others like me: Tamil society is complex and should be represented as such. As Audre Lorde says, if I don't define myself for myself, I will be crunched into other people's fantasies for me and eaten alive.

However, I am nervous. To fully embrace my Tamil and queer identities, I need to make myself visible. I need to be visibly Tamil in queer spaces, and dare to be visibly queer in Tamil spaces. I don't want other people to have authority over my Tamilness or my queerness. I know this community has not been made for me.

But I am not going to apologise for being here. I am not going to apologise for existing.

I WAS BORN THIS WAY

Carly Findlay

I came into this world at the Mercy Hospital in Albury, after a gruelling 32-hour labour. I was born with the rare, severe, genetic skin condition ichthyosis – diagnosed with erythroderma at birth, and rediagnosed with Netherton syndrome after genetic tests when I was 10 years old. I came out red and shiny, but I don't think I was in pain immediately.

Ichthyosis (*ick-thee-o-ses*) is a rare genetic skin disorder, which affects approximately one in 200,000 newborn babies. Since it's a genetic mutation, it isn't contagious – you can't 'catch' it. Ichthyosis causes the skin to build up and scale, and makes it extremely dry, among other problems.

Most types of ichthyosis are present at birth, and are lifelong. Currently, there is no cure, only treatments.

I am red and scaly. My skin gets itchy and sore. My face is the reddest part of my body because it is exposed to the elements. I get infections easily – generally on my legs, but sometimes on my face. Sometimes my infections result in hospital stays where I am bandaged up like a mummy. Infections can make me very sore.

My skin condition affects lots of other things in my body. My eyes, ears, digestive system, temperature and metabolism are all affected to a degree. I see lots of doctors!

My parents met at a party in Cape Town, South Africa, in 1978. Dad grew up in Nottingham, England, and went to South Africa to work as an engineer in 1976. Mum grew up in what would now be called commission houses in Cape Town. They kept their courtship secret, trusting only close family and friends, because my mum was classified as a coloured South African, and my dad is white. Apartheid kept them from being together in the open. They were almost caught on two occasions – when Dad's car broke down on the beach and they had to seek help from strangers, and when the police visited Dad's flat to tell him his car had been run into. Mum hid on Dad's balcony, which overlooked the rocks and sea. Both times, Mum could have been jailed.

In late 1980, Dad proposed to Mum by saying they were going to Australia to get married. Dad had found a job in Sydney. Not so romantic – but the most practical option for them to continue their relationship legally and publicly. They had a pre-wedding honeymoon in Sri Lanka, Singapore and Thailand, and arrived Sydney in January 1981. It was a condition that they got married within a month and Mum had to find work soon after, or they would have needed to return to South Africa. They did both. They married in Centennial Park in February – Dad, ever thrifty, proudly reminds me their wedding cost $87. Mum found work in bank, thanks to a referral from their wedding celebrant. Dad found a job at a car parts manufacturer in Albury, country New South Wales, in October of that year, and so they moved to Albury. I was born in 1981 in Albury – population 37,350 at the time. Albury was then a small rural city surrounded by tiny farming towns.

*

Before I began writing this book, I asked Mum what she thought when I didn't look like her or Dad. 'To be honest, I saw you were red, I asked what was wrong, but I was too tired to even wait for an answer,' she said. 'You were on my chest straightaway, which was good. We got to bond. You weren't agitated.'

Mum said it was a while before she learnt anything about my diagnosis, because she was so tired. 'I went to sleep for eight hours. You were in the nursery in the humidicrib, with Dad by your side.'

The doctors and nurses hadn't seen a baby like me before. The obstetrician sent for the paediatrician that night, and he came with a dermatologist. The dermatologist diagnosed me straightaway, though he told my parents my skin should be perfect by the time I left the hospital.

I stayed in hospital for eight days after birth, but I contracted golden staph, which we now know is likely because my skin is susceptible to infections. This isolated Mum, because she wasn't able to have any visitors apart from Dad. She asked to go home before the 10-day period, knowing I'd receive the same care in the home.

At this stage, when my skin hadn't got 'better' – I was still red and scaly – the dermatologist accused my parents of not looking after me properly. Mum and Dad were very angry, and we didn't see this dermatologist again.

When I was born I was prescribed Sorbolene (a water-based cream) to my whole body, and Sigmacort (a mild cortisone cream) to infected areas. I used Sorbolene until late primary school, but it left me with a patchy, red and white face. Mum used to feel sorry for me, using a visible cream on top of my bright red skin. How embarrassing! Then I switched to paraffin-based ointment, which I've applied to my whole body twice a day ever since. I much prefer paraffin as it absorbs into my skin and leaves me feeling moisturised for a good portion of the day.

*

My parents are very resourceful. They just got on with it. 'We had to,' Dad says. They didn't blame themselves or anyone about my ichthyosis, nor did they sit around moping. They were new to the country, new to a small rural city, newlyweds, without family help, and just had a baby with a skin condition so rare and severe it was unfamiliar to most doctors.

But Mum's always optimistic. 'I wouldn't call it difficult. I didn't know what to expect. So I just took it one day at a time,' she says with shrug. 'The doctors did their best. I didn't think of a cure at the time.' Mum always maintained 'There's nothing wrong with Carly,' and the questions and comments about my skin didn't get her down.

Mum and Dad didn't get any counselling, although Mum was referred to a social worker – and at the time, Mum thought the social worker wasn't experienced or old enough to know what it was like to care for a baby with a serious illness. In hindsight, she realises that the social worker's advice – to be around positive people and to take one day at a time – wasn't negative, but encouraging.

The nuns from the hospital visited regularly to provide assistance around the house, and gifts at Christmas time. The care the nuns gave my family is the most positive experience I've had with religion. They didn't push religion – they were hands on. We visited them regularly as I grew up – my parents had a lot of respect for them. But a priest from another denomination told Mum and Dad they needed to go to church and needed to be saved. It was only then I could get better, he said. 'I threw him out the house without dinner. I told him where to go. I still believed [in God] then, but he put me off,' Mum says. Later, I was sent to Sunday school and youth group, but was still told that if I was alive in Jesus' time, I'd be treated like a leper, and that my parents are black and white, so I'd paid for their sins.

Mum says I was a happy baby, laughing and giggling. It wasn't all sadness. But when I was sick, I was sick. More often than not.

I spent a lot of time in the Royal's Children's Hospital in Melbourne – from when I was a few weeks old – because the skin specialists were there. But there were other problems too – I was born with a heart murmur, arm paralysis and dislocated hips. At one stage, I suffered a seizure on the day I was due to be brought home from Melbourne – and my parents had to leave me there. The doctors were not sure how long I would live, (even today, babies with some types of ichthyosis have a high chance of infant mortality.) The hospital was a long way from Albury.

Mum never grieved for a 'normal' life. She did hope I wouldn't suffer. It was hardest when I was very small – I couldn't tell my parents how my skin was feeling or ask for pain relief or temperature control, so they couldn't help me. At times, Mum asked Dad why I had to be in so much pain. But I never saw it – I only experienced positivity and encouragement from them.

In 1983, we moved to a new home in Walla Walla, a tiny country town 30 minutes from Albury. The summers were scorching hot and dry, and the winters were frosty. It was a farming community – sheep and cattle were raised for slaughter, and wheat would be harvested yearly. Most people were white and Christian and worked on the land or within Walla Walla. Mum and Dad moved into a tiny weatherboard house on half an acre, with a garden abundant with vegetables and sunflowers. I had a very happy time at home with Mum and Dad – sourcing photos for this book reminded me of that I had love and encouragement and never went without.

*

Mum and Dad never invited the media into our lives – even though we'd see stories about disabled kids on *60 Minutes*. 'You were Carly, you were not an object, you were not a spectacle', Mum says. (I see a lot of parent's taking their kids' stories to the media now – and I cringe because so often the kid hasn't consented, and doesn't know the reach and implications of the media.) But they did expose me to other kids with more serious impairments like burns and cancer so I could gain some perspective. The head dermatologist at the Royal Children's Hospital (a doctor I still see today) recommended this.

My parents received a lot of advice. Everyone had a cure to suggest, everyone thought they knew more than my parents. Like Percy's Powder (bought from the side of the road in Porepunkah). We didn't know the ingredients then but Google tells us that Percy's Powder is now available in online health stores, and the ingredients are magnesium, potassium and iron (all as sulphate). It tasted like mud and did not make one scrap of difference to my skin. Mum said advice from others was well meaning, but it did get tedious, especially as I became a teenager. 'If it wasn't getting better by then, it would never get better,' she says. Most of the advice-givers had limited knowledge of ichthyosis. They only saw me outside of the house (at my relative best), and for all they knew, it was merely cosmetic. A lot of people pushed their pyramid scheme products – and they still do, years later, especially on Instagram. (People selling face creams and scented oils find me, I guess via hashtags like #ichthyosis and #skinconditions, and offer me products that will supposedly help me. Only, they're not doctors, and their products are very much cosmetic.)

My parents chose not to have any more children because I was a 24/7 baby. They felt they wouldn't able to divide their time equally – Mum had seen it happen to other families in hospital. Mum personally wouldn't have minded having another child to give me a companion, though. I did adult things and had adult conversations because I didn't have a sibling. Other children and some adults told me that if I had a sibling, it would be better if they had ichthyosis, so they could empathise with me – but they don't know what it's really like to live with the condition.

*

My earliest memory of knowing I was different was when Mum took me to daycare one day when she had an appointment. I had just turned three. I had been with other children when I went to playgroup occasionally, but I don't recall being teased or avoided, because the kids were used to me. These kids at day-care rode around me on tricycles, pinching and punching me.

I wanted to change how I looked. I didn't want to be red any-more because I thought then kids would treat me better. And looking back, I didn't want to be in photos because it would confirm I was different. There are a few photos of me at various ages scattered around my parents' home – mostly milestones like school and university graduations. In my early years, I was hesitant about smiling for the camera – sometimes I'd just screw my face up or shut my eyes. l didn't think I was worthy of having my photo taken when my face was different from most people's anyway. It was internalised ableism. I didn't like how I looked. But looking at the photos decades later, I wish I could have seen myself through Big Carly's eyes. So cute. So worthy of smiling for a photo.

I felt alone for most of my school years. Most kids don't want to hang out with someone who looks different. I tried to tell them about my skin and cream, but it just grossed them out. I was called names and laughed at. They wouldn't touch me, sit near me, sit where I'd been or hold my hand. They wouldn't touch me when we played heads down thumbs up. And I wasn't fashionable wearing a bee net over my hat – to prevent the flies from getting into my ears. Mum discovered flies buried in my ear when she was doing my hair when I was four. The flies were attracted to the smell of infected skin in my ears, and became trapped. I was operated on to remove the flies – and for a few years I wore a net. This contributed hugely to my low self-esteem. I felt repulsed that only flies wanted to get close to me, and that I had to wear such a daggy contraption to stop them. I looked like a junior beekeeper who hated the outdoors.

Aside from being spat on, which was cruel enough, there was never physical bullying. I suppose it was fortunate that kids didn't want to touch me – it saved me from being physically hurt. It was all name-calling, laughing and exclusion. I was called 'skinner', 'redskin', 'red light match', 'traffic light' – these are the ones I can remember. I wasn't invited to many parties after the age of six – I suspect this was the age when kids had a say about who to invite and who to leave off the list. Parties were a status symbol of being fully included in school and out. And so I felt pretty special when I was invited to the occasional one.

I went to a really sporty primary school – if you didn't enjoy sport, you automatically didn't fit in. Although I was often unable to do sport or swim because of the heat or stress of exercise on my skin, teachers would make me sit and watch. I was exposed to the heat and flies anyway – and all I wanted to do was go into the library and read. Mum tried to keep me home on sports days, and thankfully she had good friends to look after me while she was at work.

Teachers didn't believe me when I told them how sad I felt about the bullying, putting the blame back onto me. How could I change so they didn't pick on me? Hear this, teachers: I could not change my appearance so the kids would accept me, but they could have changed their level of acceptance and got to know me. I hate it when people use 'kids are just kids' as justification. Those kids know what they're doing. They know how hurtful they're being. The bullying stuck with me for a long time – and occasionally, even now, I get nervous when I see groups of school kids out and about.

When I was bullied my parents would confront the kid and their parents. This of course did nothing to help make friends – no one likes the weird kid who gets her parents to defend them.

And it is hard to know how to be a good friend if you haven't got many friends. I didn't know how to treat my peers well because they didn't treat me well. I wasn't able to build trust, and probably came across as needy.

When I was nine or ten or I wanted to kill myself. I can't even say those words without a lump in my throat. I had had enough of being different, and the kids were saying I got special treatment from the teachers – being able to sit out of sport or spending lots of time away from school – both of which were not special at all. I never attempted suicide, I just told Mum. I feel so sick at the thought that I can't recall the moment I told her. Mum panicked, and called the paediatrician straightaway. They referred me to a child psychiatrist – I went to two sessions with my parents, and three alone. While the psychiatrist helped (I actually have no memory of these appointments), it was Mum who rebuilt my self-worth. Mum tells me that although the bullying continued, I had a better outlook. She taught me it was important to have self-respect, and not to worry what others thought, but she never justified or made excuses for other people's behaviour.

My social landscape wasn't completely barren. Due to my parents' work hours, I stayed with the Milnes – a large family – before and after school, and made friends with them. They ran the local pub, and it was quite an adventure. It was a really bright spot – I felt welcome and safe. They were a jolly, inclusive, and loud family – they liked horseracing and sport – very different from me. In the mornings, Mrs Milne would make us all a chocolate milkshake in the pub kitchen, and in the afternoons, Mr Milne would let us go behind the bar and help ourselves to chips and Coke from the machine. Their daughter Brigette was in my year at school, and I've recently reconnected with her. She told me she would always try to include me, but would get frustrated that I couldn't join in the outdoor sports and swimming, and wished I could. This gave me a new perspective – maybe some kids wanted to include me after all. And maybe I was so fed up with the bad experiences that I couldn't see the good.

*

As a result of being bullied and excluded, I spent a lot of time indoors, reading and being creative.

Dad was my mate. We spent hours making cheeses from playdough – he taught me the names of exotic cheeses as he shaped the playdough into rounds and wedges. Cheshire, Stilton, Swiss, Brie. And on Saturday nights we'd feast on real cheeses.

He was an engineer and so a lot of the projects were hands-on and messy. I'd spend time with him in the shed – making puppets, painting rocks, making rafts out of Paddle Pop sticks, and hammering nails into wood. I didn't seem to mind having to clean the paint off my hands with turps, even though it stung a little.

He built me a guinea-pig house – a double-decker palace – for five guinea pigs. We bought two from the pet shop when I was about eight. We were assured they were two males. But Cuddles and Dinky were a male and a female. It should have been obvious they were mating when they spent a lot of time sitting on each other. A few months later, three babies were born – Tiger, Rabbit and Mouse. It was my job to feed the guinea pigs, brush them and clean their cage. It was fun for a while, but they gave me worms. I'm sure this happens to most kids who keep rodents!

Dad is creative – good at storytelling. Every Sunday morning I'd get into bed with my parents, and Dad would tell me stories about Tippy the Elf, who lived in the park next to our house, as well as Marmaduke and Joe, who drove their red lorry around town, delivering things to shops. When I got to primary school age, I'd help tell the stories with Dad, taking them on tangents.

Mum and I would also make up stories, elaborating on fairytales, while she combed the scale out of my scalp. That was a nice time to bond – we talked about our day, and had a chance to be creative. As painful as it was, I cherished this time, although Mum cooked dinner before she did my hair, and the chilli residue on her fingers stung my scalp. Mum couldn't understand why it was stinging. She'd also get annoyed with me because I'd complain when my scalp was so cold on a Saturday morning when we went shopping – she didn't realise how much ichthyosis affects my temperature regularly. (Having my scalp combed at night didn't affect me temperature-wise as we wouldn't go out afterwards. But going out in the morning just after my scalp was combed really hurt!)

I would stay up late reading on Friday and Saturday nights, devouring whole books at a time. I loved to read. I read books from a very early age – my first memory of reading is of the *Sesame Street Dictionary*. Once a week the Mobile Library (a truck filled with books – how fun!) would come to my little town. I'd go there after school, reading books on the floor, and borrowing a big pile for the next week. It transported me to other worlds.

My parents bought me a personalised Cabbage Patch Kid book to accompany my Cabbage Patch Kid – Lisa Jacqueline. How exciting to have a book that was about me! The illustration that represented me didn't look like me, though – now I would love it if it did, but back then I rejected my red appearance.

The *Baby-Sitters Club* books were a staple in my final years of primary school, and every month I'd buy one from the Scholastic book club. Mum thought they were too old for me when I talked about boys snapping Stacey McGill's bra strap, but then I read them anyway. It was the same with *Sweet Valley High*.

Craft was another pastime. I'd spend a lot of time hand-sewing Barbie and peg doll clothes, creating animals from gumnuts and leaves, and knitting with a bobbin. I developed some skills in keeping house too – my parents were far from giving me special treatment – so I had to learn how to cook and clean. I enjoyed cooking much more than cleaning as a kid – and that hasn't changed as an adult!

I was luck my sore skin afforded me so much time to read, write, create and imagine. Yes, lucky.

*

I asked Mum and Dad what advice they have for new parents. Mum encourages parents to take one day at a time. She also said that they need to show their child respect, and teach their child self-respect – even before self-love. She is matter of fact when answering strangers' questions, but gives parents permission to be rude if the questioner is rude.

Dad is ever practical. Stoic even. Carry on as normal, he said. 'Accept that skin debris and cream-tainted walls, books, phones and TV controllers will prevail. Buy a decent vacuum cleaner and commercial-grade washing machine. Tiled and timber floors are preferable over carpet.'

Both my parents believe in good doctors over naturopaths and herbalists, and discourage looking for a miracle cure and comparing whose child has it worse within support groups.

POWER

Hope Mathumbu

The sharp sting on my thigh brings my mind back to the present, and I look up to see Mama's face glaring at me disapprovingly as Pastor Mnisi continues to scream into the microphone, beads of sweat trickling down his forehead. Naledi's smirking face pops out from behind Mama's shoulder, and she shakes her head at me in feigned disapproval. It's been two hours now, and it doesn't seem like we are any closer to the praise-and-worship part of the day. These visiting pastors always have to make a show of it, as though we have all the time in the world, like in Africa.

Jenny's birthday party started an hour ago, and Mama promised to drop me off in Collingwood to celebrate with her. I don't want to miss out on lunch because Jenny's mother is making hotpot and I don't know what that is. It doesn't matter to know – all the food that Jenny's mother makes is the best. Jenny thinks it's funny that I never had an Asian friend or Asian food before. Specifically, as she keeps telling me, a Vietnamese friend and Vietnamese food – because Asia is not a country, just as I keep telling her Africa isn't.

To be honest, this is also the first time I have had other African friends before, from countries that aren't right next door to my own. I never knew black people could be Muslim until I met all my North African friends. When I asked Papa about this over the phone, he struggled to explain it, and told me to make sure I keep going to church and pray for all my friends.

The phone card ran out of money before I could tell him I would.

Pastor Mnisi's voice has softened a bit now, and the band has started to play. Oliver is on the keyboard today, and my heart flutters with joy. I have never seen a man with relaxed hair before, almost to his shoulders. Each week he wears a perfectly ironed colour-coordinated suit with a matching tie, bowtie or handkerchief in his pocket. We have been going to this church for two years, and I have never seen him wear the same outfit. Today he is in purple, like the singer Prince. Naledi says he is gay, but I don't think so because he is always talking to women and laughing with them. Sometimes I see sesi Violet touching his hair and giving him advice, though God knows what she could possibly be telling him because she is always wearing the same old boring cornrow style, like me. Mama says it's too expensive to get our hair done the same way we did back home. Even though it's embarrassing, there are also not many black people in my day-to-day life to notice, and most of my black friends at school have their hair covered anyway, so I am some kind of novelty to people who don't know anything about how impoverished this two-month-old styling really looks. Sometimes I wonder if Mama is just punishing me and trying to keep me humble.

I don't understand how Oliver can have such perfect hair and clothes, and we have nothing. If my friends from home could see us now, they would be shocked. If Papa could see me now, too. Saying goodbye to him was the hardest thing I have ever done. It's only the second time I have seen him cry like a baby: shoulders shaking, and the pain rising out of his throat in uncontrollable wails. The first time I saw Papa cry was when my brother, Tinyiko, died – his only son. When he cried for us like that at the airport I knew I was loved. I knew it didn't matter that people pitied him for losing the continuation of his bloodline.

I promised myself that I would never get married, but find a way to have a boy-child that could continue the name. Zalabantu! If what sesi Violet tells us in youth Bible study is true, God probably won't like this plan to continue the bloodline. Auntie Grace has two children out of wedlock to different fathers and she still comes to church like there is nothing wrong. Mama sometimes offers them a lift home from church, but never goes inside the house like when she offers other people lifts.

I once asked Mama if I could make extra money babysitting Auntie Grace's kids now that I am fourteen years and nine months old. She smacked me across the head and told me that I am too young to know anything about looking after babies and that Auntie Grace's house isn't the best place to learn, either. I asked Naledi why Mama was so weird with Auntie Grace, and she just laughed and told me to mind my own business. I told her that nobody at church ever minds their own business, and she laughed again and said that's why they are all doomed. I have to remember to tell Dad about that.

The band is in full swing now, singing my favourite song: 'There Is Power in the Blood'. To Mama's joyful surprise, I stand up and lift my hands to the sky, singing along. I catch Naledi's disgusted eye and start to shake myself up and down to the tempo, singing, 'Lord send the power! Lord send the power!' I feel ashamed of myself for thinking that the only power I need is to survive this final hour so I can get to Jenny's birthday. The muscles in my stomach grind in unrelenting hunger, and I shake myself harder to the music.

Pastor Mnisi's voice booms through the microphone: 'Yes, send us the power, oh Lord, the power to transform ourselves through your sacred blood. The power to claim everlasting victory on this earth in your holy name. Yes, Lord, send the power!' A lot of things changed when I got my blood, and none of them involved more power or victory. In fact, Mama told me that I wasn't allowed to play sport anymore because of my blood, so I joined the debating team. I am surprisingly good at it so far.

The beat quickens, and I feel the blood rush to my head as I scream to the Lord for more power. The bass from the music reaches from my toes, and spreads right up my body and through my chest as I jump up and down in pure manic joy. I am so caught up in the celebration that I fail to notice the gradual dimming of my surroundings, as my body shuts down and drops to the floor. 'Sagwadi, Sagwadi?!' Sharp stings across my cheeks bring my mind back to the present, and my eyes open to see Mama's scared face looking down at me. Pastor Mnisi's triumphant face pops out from behind her shoulder, nodding in approval. 'It's okay, Mama, she is fine. The Holy Spirit has moved her today.' He kneels beside me and reaches his clammy hand forward onto my forehead, and I am overwhelmed by the sour smell of sweat and Old Spice. I close my eyes and think of my own father, who wears Old Spice, but doesn't sweat as much. I surrender to the cacophony of voices in prayer around me, as I am baptised by the occasional spittle from Pastor Mnisi as he speaks in tongues. I am grateful for the noise, as I feel my stomach twisting in agonising hunger. While I am here, I may as well whisper a prayer of my own.

God never answers my prayers the way I need them answered. After the service, people flock to Mama to compliment her outfit, and her God-fearing daughters. Naledi is obviously irritated at all the fuss, because she wishes she could have been the star of the show today. Sesi Violet invites Mama to lunch at her house and mentions that Pastor Mnisi will be attending before flying home later in the evening. Mama accepts the invitation and says we will all go to Frankston to sesi Violet's house.

I realise that not only have I missed Jenny's birthday, but I have also missed tonight's episodes of *Big Brother* and *Charmed*, because Frankston is on the other side of the world. As we walk to the car, I try to softly whisper to Mama that she promised to take me to Jenny's birthday, but she pretends not to hear me. As we are about to drive off, Oliver rushes to the car and asks for a lift to sesi Violet's house, where he too has been invited to lunch. I thank God for his small mercies as Oliver slides into the backseat beside me, smelling sweeter than any other man I have ever met. I catch Naledi's eye in the rear-view mirror as I try to hide my smile.

FOUR STAGES

Rafeif Ismail

Two months ago, my paternal grandfather passed away. It was a Wednesday, usually my favourite day of the week – now always a reminder that it has been (x) days since he left us. The worst thing about grief is the forgetting: those split-second eternities when you are caught between dreaming and waking. Those moments in between heartbeats, as you draw in a breath, before it leaves your body with a sob. The space of a step when suddenly the weight of memories makes you stumble. I still forget there is a gaping hole in the universe in the shape of his smile.

My grandfather, my Baba Jidu, as I'd called him ever since I could speak, was not my first family member to pass away. He was not even the first grandparent – my maternal grandmother died in 2009, and ten years of grief lines have yet to fade from my mother's face, but she moves forward because that's what Black women do.

Grief in exile is a funny thing. There is no 'closure'; there is no room to contemplate the enormity of the loss. Often you're too busy consoling everyone else, making arrangements, keeping up a façade of normality.

Grief in exile is complicated, because it's hard to know exactly what you're grieving for.

1. Shock

The day we run is like every other day. The adhan carries through the town, calling people to prayer. My mother wakes and waters the plants, makes breakfast and packs our backpacks. We leave our house as though we're just going to visit relatives. We do visit relatives. My younger brothers are a toddler and an infant, and I'm nearly six years old as I hug my maternal grandmother for the last time, as my oldest *khalo*, maternal uncle, cries. All of our goodbyes are filled with tears. We get into a white truck with only the clothes on our backs and a few possessions, some photo albums. My father travels separately; he joins us in Khartoum.

When we get to Cairo, it's a whole new world. I taste apples for the first time: sweet, and slightly overripe, but not so much that they have lost their crunch. Apples become my favourite food, though I miss the taste of fresh sugarcane and guava, the taste of home.

We thought it would be a year, maybe two, before we could go back home. In Cairo I have the same dream every night for months, of walking down a new street, turning a corner and finding myself near my family home, of hearing the clamour of voices, a cacophony of chatter, singing, debate and laughter.

I had never been outside Sudan, never seen people with skin paler than Nile soil, never thought my Arabic was not Arabic, never doubted who I was and how I was, until Egypt. Years later, I find out that my paternal great-grandmother thought her husband was a ghost lost in the desert the first time she saw him: the brown-skinned Turkish soldier who deserted his post during the occupation and fell in love in the land his people conquered. I wonder if my late grandfather had questions about his identity, if he ever wanted to know his father's homeland, what he thought about being born in a country under occupation. I will never get to ask those questions.

My grief is mixed with anger, to have lost nearly a lifetime that could have been spent with family. Seventeen years of knowing family, learning language, learning history and culture, learning self, gone. To have had seventeen years *stolen* from my family is a wound I will always carry. The blame lies at the feet of the Bashir dictatorship, alongside the bodies of loved ones lost or buried, alongside villages and towns, burnt; so many lives and lifetimes, stolen. The blame lies at the feet of every single person who benefited from the exploitation of Black lands and Black lives. The spectre of pre-colonial Sudan is not far from my life – my eldest *amo*, paternal uncle, was born four years after independence. Most of the elders in my family, in my country, spent the majority of their lives in lands occupied. It's hard to find an identity in the midst of all that confusion. It's even harder when elements of your identity seem conflicting at first glance.

In Australia, the question I get asked the most is, 'Where are you from?' In other words, explain why you are Black, and existing in this space. Or, more rarely, 'I hope to find a common connection.'

Most conversations go like this:

'Where are you from?'

'Perth.'

'Where are you really from?'

'Sudan.'

'But you don't look Sudanese.'

'But you can't be Sudanese.'

'But you're not really Sudanese.'

There is no single way that all Sudanese people look, act or speak. Just as Blackness is not monolithic. The homogenisation of Sudanese people further erases cultural and ethnic groups that have been purposely written out of our collective history. Genocide isn't just about the violence; it thrives on the silence around it.

In my first year of 'mainstream' school in Australia, after the intensive English centres deemed my progress in the language satisfactory, 'Where are you from?' was the first question my teacher asked me, before even knowing my name.

Around that time, I began to learn a universal truth: Black girls are seen as women before they are children, objects before they are human. 'Growing up' isn't an option when you are already grown in the eyes of the world. A school uniform does not protect you from white women touching you without consent as you're walking down the road. It does nothing to stop the gazes of older white men following you, or comments about how 'well developed' you are. A school uniform does not protect you from the idea that, for you, the ages twelve, fourteen and sixteen are not 'too young'. That then you are 'old enough'.

As an adult, I am very particular about my personal space; I cannot stand being close to people, and I am always hypervigilant in crowds. Being able to say 'no' and 'don't touch me' have been the most liberating things about the last few years – there are indignities adults will inflict on a Black girl child, especially in public, that they wouldn't dare with someone who can speak back. I relish being able to take the train without using a schoolbag as an insufficient shield, and to stand in spaces without trying to make myself small. I love being able to speak with friends and know that they respect my space and boundaries. For the first time in my life, I do not blame or despise my body, having realised that every instance of violence inflicted, whether macro or micro aggression, was not my fault.

2. Guilt

How do you live with yourself when you are alive while so many are dead or dying? There is survivor's guilt when you make it to a new country. Knowing that people around you sacrificed, and were prepared to sacrifice, their lives, their world, for your survival is a heavy burden. The only difference between me and the people imprisoned in offshore detention is luck. If that white truck had been stopped, if the security forces had raided our house again the night before, or just after we left, if my father had been stopped before boarding the plane, things could have gone differently. A billion possibilities of what could have gone wrong still go through my mind. It is luck that has us treated as marginally more human than our siblings of circumstance in onshore and offshore detention.

In 2017, I went back to my first primary school here, an intensive English centre where some teachers discouraged me from speaking Arabic. I was supposed to speak to students, to somehow 'inspire' them. As I stood in the front of the room, I felt too old and far too young to be in this position. A blink of an eye ago, I was sitting in the same spot, picking up every third word in English and thinking that adults had all the answers, waiting to feel safe or saved. But at that age, I had not seen anyone who looked like me, spoke like me, lived like me.

My first question to this group of children was, 'What's your favourite superhero, and why?'

They had a multitude of answers to the whos, but the whys were pretty similar:

'Because I want to change the world.'

'Because I want to make my family safe.'

'Because I want to help save people.'

'Because I want to be brave.'

Children of diasporic heritage are aware of the reality of the world around them. Not understanding something and being unable to communicate your understanding are completely different things. We rarely give an opportunity to those who are affected the most by the life-altering circumstances of migration, forced or otherwise, to speak or find a common language.

My favourite superheroes growing up were *Superman* and *Wonder Woman*. They were both far away from home. They couldn't return, yet they tried to make a better world where they were. Comics were the only commonality I could find between Egypt and Australia, and I would sit and read them day after day, during recess and lunch. It's how I learnt to read English. In those early years, I imagined myself an alien abandoned on a foreign planet. I would daydream about Amazons teaching me how to defend myself, about finding people who could understand what I could not yet put into words. About returning home.

3. Rage

'Don't open the doors to strangers,' my mother warns. My father tells me to make sure all the lights and the televisions are on. They're only leaving for two hours, yet I double and triple-check every lock in the house, close every curtain, and wait. This is Australia, 2018. We have been here for fourteen years.

Late at night, when I am unable to sleep due to stress or distress, I walk around my house. I look into my siblings' rooms, look in on my parents, to make sure they are okay. I check every lock in the house – twice, three times, and again, until my thoughts stop racing. There are occasions when I hear a noise in the backyard and stay awake until dawn, counting the exits, the distance to the front door, how long it would take to break the windows. Should I text my siblings to run? Back home, if you were sleeping inside, you heard the *thump*, *thump* of the Kalashnikovs on the shoulders of soldiers before they broke down the door, if you were lucky. If you weren't, you'd wake up with the rifles pointed at your family. In Sudan, we slept under the stars. Every night, my parents would drag our mattress out into the courtyard, put my siblings and me between them and shield us even in sleep. Noises meant raids, meant disappearances, meant strangers. They meant pretending to sleep, practising that instinctual *if I don't see them, they cannot see me*.

I still freeze when I wake up, to listen and wait. There are times when cars backfire, and I duck for cover. Every time someone reaches into their jacket, my heartbeat spikes. I steel myself with every ring of the phone or knock at our door. We fled the war seventeen years ago, but the war hasn't left us.

Once, after speaking at an event, I was thanked for my 'inspiring' and 'articulate' speech. It was not the first time this had happened, but it was the first time my response was not something that somewhat rhymed with 'thank you'. I was angry, in public, for the first time, because I was being cast into the mould of 'model refugee'. My life was being used as a tool to assuage white guilt – to provide absolution even as my across-the-world siblings and I struggle through the shackles of white supremacy. My experience and existence are not teachable moments for those who can step in and out of power. We escape wars just to end up bound by different chains.

4. (Re)Building

With the death of my grandfather came the death of a dream. You see, I had always thought that one day I'd go back home. It has been seventeen years since I stepped foot on Sudanese soil, but there was always a part of me that believed we would go back after it became safe. There was always a part of me waiting to complete a childhood there. That part waited and waited and waited, even as hope crumbled with each passing year, with each grave of a family member or of a friend who might as well have been family. With each act of violence.

That part persisted somehow – a dam to keep at bay a flood that has been gathering since I was five years old – and with this last death, my grandfather's, the dam has shattered and I am left trying to wade through torrents of grief and rage.

Sudan was family, it was laughter, it was never being alone, it was being blanketed by unconditional love. It was the scent of *bakhoor*, the taste of sugarcane and guava, the lanterns lighting the street during Ramadan. It was Mustafa Said Ahmed's music and Mahjoub Sharif's poetry. It was also police cars at our doors, in front of our school. It was the marks of lashings across my father's back, relatives in hiding, being spoken of in code. My mother risking her life again and again for her children. It was like living in the middle of a storm, praying to not be hit by the debris.

Egypt was a flood of change, unexpected and terrifying – a deluge that carried us all the way to Australia.

I'm still trying to figure out what Australia is.

It has now been (x) days since my grandfather passed away. I go through the motions each day, and try not to regret what I have lost. I am learning, slowly, that grief does not dwindle by the day, but that the capacity to deal with it expands.

As I write this it has been 6210 days since I was last home.

And I am still trying to find a way to exist in this world.

I have spent 5294 days in Australia, and I am finally learning to grow into myself.

A PORTRAIT OF THE ARTIST AS A YOUNG LARRIKIN

Lech Blaine

An artist doesn't happen by accident, and neither does a larrikin. My parents met at a backyard barbeque in Ipswich, circa 1979.

Mum was a nervous bookworm and a financial clerk for a department store – a bush poetry enthusiast with a permed mullet who shunned make-up, dresses and jewellery. She was allergic to public speaking and physical exercise.

She said, 'Slow and steady finishes the race.' She said, 'You're not playing for sheep stations.'

She said, 'You don't need to win anything to have fun.'

Dad was a 130-kilogram cab driver with a mullet and a handlebar moustache who had never read a novel in his life. A rugby league coach and a former professional gambler, he let off steam at weekends by punting large sums on thoroughbreds and greyhounds. He peppered his enemies with sledges and sculled beer from a saucepan. Beating people was the meaning of life.

He said, 'If you're not first, you're finished.'

He said, 'You need to risk it to get the biscuit.'

He said, 'Never trust a bloke who doesn't drink.'

I have her to thank for the vocabulary and him for the ego. Both dropped out of high school before Grade Nine to support their families. Dad dreamed of being a rich businessman.

Mum dreamed of raising a big family.

After tying the knot, Mum suffered six miscarriages. The pragmatic battlers became foster carers instead and relocated to the bush in pursuit of a cut-price Australian dream. By autumn 1991, they'd leased three rundown pubs across country Queensland and accepted six permanent foster children under the age of twelve. This brood sometimes blew out to ten or eleven.

'One more try,' said Mum, who had started taking a shady oestrogen-replacement drug from a rogue fertility doctor at the age of thirty-eight. It was manufactured from the urine of pregnant mares.

Secretly, she daydreamed about a baby girl named Amy Blaine, another shy female, and a rare example of her personal preference prevailing over that of her cocksure husband.

'Let's hope the piss came from Phar Lap's granddaughter,' said Dad, craving a biological son who could run the hundred metres in under ten seconds.

On 22 January 1992, I arrived to great fanfare, surprisingly alive, a miracle child with a full-blown god complex. My mother emerged from a C-section to see her first breathing baby wrapped in a pink sheet. The hospital had run out of the blue ones it used for boys.

'It's a girl!' she cried.

'Nope,' said Dad smugly. 'It's a boy.'

According to my eldest brother, Trent, it went back and forth like this: *It's a girl! It's a boy! It's a girl! It's a boy!*

Mum gestured desperately. 'Why would they give a pink sheet to a boy?'

Dad unwrapped the sheet to expose the only evidence that mattered, his prize for a lifetime's supply of bad luck. 'My kid's got a dick!' he roared.

My father won naming rights and named me after his doppelgänger, Lech Wałęsa, a fat battler with a thick moustache. Lech was a revolutionary trade unionist and the freshly elected president of Poland. My pop John had been a blacksmith on the Ipswich railway and vice-president of the Queensland Ironworkers Union – this was why a bartender in Wondai dedicated his long-awaited heir to Eastern Europe's great emancipator.

At the age of sixteen, my father had shattered his hip at the Ipswich meatworks and spent six months in hospital. He never played rugby league again. That bitter winter, Dad's brother George won the Bulimba Cup for Ipswich as a goalkicking fullback, and his sister Rita gave birth to a blonde bombshell named Allan Langer.

After Allan dropped out of high school, my mother got him his first job, as a furniture removalist, while my father was still getting laughed out of clubhouses across Ipswich for suggesting his 166-centimetre nephew would play football for Queensland and, one day, Australia. 'Are your eyes painted on?' they said. 'He's a friggin' midget!'

Dad had a history-making chip on his shoulder. He was pissed off about missed opportunities, and craved greatness in the next generation of the Blaine bloodline. Allan Langer was a part-time athlete and full-time council worker when selectors picked him to play the first game of the 1987 State of Origin. 'Alfie' starred from the get-go, picking up Man of the Match in the series decider.

Nineteen ninety-two was indisputably the happiest year of my father's life. On the fourth Sunday of spring, Allan Langer captained the Brisbane Broncos to the first of consecutive premierships against the St George Dragons, whipping the cream of Sydney's establishment.

'You little beaut-*ay!*' Dad sang while feeding me mashed bananas and himself a Johnnie Walker and Diet Coke. That scruffy Australian battler was the father of a son and the uncle of a gun.

My parents sold the lease of the Wondai Hotel. Mum got paid a few dollars an hour to be a 24/7 psychologist to six children. Dad got a part-time job as a bartender at the Wondai

Bowls and Golf Club. They ploughed their life savings into a cheap acre of red dirt, where they planted a removable home that used to be a maternity hospital.

Every Sunday for a month, my brothers filled the tray of a one-tonne Falcon ute with turf from the Murgon Meatworks. My father drove the cargo home so they could mask the drought-stricken earth around the house.

At night, Mum and Dad checked my cot as though it harboured a million-dollar bill. During the day, six overprotective foster siblings studied every burp, piss, fart and shit with wonder and unspoken envy. 'Mum,' they cried, fighting over me. 'It's my turn to hold him!'

The slew of days and nights turned me into a toddler, but my novelty didn't wear off. I remember an island of green grass in an ocean of red dirt. The sound of buzzing flies and squealing springs on a trampoline. The scent of beer on Dad's thick, tickling fingers, and the whiff of menthol cigarettes from Mum's insistent kisses.

'Mummy didn't have any babies come from her tummy until a little boy named Lech Jack Thomas,' she cooed, a lullaby that never grew old. 'Everyone was so happy the day that Bubby Jack was born, but especially Mummy and Daddy. He made up for the sad times, because his face made Mummy feel warm and fuzzy in the tummy.'

The adoration was unsustainable. I'd never be loved so unconditionally again. This set me up for daily heartbreaks in the real world, where no one responded with quite the same level of amazement.

We moved to Toowoomba in 1996. My father bought a cheap hotel lease. My mother – who didn't want to leave the bush – ferried six foster children in a small bus. Dad and I drove separately. I sat in the front passenger seat of a black Ford Falcon with a moon roof. We passed farms that hadn't yet been subdivided, and the slight bend in the highway where my life would spiral out of control.

Toowoomba was treated to its wettest year since 1893. I remember pissing rain and hissing winds. The Country Club Hotel was stubbornly rundown, a fitting reflection of the suburb, Mort Estate, which was filled with boarding houses and council flats. The customers were tradies and railway workers with loose bowels and foul mouths. They drank cheap schooners until the sun went down. Then the shot glasses came out and their red necks got hot underneath blue collars.

'Oi, two-pot screamer,' my father declared to a man speaking lewdly to the barmaid during happy hour. 'Pull your head in, before I do it for ya.'

I was forever running from the publican to the bookkeeper. In the office, my mother kept a secret stash of sweeties: milkos, strawberry and creams, chicos and pineapples. She raised seven kids while speed-reading half a dozen novels a week, and could recite 'The Man from Snowy River' and 'Clancy of the Overflow' verbatim, like a bush poetry jukebox: '*... the hurrying people daunt me, and their pallid faces haunt me, as they shoulder one another in their rush and nervous haste.*'

We had matching hazel green eyes and generalised anxiety, but my mother was never the same after moving to the Big Smoke. She didn't like the density of bodies and the condescension of rich agricultural types from old money. During the wettest year since Federation, mosquitoes provided a convenient alibi for clinical depression – she blamed lethargy on Ross River fever.

Although Dad had the gift of the gab, he was minimalist, not a chatterbox like me.

He said, 'Life's a mixed bag of shit.'

He said, 'Death's a one-horse race.'

He said, 'Pity's the last straw of pride.'

My father's poisons of choice included steak-and-bacon sandwiches, snags, rissoles, T-bones, lamb cutlets, rib fillets, deep-fried potatoes, meat pies and sausage rolls. I never saw him eat so much as a chicken nugget or a fish finger, such was his fidelity to red meat.

'Chicken's for women,' he told me. 'Fish is for Christians.'
'What about salad?' I asked.

'Do I look like a friggin' guinea pig?'

Upstairs, when he took a rare break from the bar, a drape of flab hung from the bottom of his Jackie Howe singlets, worn with footy shorts and thongs. His heels cracked under so much weight and yellowed from the application of Rawleigh's Antiseptic Salve, giving him a perpetually sterile scent. *For man and beast*, it said on the tin.

One Sunday afternoon, the licensee evicted a trio of skinheads because a member of the gang was underage. A few hours later, I was bouncing a football around the plastic-wrapped pallets of XXXX Gold and Victoria Bitter. The nu-metal enthusiasts returned with reinforcements.

'Fuck you and your grandson,' said one.

I was five. My father was nearly fifty. Half a dozen heavily tattooed teenagers stood on the footpath.

'Say that to my face, ya Nazis,' he said, so they did.

Dad went for a quick knockout but missed, before tripping backwards on a gutter. The punks kicked the shit out of him within touching distance of me. A plasterer rushed out from the bar and king-hit the ringleader.

Afterwards, we sat in the coldroom waiting for the police to make a routine visit. My father applied a cool can of VB to a bleeding eye socket. I was mesmerised not by violence, but by the sight of a humiliated tough guy.

'I'd love to see them throw a punch one on one,' he said. 'A bunch of gutless wonders.'

That year, he suffered a life-threatening heart attack. In the hospital's smoking area, my mother's hands were shaking. 'What's wrong, Mum?' I asked.

'I'm worried, honey. Dad's heart is in a bad way.'

I'd never set foot inside a church, but I spent the next week praying to God and negotiating Dad's entry to heaven.

'What happens after we die?' I asked him.

'Sweet stuff-all,' he said. 'We'll be meat for the worms.'

Dad came home in a hospital bracelet, compression socks and with fresh scars on a shaved chest. I whipped myself into panic about the fact one day he'd be dead. The interesting thing about my routine retreat into the master bedroom between midnight and sunrise is that my tough-as-nails father didn't tell me to grow some balls.

'You're a big boy now,' said my mother.

But Dad pulled my small body into a stomach that just kept going, a grizzly bear harbouring a koala. 'Leave him alone,' he said. 'He isn't doing you any harm.' I knew that I'd rather cease breathing than be alive without him.

*

In 1998, I was a six-year-old obsessed with professional wrestling and rugby league. My parents had paid $70,000 for a dilapidated worker's cottage. Firewood was piled in a dead garden bed beside the ping-pong table in the carport. I wasn't strong enough to lift the axe, so I watched my brothers chop kindling atop a metal plate on the concrete driveway, limbs thick with muscle.

'You don't pee sitting down, do ya?' they would enquire when I burst into tears if they didn't hand over the Super Nintendo control.

'Mummy's boy!' my sisters would sing whenever I ran to the matriarch after a disagreement on the trampoline.

'Are you a man or a mouse?' my father would ask.

'I'm a m-m-man!' I cried in my high-pitched stutter, an impediment that appeared whenever I got flustered.

At the 1998 NRL grand final, I was dressed from head to toe in maroon and yellow, as the Broncos defeated the Bulldogs 38–12. Allan Langer was made captain of Australia. On TV, I watched the haka being performed by enormous Kiwis. Luckily, my father had X-ray vision for the internal organs of other men. He pointed at the biggest, meanest rival forward.

'Relax,' he said. 'That guy's got a heart the size of a split pea.'

Meanwhile, during pre-season training for the under-sevens, it became tragically apparent that the Blaine rugby league gene had gone on strike during my conception.

'You're gonna catch a cold out on the sting!' yelled my father, the team manager. 'Take a run up the guts.'

After winning four grand finals in seven years, Allan Langer dramatically announced his retirement, relocating to play for a team in the north of England.

In the second season, my puppy fat was no longer adorable: I was certifiably obese, thanks to a strict diet of steak sandwiches, while the other boys were even leaner and more bloodthirsty than before.

My brother Steven carried all of my father's athletic expectations. He won St Mary's Best and Fairest over Johnathan Thurston and Jaiman Lowe, two future NRL stars. Dad brought his prized horseracing binoculars to Steven's games and made me magnify my brother's textbook defensive style.

'See how he creases blokes with the point of his shoulder?'

'Yeah,' I said.

'No hands! Imagine they've been amputated off.'

The issue, in his words, was I had *shoulders like a brown snake*. I couldn't sleep before my final game of the season, visualising a boy with bleeding shoulderblades. I volunteered to warm the bench after suffering a panic attack in the dressing sheds.

'What's wrong with ya?' asked the relieved coach, who was forced by protocol to rotate the weaker players with the best.

'I don't feel good in the guts.'

'Ya got the runs?'

'Yeah.'

My father knew I didn't have diarrhoea, but he played along with the charade. We left before the half-time siren. He'd spent thirty years coaching rugby league players and had seen enough to know that his son wasn't one.

'Next year you should go back to playing hockey with your

sisters,' he said. 'Don't do something unless it's fun.'

At home, I flung my underwhelming body onto my bed. The anguish blared from both lungs like a full-time siren. Mum rushed in from the Hills Hoist and hugged me. 'What's the matter?' she asked.

I told her that Dad wanted me to retire from football. 'I've got a heart the size of split pea,' I said.

My mother tried to comfort me without betraying an underlying glee that I was more like her than my father. 'Don't be silly. You've got the biggest heart of any little boy that I've ever met! It's a blessing to feel all of those feelings.'

'Why can't I crease people like Steven?'

'Because you aren't Steven. You're *Lech*.'

Without denying the possibility I might one day play halfback for the Brisbane Broncos, Mum explained that everyone was born with a different gift. 'You've got a brain that's wider than the sky,' said the stay-at-home poet, plagiarising Emily Dickinson. 'It's deeper than the sea.'

'I don't want a big brain. I want big guns!'

'I know, baby. But one day you'll work out that all the muscles in the world aren't worth an imagination like yours.'

Quitting rugby league heralded my improvised identity as an extroverted bookworm. On the way to cricket practice, my father and I ate sausage rolls smothered in tomato sauce, washed down with strawberry milk. I covered my nose with zinc and bowled leg spin off three steps like my hero Shane Warne.

'I smell b-b-blood, fellas!' I spluttered, while glowering at the puzzled batsmen like they were on death row.

On Sunday afternoons, I went to Toowoomba Library with my mother, who generally dressed in second-hand jeans and sneakers from Lifeline, where she volunteered twice a week.

'Don't sweat the small stuff, baby,' said my mother, despite logging the most prosaic facts about me in a diary.

'Why do you write all that stuff?' I asked.

'Because I don't want to forget anything.'

Mum preferred to write down arguments over shouting them. I grew up hearing her read other people's perfect sentences to me. And slowly but certainly I was converted to a life of reading and writing, just as she had been.

Dad sold the pub and bought the corner store across the road from my public primary school – a man who lived a hundred kilometres an hour trying to stay alive by slowing down. It was the worst financial investment of his life. Families started fleeing the suburb due to a series of ghastly murders. The reluctant shop-keeper spent his new career bartering with junkies over the price of Chiko Rolls, selling *Hustler* to underage teens and putting cigarettes on tick for destitute pensioners.

I was delighted by the development, because we'd never spent so much uninterrupted time together. Dad studied form guides and made calls to the TAB, but the bets were bad more often than good. To improve his mood, I peppered him with the names of athletes and politicians from encyclopaedias. John Curtin and Don Bradman. Martin Luther King and Muhammad Ali. Nelson Mandela and Imran Khan.

'Taking it easy's for wimps,' he said.

Dad loved the Beatles, the Australian Labor Party and the Maroons, Queensland's rugby league team. He delivered sermons on a holy trinity of duos that made the skin on my forearms tingle: John Lennon and Paul McCartney, Bob Hawke and Paul Keating, Wally Lewis and Allan Langer. 'They were better together,' he said. 'Like you and me.'

But it was clear that he preferred Lennon's dark charisma over McCartney's choirboy perfectionism, Hawke's common touch over Keating's intellect, Langer's enigmatic brilliance over Lewis's persistent physicality.

'Who would ya rather have a beer with?' he asked a nine-year-old who had never tasted alcohol.

'Hawkie!'

'There's your answer.'

'What was Keating like?'

Dad, that 140-kilogram totem of masculinity, would pucker his lips and swivel his wrist in the air, insinuating that Keating was a sheila. 'Bloody good treasurer. But he'd rather be at the Opera House than Belmore Oval.'

My father preferred doers to thinkers, loose cannons to tall poppies, larrikins to wowsers. He wanted me to be brilliant without thinking I was better than battlers like him.

'Why did you call me *Lech*?' I asked, never getting sick of the gleam that appeared in his tired eyes.

'Lech Wałęsa is a hero. Trade unionist like your Pop. A sparkie who rewrote history. Because people believed in the rights of the worker! That's what we need, mate. A Lech Wałęsa – or a Lech Blaine – who stands up for the battlers. Unlike that rat Little Johnny Howard.'

He burst into an anthem for the proletariat. '*Solidarity forever! Solidarity forever! Solidarity forever!*'

'*For the union makes us strong!*' I chimed in.

*

As a teenager, I spent a rainless wet season working in the bottle-o of the Bernborough Tavern, Dad's most profitable business yet. It was named after a famous dead racehorse and situated on the main strip of Oakey, a glum town in the guts of Pauline Hanson country. My job was to restack cartons using the forklift and wrap tallies in newspaper to keep them refrigerated.

It was the unforgettable summer of the Cronulla riots. I was the closest source of XXXX Gold and Bundaberg rum and Coke cans, as Alan Jones – Oakey's most famous national export – whipped the local neo-Nazis into a frenzy.

'I'll tell you what they should do,' said one deadbeat regular. 'Round all these shitskins up and drown 'em.'

'You're a Nazi!' I said. 'You're a poofter,' he spat.

Each day, the clearest dissenting voice of compassion was a

refugee advocate named Ian Rintoul, who defended boat people on the news. I tracked down his Hotmail address, and we became pen pals. Rintoul sent reams of socialist magazines featuring diatribes against the Iraq War and offshore detention.

'There's no difference between Labor and Liberal,' I said to my father on the way home one night.

'That's real easy to say,' he said, aghast at my rising nihilism. 'You've never worked a hard day in your life.'

That year, 2006, the culture war between us engulfed the whole district. As dams edged towards empty, the mayor – an environmentalist named Dianne Thorley – tried to introduce recycled sewage water. Due to her short hair and a gruff voice, she was accused of being a lesbian. Clive Berghofer, a real estate developer, joined forces with Lyle Shelton, a Pentecostal on council. Their slogan was simple: *IT'S OKAY TO VOTE NO*.

'We are known as the Garden City,' said Berghofer, a high-school dropout who'd subdivided 10,000 blocks of land. 'Now we are the Shit City or Poowoomba.'

After the release of *An Inconvenient Truth*, which I watched with self-righteousness, 62 per cent of my home town voted no to recycled water based on fake news funded by a megalomaniac millionaire. Capitalism and Christianity waged a scatological battle against science.

I can't wait to escape this place, I wrote to Rintoul.

*

On a Sunday afternoon, 'This Charming Man' by the Smiths jangled as I served a farmer, who suffered an anaphylactic reaction.

'Are you one of those faggots?' he asked.

Mercifully, the door to the front bar swung open, revealing my brother John. 'What's goin' on?' he asked, detecting the tension from the customer's disgusted lips and the attendant's blushing cheeks.

'He called me a faggot,' I said.

'Why don't you call *me* a faggot,' he said, before landing a clean punch on the customer's chin. 'Ya faggot!'

A feeling of safety and shame followed the quarrel. Did my reliance on John's muscle make me any better than the bigot? 'Thanks, mate,' I said.

Morrissey kept whining. John slapped the laptop shut like it contained a virus, and put my pink-tipped copy of Plath's *The Bell Jar* in the drawer with the porn magazines. 'Cut that shit out around here,' he said.

My mother had recently brought home a second-hand hard-cover called *Treasury of Great Short Stories*.

Hemingway bored me, but I loved Fitzgerald, because he allowed the kinds of emotions that I'd learned to repress to erupt above the surface. Joyce's 'The Dead' led me to *A Portrait of the Artist as a Young Man*, which I borrowed from Toowoomba Library. In the bottle-o, I suffered the rapture of having my specific alienation captured by an Irish stranger ninety years earlier. My Grade Ten English teacher, Mr Shaw, was a wisp of a man with a feminine inflection. He suggested that I enter a statewide writing competition. I won with a short story about a woman who dreams of murdering her father, the philandering prime minister.

'This isn't a little hobby,' he said conspiratorially in the hall-way after school. 'A university degree in literature and writing could turn you into something special.'

I had sixteen aunties and uncles, and ten of them hadn't made it past primary school. Only one had reached Grade Ten. To compensate, my father wanted me to study something magnificent like law or economics.

At the halfway mark of Grade Ten, on the way home from a careers seminar with my feuding parents, I announced that I intended to study English literature.

'That's exactly what I would have done!' said Mum. 'Don't worry about money. Do what you love.'

In the rear-view mirror, a king saw his legacy disappearing. He was appalled that I was becoming a nervous bookworm who preferred creativity and solitude to popularity and profit. In other words, my mother's son.

'I thought you wanted to be the PM,' he said.

'You can't just *be* the prime minister.'

'There's no point pissing in from outside the tent.'

The 2007 election provided us with an opportunity to reconcile. We handed out how-to-vote cards for Labor at one of the most right-wing polling booths in the country. 'Your face will be on the signs one day,' said my father, trying to reignite my political ambitions.

That night, I wore a Che Guevara t-shirt and red Converse to Sizzler for dinner with John and Dad. Dad proposed a toast during the cheese-bread entrée. 'To Mr Howard,' he said. 'Suck shit, dickhead.'

John was only twenty-four, but he had three daughters and a mortgage. He was my father's second-in-charge at the family business, and one of 'Howard's battlers' – a new generation of working-class conservatives.

'Kevin Rudd will fuck this country,' he said. 'You may as well open the floodgates to boat people.'

'You sound like Pauline Hanson,' I said.

'She says what a lot of people are thinking.'

'So you're a Nazi now, too?'

John's feelings came from his mouth in a stream, and I could tell that he'd been dwelling on them. 'Do-gooders are ruining this country,' he said. 'Everyone's a racist nowadays. And it'll be people like me with real jobs who pay for all the damage. While smug pricks like you are jerking each other off at university.'

I tried to hold back the tears that welled in my eyes whenever I got into a fight with the men in my family.

'*Solidarity forever*!' my father sang, aiming to inflame John, or to induce a truce between the two of us. But I knew he had more in common with his tough bartender son than with me, and that

Kevin Rudd had more in common with John Howard than with Nick Cave or David Malouf.

'For the union makes us strong,' I whispered.

Deep down, the only people I felt solidarity with were my favourite musicians and writers. I wanted to be an artist, not a son, brother, mate, Australian, *larrikin*. But in the dusk of John Howard's reign, when the mundane suffocated the sublime, my dreams felt like treason.

From *Car Crash*, 2021

ST LOUIS

Oliver Reeson

When I was twenty-one and had just discovered the possibilities of writing as art, I heard a Harold Brodkey short story called 'The State of Grace' on *The New Yorker* fiction podcast. In it, the narrator recounts his teenage years in St Louis, particularly times spent babysitting a young boy named Edward. The protagonist prides himself on being able to invent games that were 'wonderful to [Edward] – like his daydreams, in fact'. Yet always, despite Edward's ferocious, trembling love for him, the narrator holds the boy at a cool distance. It is only later, from the vantage point of adulthood, that he experiences regret. 'Really, that's all there is to this story,' the narrator concludes. 'The boy I was, the child Edward was. That, and the terrible desire to suddenly turn and run shouting back through the corridors of time, screaming at the boy I was, searching him out and pounding on his chest: Love him, you damn fool, love him.'

On the podcast, American novelist Richard Ford reads the story and says that Brodkey 'became a kind of perfectionist, which is a bad thing to be if you're a novelist, [but] it's not such a bad thing if you're a short story writer'. Brodkey's novel *Party of Animals* was famously delayed (it took nearly thirty years to be published), and though he was once the talk of New York for his perfect short stories – the great potential, the wunderkind of the city – that wait came to be considered a great sadness. How dare this writer make New Yorkers believe in something and then make them wait for it? His critics spoke of him like he was a grifter, and their impatience with him transferred onto his characters. 'Brodkey is so fixated upon the tragic memories of his childhood and youth that he has virtually no sense of proportion about them. In one story after another, he offers up pages of gratuitous detail, straining, it seems, to squeeze every last drop of significance out of every last inane particular,' wrote Bruce Bawer, reviewing the 1988 collection *Stories in an Almost Classical Mode*.

Harold Brodkey did not grow up queer in Australia and, depending on your view of queerness and its relation to time and self, one might not even be able to say that he grew up queer in America. He died of AIDS in 1996, and although he contracted the virus from a homosexual relationship he never considered himself a gay man – nor, presumably, a queer man. The narrative Brodkey told of himself was that he was a married heterosexual man whose romantic life was separate to his sexual one. That is – or was – his story to tell.

I don't consider myself to have grown up queer in central New South Wales or central Queensland as a child, or Brisbane as a teenager, though these are the places I lived, grew older, fucked in. I began to grow up as a queer person in a doctor's office in East Brunswick when I was twenty- five, when I cried asking for a referral to a gender therapist. In this moment I admitted for the first time that my disconnect from my body was not – as I had often posited lamely to confused romantic partners – so much to do with the surgery I'd had for breast cancer, or with being asexual, but more with that fuzziness that had persisted since my teenager years. Since I'd stepped out of the seemingly genderless space of childhood and into the heavily gendered body of a teenager going through puberty. I had never spoken about it before, but as I entered adolescence I checked out of my body indefinitely. I told myself that this was what puberty was like for everyone, but over the years it became increasingly obvious that this was not the universal experience I had imagined it was.

In high school I had no concept that I might be transgender.

I thought, for a time, that I might be gay. In Year 8 English we were taken on an excursion to the Roma Street Parkland in Brisbane to see Shakespeare's *Twelfth Night*. When Olivia tried to seduce Viola (disguised as her brother Sebastian), I felt the melodramatic and engulfing narrowing of my world. I sat in the sunlit amphitheatre in my Catholic school uniform (tartan and large, totally unfit for Queensland weather) and the pubescent voice in my head couldn't utter anything more than *That's really cool.* This feeling never culminated in any real life crushes, but I still knew that it was the start of something significant, and I remember one night praying to God that I not be gay. *I can't do it*, I said. *I don't know how*.

At times since then I have considered myself a dyke, asexual or pansexual. 'I never really came out,' I used to tell people proudly. 'I just started kissing people and never called it anything. My family didn't care. I'm really lucky.'

More honestly, I never came out because I didn't have any words, no story yet, for why what was happening in me didn't match exactly what was happening in almost everybody else. I would only understand it later in life, as I shuffled through old memories of adolescence. In all of these I have no consciousness of my body. Memories of my youth are of my mind and of a vague feeling of discomfort, like when you don't get enough sleep and your body feels like something you are merely wearing, like clothing.

Like Brodkey's protagonist, having lost my childhood, my most comfortable moments were when I didn't feel looked at. 'It was comfortable for me in the back room, alone in the apartment with Edward, because at last I was chief; and not only that, I was not being seen. There was no one there who could see through me, or think of what I should be or how I should behave; and I have always been terrified of what people thought of me, as if what they thought was a hulking creature that would confront me if I should turn a wrong corner.'

In my early twenties I was unexpectedly diagnosed with breast cancer, and thus was forced to confront the idea of my body: that I had one, that I needed it to live, that it was malleable, and that I belonged to it and it to me. It is only now, as I move into the later part of my twenties, that I am growing up. I have started testosterone therapy and I feel, suddenly, like the teenager I never was. It is as if my physical self is coming into focus, and not just when I look in the mirror. It's as though my mind is one image and my body another, and they are circling ever closer to one another, closer to something unified and clear.

I have a crush on someone, in the dizzying, disorienting sense, for probably the second time in my life, and I have no idea what to do with it. The other night she asked me about the ways in which I feel like I'm going through puberty. I told her I had always found people beautiful but now I find them hot. I find myself wanting to touch their skin or kiss their shoulders. When we talk, my voice breaks when I laugh too loudly or talk too fast, and she laughs at me and asks me why I hate it happening. I say I don't know. I do like the way it signals my growing up, but I feel residual discomfort with the notion of being noticeable.

Mostly, I feel lucky and grateful to be alive in a time when I get to claim who I am, when I can realise something was missing from my life that I deserved to experience and can correct it. Although I *am* correcting it, I think often of the missed opportunities. The incorrect explanations for myself I held for some time. Were they lies, even though I had no concept of the truth? Should I have realised earlier? What if I had had top surgery as a teenager? Would I have developed breast cancer in the residual breast tissue? Or would I have escaped something I never should have had in the first place? Sometimes I want to run back through those corridors of time and pound on someone's chest – but whose? Not the child version of me, who felt genderless and therefore comfortable; not me as a distant and confused teen. No one is at fault, yet the urge to turn and run back towards myself remains.

I have come to view all identity as a sort of constant growing up, a perpetual becoming, a continued reinvention. Our concepts of identity, the categories we use to understand it, are after all simply stories: powerful and important, but not above questioning. To approach them with an expectation of perfection is to stall us, stop the motion of becoming and therefore halt the identity and let it evaporate completely.

I wonder if Brodkey's perfectionism was connected to his choice not to identify as queer. There are countless other factors, of course – he lived in a different time. But the feeling of being adrift, isolated, because you don't have the language to articulate your life perfectly, pervades so much of his work that it gives me pause. It is both heartbreaking and deeply familiar to me.

I want to tell people all the time: there is no deadline for growing up, no submission date for your life's narrative. You can work it out now or later. You can reveal yourself in parts, or as a whole, and make revisions. For better or worse, sooner or later, life conspires to reveal you to yourself, and this is growing up.

Harold Brodkey was a writer with a highly American, masculine intellect. His success, the pressure for him to deliver, the notion that he was gifted – I recognise these as stressful at the same time as I criticise the effortlessness with which they were afforded to him. There were other geniuses at the time, non-male, who could not keep people waiting so long, not piss off their audience so deeply, and still be allowed to publish. As someone who is critical of masculinity and its easy topple into toxicity, I am self-conscious about relating to his work. I relate to it not because I understand the experience of being a man or a teenage boy in America, or because I wish to have been one, but because I recognise someone who couldn't allow themselves to be seen and didn't know why until later in life.

When I look back on my own life, I feel the weight of not realising earlier who I was, of being scared to tell the whole story. And yet, how could I realise I was a non-binary person when I did not even know of the concept until I was already an adult? How could I have grown up as a non-binary person when it was not a story I had ever heard?

Ahead of the release of Brodkey's second novel, *Profane Friendship*, a gay love story released three years after his first novel and two years before his death, Ian Parker wrote: 'Some people publish a novel, are saddened or pleased by its reception, then go on holiday, then write another, have children, write another. Life goes on. But imagine a writer who did not do that. Imagine just one novel; imagine its publication and reception expanding to fill a lifetime; imagine a vast, ridiculous, exhausting palaver going on for twenty-five years – great advances, sneak previews, mistaken newspaper reports of this novel's arrival. Think what this does to your understanding of a normal relationship between writer and reader, between writer and writer, your idea of reputation.'

You can't choose to opt out. If you don't tell the story, others will fill in the gaps for you. Brodkey's story is sad because of its undercurrent of persistent repression. It speaks to me of a heteronormative world that understood and validated his talents but would never allow him the narrative devices his own life needed. Of course, I am projecting – our lives barely overlapped; I can't claim true insight.

'There is a certain shade of red brick – a dark, almost melodious red, sombre and riddled with blue – that is my childhood in St Louis. Not the real childhood, but the false one that extends from the dawning of consciousness until the day that one leaves home for college. That one shade of red brick and green foliage is St Louis in the summer (the winter is just a gray sky and a crowded school bus and the wet footprints on the brown linoleum floor at school), and that brick and a pale sky is spring. It's also loneliness and the queer, self-pitying wonder that children whose families are having catastrophes feel.'

In the opening of 'State of Grace', Brodkey talks of the red brick of St Louis as his childhood and I think of the red brick of the first home I remember living in, in Muswellbrook, New South Wales, where I was born. I wonder if it is the same shade. Instead of being laced with blue, I remember it as being highlighted by the pale orange of the cumquat trees either side of our front door. I recall my childhood in that home not as sombre, but as sharp and free, as running naked in the yard and playing with my brothers and learning to hold their guinea pigs and rabbits and wrestling with their friends. I remember the Christmas when I asked my family to call me Peter because Chloe had gone on holiday with her real family (Some mix-up! Can't remember the details) and my family went along with it, or at least indulged me for as long as I needed this. Perhaps my memories of those bricks are gentler because my childhood there did not stretch, as it did for the narrator of Brodkey's story, until I left for college but, instead, until my dad's job moved us on, as it did every few years. In high school, there are brick buildings once again, a dark red, definitely tinged with blue this time. I went to a Catholic high school, and it's here where Brodkey's sombreness really hits me. My memories of this time are fuzzy with blue, smeared with it.

I don't believe, necessarily, that people are born queer, or that I was born trans. That is not my experience or story. I think I was born free from anything and then stories accumulated on me and some of them turned out to be incorrect. I made my own attempts to write convincing stories too: asking to be called Peter; mistaking the queerness of Shakespeare as relevant to my sexuality rather than my gender (the story I could use to understand my response at the time versus the story I can use to understand it now). None of these stories was objectively true, then or now, but the more I learnt the more I had at my disposal to understand myself. All identities, queer or not, are fictional stories. The importance of queer storytellers is not in how they prove their truth, but in how they prove it is necessary to tell our stories in a way that makes us comfortable.

For queer people, adolescence often stretches beyond the teenage years. I think of familiar queer aesthetics – delicate-featured trans men, butch dykes in patterned bow ties, hairless twinks. Most of my queer friends, in their twenties, live life with the fervent excitement of delayed adolescence, of ascending to yourself long after puberty has passed; of needing to regress to progress, to go back to your adolescence in order to grow up, telling the story correctly this time.

I have two older brothers and although my mum longed for a daughter, she was so certain that I would be a boy that when I emerged into the world and was handed to her, she looked up at my father and said, 'Robbie, what's wrong with his penis?' He looked down at her and replied, quietly, 'Kim, it's a girl.'

In queerness, growing up isn't confined to childhood. The gift of being queer is in the close contact it gives you with the nature of identity, the great many possibilities for becoming and for telling stories. Queerness is the red brick – that heavy, strong thing that reflects the light we see around it.

DON'T TOUCH ALCOHOL

Sara El Sayed

Australia was closed on Sundays. A ghost country. The streets were empty of cars, garbage and people. We had sixteen suitcases, each tagged with red, white and blue ribbons that aunties had plaited for us. I looked out the window of the maxi taxi as we drove away from the airport after our twenty-four-hour journey and did not see a single thing move, aside from the road. We had entered a still image. A billboard of Australia. We were in The Down Under.

Our guardian, the taxi driver, had a neat beard like Baba, and wore a turban. Baba had been bald since at least his wedding photos. The driver and Baba spoke back and forth, neither understanding the other's accent. But both were laughing as if they understood something much more important. Or, more likely, nothing at all.

It was January 2002, and it was hot. The air-conditioning hardly reached the back seat. Nana, who was sitting in the middle row of the taxi next to Mama and Aisha, turned to Mohamed and me.

'Remember,' she said, 'Australia is where kangaroos live. Tell me if you see one.'

'I saw one! I saw one!' said Mohamed, his fat hand pressed against the window, his breath fogging up the glass. 'It was hopping near the road!'

He was a liar. I looked for the whole trip and didn't see a single one.

*

When we first arrived in Morningside, named for the nineteenth-century sunrises hitting the hills, Baba booked two rooms at the Colmslie Hotel, named after the house of a colonial aristocrat who delighted in horseflesh. In the hotel, Mohamed and I were in one room with Nana; Aisha was in the other with Mama and Baba.

Across the road was a small shopping complex, of the blandest colours and geometry the 1960s had offered. The place echoed with the emptiness of absent churchgoers and Sunday late sleepers. The lights in the supermarket were off. A mat sat at the door of the butcher, imprinted with a deceptive welcome. We were still in our clothes from the plane, Aisha's spittle encrusting Mama's t-shirt. 'Does no one eat on Sunday?' Mama said.

A produce store had its roller doors up, and there was a man inside, sweeping the floor. Baba approached him.

'Hello. You are open.' He said this as a question, but it sounded more like a command.

'No,' said the man. 'This is closed. I'm the cleaner.'

'But you are open,' said Baba.

'No, I don't work here. I am the cleaner of the complex.'

'But you are working here. I need to buy food for my kids.'

'I can't help you, sorry.'

My father didn't understand. 'I need food!'

'Fine,' the startled man said. 'Take it.'

Baba started gathering food in a basket. He took it up to the counter. 'I pay here?'

'No. No one is here to take your money.'

'But you are here. I have to pay.'

'I don't work here!'

'I have to pay. I am not a thief.'

'Fine. Give me ten bucks.'

Next stop was a nearby petrol station, whose counter housed a lady clad in hi-vis. He bought some bread, milk and five semi-frozen meat pies.

'What time … do you go home today?' he asked the lady in his halting English.

She looked disturbed. 'Excuse me? I'm not telling you that,' she said.

'No, no.' Baba was embarrassed. 'What time do you stop work here?'

'Oh. Do you mean what time do we close?'

'Yes. Sorry.'

'Four pm.'

'Okay. Sorry.' He watched her scan the meat pies one by one. 'Are these beef?'

'I think so,' she said.

'Are they halal?'

The lady looked at him, confused.

He coughed and rephrased. 'How were they made?'

'Do you mean how do you cook them? You just warm them in the oven.'

'We have no oven. We are at Colmslie.' He pointed out the window.

'Oh. A microwave will do.'

The hotel held two appliances we had never used before. One: a toaster. Mohamed and I were fascinated and kept making toast. We didn't have square bread in Egypt, we had shami – a round flat loaf, which people in Australia like to call pita bread, or Lebanese bread, or *wraps*. We'd toast shami in the oven, or on a naked flame on the stovetop. I'd watch Mama flip the bread over with her fingers, not feeling the flame. But Australians didn't use stoves with flames, Baba said. They used stoves made of plastic and electricity. Australians only cooked with fire for fun, when they went camping and pretended to live like cave-men. They didn't wash their assholes, either. No one owned a bidet. We each had four showers a day in the Colmslie.

Two: a microwave. We had never used a microwave before – and Baba wasn't about to start the day we arrived in a foreign country. When he got back from the petrol station, he bit into the cold pie. He spat it out. 'Eh da? Yuck.' But he ate the rest of it so as not to waste food.

*

Back in Egypt, Baba was an engineer and an architect. In Australia, he was nothing. He started taking cash jobs, laying bricks.

'I am an educated man,' Baba said, 'but for my family I will do anything.' The difficultly manifested physically. In his back, when he lifted loads. In his fingers, which calloused and formed a tough skin. In his mouth, as he tried to connect.

'Can I get you anything while I'm at the shop?' he asked the other workmen on smoko. He thought fetching their lunch would make him some friends.

'Just a pie and a ginger beer for me, thanks, mate,' said one, a greasy-looking man in his twenties.

'Sorry, mate,' Baba said, uneasy. 'I can't buy those sort of things.'

'Huh?'

'Beer things. It's against my god.' He pointed to the sky. Baba took his religion very seriously. He never drank alcohol. Was never in the vicinity of alcohol if he could help it.

'No mate, it's not beer. It's ginger beer. No alcohol,' said the guy, laughing.

'I don't do this. I won't buy it.'

'It's just a soft drink.'

'I won't fall for a trick, mate. Beer is beer. I know what beer is, mate. I can buy something else.'

Despite his difficulties in making friends, it wasn't long before Baba found a position as a foreman. He soon had an esky for a lunchbox and a hard hat without a scratch on it. He was working on a site in Hamilton – a skyrise apartment building near the wharf. Once it was finished, it filled with occupants almost immediately. Baba was immensely proud of himself. They started work on a second building to face the first. By then, the group of tradies he worked with had earned themselves a reputation with Baba.

'Every time a lady or a girl walked past the site, they go crazy,' he said. 'The boys point and stare, like monkeys. I don't understand this. Because some of them have beautiful wives and girlfriends who come by and drop off their lunch. Then they go and do this staring thing. It's not good. It makes the new residents unhappy.'

One lady complained to Baba's boss. She said their ogling was making her uncomfortable. His boss came to the site and handed Baba an envelope.

'Don't look inside, but take this up to the lady on the fifth floor,' he said.

'Why can't I look?' said Baba.

'Because you if you look, I know you won't want to take it to her.'

Baba looked inside. It was a Beer, Wine and Spirits voucher. 'I don't want to be involved in alcohol,' said Baba.

'It's a gift,' said his boss, 'a peace offering. To make her happy. From me to her. Not from you. You're just delivering it. Can you do that for me?'

Reluctantly, Baba made his way up to the fifth floor. He knocked on the door and was greeted by a young woman who looked like she was on her way to the gym.

'Hello. Peter sent me to make you happy,' said Baba.

The woman turned red and cross. 'I've had enough of this crap. Fuck off,' she said, and shut the door in his face.

Baba was embarrassed. He'd said something wrong, but he didn't know what. He gave the envelope back to his boss and resolved never to touch anything to do with alcohol again.

We moved from the Colmslie to a modest three-bedroom,

with a landlord who lived next door. The house was beneath a flight path, and the whirr of planes, with time, would come to remind us of the ocean.

The landlord was a nice man with two kids and a new wife. He would peek over the fence every time we were in the yard and ask us what we were doing, in a friendly way. We didn't meet our neighbours on the other side at first. We could hear and smell their chickens, which strutted around their garden, and we could see the Australian flag that flew from the thick pole that sprouted in it.

During our first week in that house, I watched an episode of *Hi-5* where Kelly uncovered a time capsule she had supposedly buried when she was a little girl. I decided that I, too, would make a time capsule. As we had just moved from across the world, we didn't have many things we were willing to part with. But I was determined to capture our family as we were – a new start, in a new house, in a new country.

In the dining room, my mother's arms were stuck to the plastic gingham-patterned tablecloth, which was covered with newspapers, and the newspapers covered in highlighter. Mama's latest rejection was from the supermarket, where she had applied to be a cashier.

'Do you have anything I can put in our time capsule?' I asked her. She didn't answer. I asked again. 'Do you have anything?'

'I'm busy, Soos,' she said, her eyes reflecting the vacancies. 'Anything?'

She reached across the table and grabbed a wad of junk mail. 'Here,' she said.

I thought of a place that was full of things no one would miss: the rubbish bin. I dug through and found an empty yoghurt tub. I washed it out and stuffed it in with the junk mail. Also in the bin was a box with the words *rum balls* written in cursive, still full.

If there was one thing Baba hated, it was waste. It was haram to waste food. Since that cold pie from the petrol station, I'd seen him spit out food only once – when the landlord gifted him that box of rum balls on moving day. He put a ball in his mouth and read the box, saw the word rum, spat it out, rubbed his tongue with a baby wipe and rushed to the bathroom to gargle. He did this with the same energy one might lick the salt off the back of their hand, down a shot and suck a lemon.

I took two rum balls out of the box and put them in my time capsule.

The ground in the yard was hard and dry, so I dug a hole in the loose bark that sat at the base of the tree on the nature strip. The time capsule was a box of us. This is the story it told: we liked yoghurt, because the yoghurt tub was licked clean; we received junk mail, because we finally had a mailbox; and we never, ever ate rum balls, because we were Muslim.

'Excuse me,' called a voice from behind. The lady from next door, the chickens-and-flagpole side. She was wearing horse-riding boots, and her hair was coiffed in a ponytail that pulled her forehead taut. She looked like she would smell overwhelmingly perfumed if you hugged her. She must have been watching me burying the capsule, but had kept her distance. When she spoke, she sounded polite: 'Your rubbish doesn't belong on our street.'

From *Muddy People*, 2021

COMING IN

Joo-Inn Chew

Michelle stares at me like I'm an alien. 'If you don't say, you can't play,' she insists, and pouts her strawberry-glossed lips.

Kylie and Debbie nod, ponytails bobbing in agreement.

It is dim in the cubby and it smells of Vegemite sandwich. There's not enough room, so the baby's cot is on top of the fridge, and I'm sitting on the stove. Through a gap in the stick wall there's a glimpse of blue sky and scraggly gum trees.

I sigh down at my dirty toes poking out of my uncool sandals. I scratch my short hair. For some reason a flash of Lisa Kennedy from Grade 5 acing elastics arcs through my mind.

'I don't have one,' I say.

Michelle frowns. 'Everyone has one. You have to have one for Mothers and Fathers. Otherwise who are you going to marry?'

'Yeah,' says Debbie, 'but you can't have Greg, he's mine. We're going to have twins.'

I pick at the scab on my knee and wish I was in the library, reading a book. Should I say Alan? He seems less germy than the others. Or Jason – but he likes to squash ants. They're all so gross. Mothers and Fathers sucks. It was better when we liked horses.

'I don't really want to get married,' I blurt out, horrifying myself. The girls all glare in disbelief. Already lips are curling, hair is tossing, mean words are fizzing on tongues. I stand up and they draw back and closer together, like I'm a bomb. The baby's cot wobbles and I don't even bother to catch it this time. It hits the dirt and the doll tumbles out onto its face, one blue plastic eye staring sideways accusingly. Probably dead. The cubby's gone blurry and I stumble over the cot with its tangle of blankets, out the low door.

I hate that I am crying. 'I don't care, I don't want to play your stupid game anyway!'

Outside it's cold and fresh. I run down the hill away from the shrieks and the dead baby and my future husband and triplets, run into the open, jumping anthills and logs, looking for a tree to climb, scaring the magpies into flight.

*

'Brad's *so* cute, but he got with Nadine at the Blue Light and my life is *ruined*.'

'She's such a slut anyway.'

'Jason said hi before Woodwork, but was that hi or *hi*?' 'You should totally ask him out, Nic. He's such a spunk.'

I hitch my short uniform up even further to let the sun bite into my thighs. Eight tanned legs lie parallel along the concrete, like long shiny coconut-scented rolls. Forty painted toenails loll at ease. Four mouths gossip or mmm-hmm, while trying not to eat too much fattening food. Four sweaty backs with trainer bra straps lean against the warm bricks of the canteen wall. Distant shouts and the crack of ball against bat float up from the oval. The air is heavy with wattle and sun-tanning lotion, and the drowsy droning of flies.

Shar strides across the netball court with her friends, and suddenly I'm wide awake. She burns across my retina like a comet. My skin is prickling and shivers ripple down to my toes. Electricity dances all over me. It's hard to sit still, hard not to run. Hard to act cool as she walks towards us. Sun is in her hair and sliding off her arms, spilling down her long legs, teasing out a sinuous shadow behind her. She stops to say something to her friend, so close I can see freckles on the side of her neck. Her voice tickles my ears. I can't look at her lips, her green eyes, the way she's laughing, or I might explode or give myself away. I stare at a wad of gum flattened into a whitish splot on the concrete by my left ankle, run my eyes round and round its rough edges, until at last she moves away and I can breathe again. My heart is skittering and blazing, faint and fierce all at once. I let myself watch her as she walks away, the way her hair slides across her shoulder and one strand lifts in the breeze. When she disappears round the corner she takes light and colour with her. The afternoon is empty and dull, a stage after a show.

Around me the others are still chatting, they haven't noticed, or maybe they're used to my silent weirdness. Now they're talking about which boy has the best bum. I make myself nod and mmm. I concentrate on acting normal. I file Shar away with the others in my secret Quite-A-Few-Crushes-But-I'm-Not-A-Lesbian-It's-Just-A-Phase file. Lots of girls love Madonna and Jodie Foster. Lots of girls aren't into boys yet. Lots of girls are too busy reading books and getting As – okay, well, not that many, but if there were more with glasses and Chinese fathers like me then there would be lots. I'm just a late bloomer. And Shar is just distractingly beautiful. It's not like I love her or want to kiss her or anything. I'm not a perv or a lemon. Those Grim Reaper ads are nothing to do with me. When I imagine rescuing her from a fire in assembly, or saving her from hypothermia in the snow when we miss the last bus, it's not like I … oh god – think about something else.

I can do this. Only ten minutes till the bell goes. I focus really hard on what I can add to the group analysis of Derek's personality and Wayne's shorts. And I keep my dangerous and delicious secret hidden under my uniform, right over my heart.

*

I wipe the steel kitchen bench again and again, even though it's shiny clean. The last elderly resident has shuffled out of the dining room, and Carol hurries in with an armful of trays. I open my dry mouth then close it again. I watch her stack porridge bowls into the dishwasher and feel my heart doing a tap dance of terror. Come on, you coward. Don't pike now. It's 1992, you can do this.

'Guess what?' I squeak.

'What?' she asks. She has kind, dark eyes and a gold nose-ring, and she is an Indian dental student.

'I'm ... I'm bisexual,'* I blurt out. And start sorting trays like a maniac, feeling my cheeks heat up the room.

'You're kidding me,' she says.

'No, really.'

The longest silence in human history ticks by. I fight an urge to hide under my apron. Instead, I wipe the pink-and-purple floral placemats, the true hideousness of which I've never taken in before. Mrs White's radio blares golden oldies from Room 9.

'Wow ... well, that's okay,' she says.

I drag my eyes up to her face and see she means it. Something in me collapses, a breaking wave of relief that washes warm tingles to my toes and salt water to my eyes.

'Course it is,' I say gruffly. I line up the water jugs. Their painted daisies and teddy bears seem about to gambol off the glass. Just seeing them frolic beside the stack of attractive floral placemats is making me grin absurdly.

Carol is staring at me.

'Um, thanks,' I say.

'No problem.'

Who knew dental students could be so cool? I skip away at the end of my shift, leaving my old skin a tattered remnant on

---

* This is true at the time. I do have a boyfriend (I have to give blokes a try, and he's a good one) but I'm in love with my best friend, and I'm about to break my boyfriend's heart in a long, messy, self-absorbed twenty-year-old way to go out with her . . . and never look back.

the mopped kitchen tiles. Outside, my new skin fizzes in the sunlight, alive to the breeze, smelling much more like me.

*

The line snakes down the block outside the Builders Arms, into the warm Fitzroy night alive with glittery grunge. Thursday is Queer and Alternative night at the pub, and it feels like everyone radical and fabulous is queuing to get in. Dreadlocked ferals and tripping ravers suck lollipops next to my lesbian separatist housemates, next to gay boys with sparkling pecs, and a sprinkling of Asian queers. Hot dykes in dog collars, radical feminists, drag kings and queens – they all let each other be tonight. There's even a sheepishly excited handful of medical and engineering students, and a couple of fellow formerly closeted survivors from high school, freed at last. Doc Martens and goddess tattoos abound.

There's lust and revolution in the air. Last week was Melbourne's first pride parade, thousands striding defiantly through the St Kilda streets – where some of us had been gay-bashed – holding hands and kissing, strangely buoyed by the cheering voyeurism of the hetero crowds. Heads high: we're here, we're queer, and we're not going shopping. We don't belong in your 'straight suburban breeders' world; we're roaming in wilder terrain outside the map, making new tribes and families, seeing more clearly from the margins.

Our love is in the spotlight in the early '90s, zigzagging between wicked and chic. k.d. lang is on the cover of *Vanity Fair* in a suit, lathered up for a buxom Cindy Crawford teetering in stilettos to shave. There are gay flicks in the cinema, and Queer Studies at uni. We go to AIDS rallies, Reclaim the Night marches and Queer Kiss-Ins. We come out to family and some of us are thrown out of home, or told to pray away the gay.

I am lucky; my parents and siblings accept my sexuality. Perhaps softened up by the long teenage years of tortured girl crushes, they are more surprised by my two-year heterosexual detour than by my eventual coming out. They see how happy I am with my girlfriends, and welcome them into the family. Still, we keep the secret from elderly and religious relatives, here and in Malaysia, not wanting to identify a devil incarnate in their midst and be fending off prayers and condemnation for eternity.

My father comes to the launch of a book I have contributed to, a collection of coming-out stories. He stands awkwardly in his hand-knit jumper and cargo pants, a lone Chinese dad in a crowd of people he once would have called fairies and poofters, just to be proud of me. He used to jeer at Mardi Gras on TV; now he drops me off at Pride March and warns me to be careful. But when I try to stay over at my lover's house, her father shoves a twenty-dollar note under the bedroom door. 'Get that *woman* out of my house,' he snarls. And we flee into the night, and I never go back.

But for now we are gorgeous radicals, uncloseted and in love, ordinary and extraordinary. Dance anthems throb from the pub doorway and my girlfriend grins at me in the streetlight, setting me aglow. A passing ute-driver rolls down his window to yell, 'Fucken homos!' The drag queens in the line blow him a kiss. The lesbian separatists muscle towards him and he drives off fast, silenced. 'Dickhead!' chorus the engineering students. And we laugh and growl and shimmy, because tonight we own the night.

*

A rainbow balloon slips loose and disappears into the wide blue sky. My daughter frowns and clutches hers more tightly. My son leans against my leg in his black hoodie and pink socks, reading *Harry Potter*. He's bored with rallies now and has only come to get his ice-cream bribe afterwards. Next to him, my partner holds a banner with the kids' donor dad. Around us, the feisty crowd listen as gay dads, lesbian union organisers, politicians and religious leaders speak with passion and honesty. A wave of cheers echoes off the buildings and the march is away.

What do we want? Marriage equality!

When do we want it? Now!

We surge down the Canberra streets alive with rainbow flags and banners. The kids skip and chant, glad to be on the move, hopeful of getting on TV and being famous at last. At the edge of the crowd, a handful of men shake placards scrawled with Bible verses and shout that we'll burn in hell. My son glances at them in confusion and I hurry him on. Another thing to explain over dinner tonight. There are too many things that are too hard to explain. Why the whole country is 'voting' on whether their two mums are allowed to get married, even after seventeen years together. Why everyone at school is talking about it. Why we keep muting the news as another politician spouts bile about the slippery slope to bestiality, or how we are not fit parents. Why their mums have been edgy for months. The stress of wondering how everyone we know, how our whole country, is going to 'vote' takes its toll. We discover things we wished we hadn't known about workmates and family, things that can't be forgotten. As a doctor, finding out my valued nursing colleagues are voting 'No' stings.

One, two, three, four, stop this homophobic law!

Five, six, seven, eight, how do you know your kids are straight?

*

It's the week after the plebiscite. The resounding 'Yes' vote has brought wave after wave of emotion. First: relief. Then, surprise, gratitude, a melting wonder. I realise I had been dreading a kick in the guts from the entire nation. Despite the confident lesbian life I am living now – rainbow family, queer community, LGBTIQA+ health work – I was still carrying around an '80s-kid view of Australia.

Believing that outside my little protective bubble the great masses disapproved, thought I was abnormal, lesser, sinful, wrong. A perv and a lemon. I hadn't dared hope that my country had moved on from homophobia to affirmation.

Now I walk around the shops, the schoolyard, the waiting room, knowing I am welcome in my real skin. I came out decades ago, but it has taken this long to truly *come in*. Married or unmarried, our family of 'Mothers and Mothers' has a place in the cubby too. Our love has come in from the fringes, into the muddle of humanity in the middle. Bringing its own radical gifts.

And somewhere inside me, an eight-year-old girl up a tree shakes out her short hair, then breaks into the most beautiful smile.

SELECTED EPISTLES

Olivia Muscat

Dear PE teachers,

I know physical activity is important. But you didn't need to try to convince me I was good at athletics. I was never going to believe you. I knew coming second out of two isn't actually a mark of talent. It just made me feel like shit. I like to win because of effort and skill, not because I'm the only competitor. And also, I really, really, *really* hate shot-put.

Sincerely yours,

The least enthusiastic potential shot-put champion that ever attended an athletics carnival,

Olivia

*

Dear creepy man on the train platform (or on the train, bus, tram, or in the shop, or wherever),

It is no concern of yours how I get dressed in the morning, how I look after myself or if I have a boyfriend. Please take the hint when I move away from you, and don't follow me to ask if I live on my own. I don't have to answer your creepy questions and I am under absolutely no obligation to be polite to you. Kindly get lost.

Regards,

You don't need to know my name, so stop asking

*

Dear person at Flinders Street Station,

I don't know what part of me walking straight towards the escalators makes you believe I don't know that the escalators are ahead of me. Don't grab my arm and try to drag me on. It's dangerous and pretty fucking rude.

Yours truly,

Just trying to get where I need to go

*

Dear random street people,

No, I am not the person you know who looks nothing like me but also happens to use a cane or have a guide dog. And no, I don't know them … probably.

Best wishes,

Olivia. Not Ashleigh or Claire or Christine or Tess or Michaela or Jordie or Cassie or Emma-Mae

*

Dear Drama teacher,

It was astonishingly hurtful when you would not let me audition to be a member of the chorus in the Year 8 school production – when you offhandedly told me you hoped I wouldn't come to the audition. I'm not sure if you realised how soul-crushing that was. Well, let me tell you: it was one of the most upsetting things that happened to me in a really terrible year.

Thank you for seeing the error of your ways (once my parents pointed it out to you, mind) and for becoming more open to creativity and improvisation, and for going on to cast me in several major roles in musicals and plays that involved me dancing and running and throwing myself across a stage. You turned out to be one of my favourite people and a truly amazing teacher and director.

Playing Ida, Malvolio and Nancy was some of the most fun I have ever had. And when people came up to me afterwards and told me that they didn't realise I was blind, it was a testament to both of us. There were some hairy moments, but that never stopped us from giving anything a go. I'm a better performer and person because of you and what you encouraged me to achieve.

In Year 12, you completely made up for that first, heartbreaking non-audition by informing me that with my acting and singing abilities, there was no other choice for the role of Nancy in *Oliver*! You just casually said it in the corridor one day and it made everything worth it. So many people would have chosen the next best actor and singer because it would have just been easier with a sighted person. You didn't, and if I do say so myself, I crushed it. We crushed it!

With gratitude and appreciation,

Olivia

*

Dear Jemima,

For so long I was reluctant to take the plunge and get a guide dog, but you are one of the best things that has ever happened to me. I'm no longer fearful of travelling independently to places I've never been before because you're crazily good at your job. And though I might occasionally get us a bit lost, I know you'll stick by my side and keep me safe. You have an uncanny ability to know exactly what I need you to find before I've even given you a command, which is a bit spooky but often comes in handy.

We've conquered so much of Melbourne, and even cities we don't live in, together. And although you do shed that blonde hair of yours everywhere and you have some pretty gross habits – and I really hate talking to random strangers about dogs – you've changed my life and expanded my world. You are 100 per cent worth any compromise.

I will love you always, my girl,

Olivia (that's me, Ma)

*

Dear fellow blind person,

Just because we're both blind doesn't mean we will be friends.

If we have things in common, and get on, and enjoy each other's company, we can absolutely be friends. I look forward to it. But our mutual blindness doesn't equal automatic best friendship. I will ignore that Facebook friend request, no matter how many mutual friends we have, until we have actually met in person, or at least had a conversation, because that's my policy, and being a fellow blindy doesn't exempt you from that. It's not a secret society.

'Till we meet,

Olivia

*

Dear every visiting teacher I ever had,

Thank you for insisting that I learn braille even though I still had enough vision to read print. Although I don't use it all the time, it comes in useful pretty often. It's a great skill to have, despite all the fancy tech that exists these days.

I apologise for being so resistant at times, and I know I'd probably be a faster braille reader now if I'd worked harder at it then. It's in my nature to be stubborn, and I couldn't predict the future. I didn't want to imagine that my vision would go and I'd need to rely on braille; I was a kid and that thought was scary. But here we are, and I'm grateful for your perseverance.

Apologies and thanks,

Olivia

*

Dear kids at school,

Primary school, high school – it doesn't matter. I know there were those of you who were completely pleasant to my face but laughed or scoffed behind my back. I don't know if you thought I couldn't tell or that I was too brainless or naive to realise, or too scared to confront you about it. But honestly, I just didn't care. It's no concern of mine if you think being blind made me somehow worthy of mockery. And guess what, I probably mocked you right back. I didn't give a shit about your approval anyway.

Bye!

*

Dear well-meaning people,

Chances are, unless I've asked you outright, I don't want, need or appreciate your advice.

Thanks in advance,

P.S. Yes. I know scientists are working on bionic eyes.

*

Dear even more random street people,

Don't touch me without my permission. Don't grab my cane. Don't pat my dog. And definitely don't argue with me if you do pat my dog and I ask you politely not to. If you say something about my cute puppy and I don't respond, don't get shitty. I've probably had a long day. If you offer me a seat on public transport and I say thanks but no thanks, don't call me an ungrateful bitch. I have my reasons. If I walk onto crowded public transport and ask whether there's a seat close by, don't just ignore me until I give up and go stand somewhere, desperately trying to both keep my balance and keep my dog from getting trampled.

Just because I don't see you, it doesn't mean I don't know you're there. When you advance on me in some misguided attempt to tie my shoelace and I pull away and tell you I've got it, don't act like I've done something wrong. *You've* invaded my personal space and made assumptions about me. I'm not in the wrong here.

Cheers,

Member of the public who deserves just as much respect as you do

*

Dear teachers, of music and other subjects,

I appreciate all the time and effort and energy you put into making me a good musician. I really do. It seemed like the easiest road, didn't it? I was a talented singer, and music is one of those pretread, ready-to-follow blind paths that appear to have the fewest hurdles. But this unwavering assumption that music was my future led me to think it was my only option, especially after I went totally blind. I cut off many other possible pathways because everyone told me music was my future. And when I got to university and found out that studying music made me want to curl up in a ball and never do anything again, I had the most enormous crisis of confidence imaginable. Every tutorial, every lecture, every singing lesson filled me with dread. I felt constantly on the verge of throwing up. And of course I pretended everything was fine.

Everyone's expectations that I would become a musician weighed heavily on me, and it was a huge struggle to wriggle my way out from underneath them. It almost completely crushed my spirit.

So, while you meant well, I wish you hadn't implied music was my only option. Because it wasn't. You took something I loved and twisted it into something compulsory, something that caused me terrible pain and fear. And only after that horrible year did I realise I had other talents, other interests, other pathways, and I was able to forge a new, more fulfilling future for myself.

Yours, in relief and regret,

Olivia

*

Dear word police,

I don't know how many times I have to tell you that it's okay to refer to me as totally blind. That's what I am. I'm not 'vision impaired'; my vision is non-existent. I'm not 'partially sighted'; there's no partial about it. I have no sight. It's gone, dead, caput.

There's no need to get flustered when I say 'totally blind'. That's how I refer to myself, because it leaves no room for interpretation. It's final. Totally blind means I can't see anything. *Because I really can't see anything* and it's kind of important for people who I interact with to know that. It's a fact, like saying I have brown hair, or size seven feet, or naturally great eyebrows. I'm not offended by it, so I don't see why you should be either.

Kind regards,

Totally blind Olivia – yes, totally

*

Dear people who assume that because my eyes don't work my mind doesn't either,

Fuck. You.

Best wishes,

None of your damn business

*

Dear Mum,

I don't think I will ever know all the things you did for me. All the battles you fought when I was too small, too scared or too sad to fight them myself. All the opportunities you made sure I was able to take advantage of. All the times people tried to knock me down and keep me out: dance lessons, Japanese classes, 'dangerous' excursions, school productions. The government told you I couldn't stay at my school if I wanted support after I lost my remaining sight. You went in there and gave them absolute hell until I got what you believed I deserved.

You always did it with such poise and professionalism, and with your signature brand of take-no-bullshit attitude.

Watching you do all that on my behalf set me up to become someone who isn't afraid to demand what she deserves. To call out injustice where she sees it. And to take absolutely zero bullshit. Of all the many gifts you gave me, this one might be the best.

You put fire and steel into my head and heart when I needed to take charge of my life and stand up for myself. But you also knew when I just needed you to wrap me up in a hug and not let go.

Because of everything you did for me while you were here, I am able to do it on my own now that you're gone. I know you're cheering me on inside my heart, and that means everything to me. I never sit around and wish I wasn't blind. It isn't a good use of my time. And most of the time I hardly even notice that I'm down 20 per cent of my five senses. Sometimes I genuinely have to remind myself that other people get most of their information visually.

But those weeks spent sitting beside you in that hospital bed, when we knew you were dying, and you could barely bring yourself to speak. When we couldn't have our passionate, ridiculous, funny conversations, or arguments, depending on the day. Then. Then, I would've given anything to see you for just five minutes. To look into your eyes and memorise every detail of your beautiful, precious, fierce face. The face that raised me, the body that held me, that was about to be wrenched from me forever.

We will never sit down and discuss all the battles you fought for me, all the times you felt that the system was beyond broken but you kept fighting anyway, all the times you came up against sheer ignorance and prejudice but you didn't back down because you loved me and believed I had something to offer the world.

I will never hear those stories from you. Yet somehow, I don't need to hear them, because they are in my blood. They live with your unending spirit inside my soul. They course through my body and spill out into every decision I make – and will continue to make.

I love, honour and treasure you with everything I have.

Forever yours,

Your first daughter,

Olivia

BULLY FOR THEM

Christos Tsiolkas,
as told to Fiona Scott-Norman

When I think back on my primary school years, it was a charmed existence. Everyone's parents worked in the same factories, and the factories were within a kilometre radius, so you knew everyone. We felt quite safe to go in and out of people's houses. We were all immigrant kids, so my best friends were Harry who was Greek, Victor who was Spanish, Zolati who was Yugoslav. All my memories of that Richmond period are outside; we played in the alleys and on the road. It was like we possessed the streets.

Then our family moved to Box Hill North. I was just shy of 13, middle of Year 8, and even though it was the same city, it was like I'd entered another Australia. I still remember the shock of walking into the classroom and seeing a sea of blond people.

My parents moved because they wanted a bigger house, a bedroom each for their two sons. The inner city was seen as quite rough then, and their friends were moving away. I remember my dad shaking: he was so upset after a parent–teacher interview. One of my brother's teachers had said to him, 'Why are you worried about John's education? He's just going to end up in a factory.' That was the expectation. So there was an element of, 'Let's get our kids to the suburbs, where there are more opportunities.'

My new school was immediately isolating. I mean, obviously I'd heard the word 'wog', and heard it used against my parents and myself, but when we were in Richmond, and we were all wogs, we were protected against the ferocity of the word. But in the first week, these three boys ganged up on me, and I remember walking past them in the corridor, them holding their noses and talking about how wogs stink.

All the rules had suddenly changed. They picked a fight, and I'm not a fighter, I never have been, and there were three against one. I remember thinking, 'Oh well, I'd better go for it', and biting one of them, and him yelling, 'What are you doing? You're not allowed to bite', and I realised I didn't even know how to fight correctly.

The bell would go for recess and lunch, and the kids would form their tribes and groups, and I didn't have anyone. So I would just go to the back of the oval and walk around and around, and get lost in a fantasy world. I was anywhere but suburban Blackburn. I was making up worlds, and dreaming of being someone else. I was making movies in my head. I would say there were two years where, if I wasn't thinking about sex, I was thinking about making movies.

I don't want to overstate the racism, because in lots of ways it was quite casual, but it was venomous. Those daily slurs were powerful. I became acutely aware of my difference. I was just becoming aware that my sexuality was – in the eyes of the world back then – abnormal, and it all came to a head. I felt like I was completely abnormal. Some weird … thing. For a boy back then, sport was one of the things that defined you, and because I was late to the school and a wog, I was always chosen last for teams. It became a symbol of where I sat in the hierarchy. It was a ritual of humiliation. I hated PE. Loathed it. I'd use any excuse to get out of it.

And I hated it because you had to strip, every time. I hated the showers. I'd started developing early, so I already had pubic hair and the rest, and they'd taunt me, 'Greeks are so hairy.'

Stupid stuff. So I became self-conscious and disassociated from my body. I saw it as smelly, as hairy, as something disgusting. That took a long time to overcome, and even now, no matter how hard I try and fight it, I still associate physical perfection with a smooth white body.

The PE teachers were real arseholes in the late 1970s. They didn't intervene; they made it worse. You could see the contempt in their faces for kids who weren't physically able, or excluded, and they'd literally say things like, 'Don't be a cry baby.' There were some kids, physically weaker than me, who were bullied terribly, and PE class was a form of torture. The teachers did nothing.

I thought I was the ugliest kid in school. School takes up so much of your time and space so those slights accumulate and you take them on. You think you're ugly, you think you're just a weak, unlovable being. I'd wonder, 'How am I gonna kill myself?' That to me was such a part of adolescence. Sitting for hours in my room at night thinking, 'If I was to do it how would I do it?' I decided I'd be behind the wheel of a car and just drive as fast as I could into a wall. That was the fantasy, something spectacular.

The first person at the school who was friendly to me, actually kind to me, belonged to this evangelical Christian sect. I realise now there was an element of her wanting to convert people. She introduced me to J.R.R. Tolkien, who I'd never read, and after I finished *The Lord of the Rings* she showed me the Christian analogies in the book and started inviting me to her church group.

I grew up Greek Orthodox, but very anti-clerical, and feeling so isolated I just jumped into that Christian world. It was a way of battling my sexual demons. And I saw them as demons – I did not want to be gay. I had no idea how you could possibly survive it. It was impossible during that period to think I could reconcile my masculinity and my sexuality.

You know, back then, it was still illegal to be gay? It wasn't talked about and if you heard anything, it was in the most derogatory terms. For the longest time I felt I had to hide myself, live that aspect in silence. And I knew about my sexuality very, very early on. I was conscious that I was different at five or six. So I tried desperately hard to be Christian. Really hard.

It was that summer between Year 9 and Year 10, and I was so ashamed of the body I was in, that I was badly hurting myself. I remember being in bed and having these sexual fantasies, and to stop myself masturbating I'd scratch and scratch my body until I made myself bleed. Poor mum. She had these bloody sheets to deal with.

Of course I couldn't talk about it with my parents. I just kept saying to God, 'If you stop making me gay, I will do whatever you want.' In the end, I just couldn't come at it. There came a point, in one of the Pentecostal bible study groups, that they started talking about the evil of books and the evil of film and, look, I'm not even sure which writer they were talking about, but they were talking about a writer I loved, and I got up and walked out and kept going.

I just remember realising, 'Oh, there is no God.' So whatever was going to happen, there would be no 'god' to save me from what my life was. Weirdly, that was liberating. I mean, it didn't necessarily change anything about my school years but, interestingly, it was only after that realisation that I began to form firm friendships, though all of them were with girls.

Being at a co-ed school saved me. I found close relationships with the girls, and I treasured those friendships. They kind of protected me from the boys, all the way through. I grew up in a time where you were either one of the boys – the jocks – or if you had an intellectual curiosity, you were a pansy or a freak. Even though the high school had a music program, there was a hostility to humanities. You were meant to do sports and be incredibly physical, and if you did really well in my favourite subjects – Art and English – well, that made you a poofter. If you like reading you're a poofter, if you like art you're a poofter. With the girls there was a safe space where you could be that. I found the girls' world fascinating, but I'm not romantic about women's friendships – I saw how girls could treat other girls. To be honest, I'd find it unimaginable to not go to a co-ed school; I'd be terrified to be with just boys all the time. I only had one male friend, and eventually he turned out to be gay as well.

The path out, in the end, was books and cinema. The books I was reading and the films I was watching were like a light going on. They presented a seductive alternative, and I knew there was a big world out there. I read all the time. I don't remember when I first awoke to the pleasure of reading, but we're talking back in primary school. I wanted to write from very early on, but I didn't know how. Coming from a very typical migrant working-class life, the idea of writing as a career had a fantastical element to it, and that continued well into my adulthood.

I remember in Year 9 my teacher, Mrs Crabtree, standing in front of the class in English and tearing up my story. She said, 'This is by Chris …' she could never pronounce my name right '… ti-ol-ka', and then she ripped it up in front of everyone. She said, 'He writes filth.' My first critic, and they haven't changed! You don't do that to a kid in Year 9. I was a very promiscuous reader, and I'd been reading a lot of Philip Roth, things like *Portnoy's Complaint* and *Goodbye, Columbus*. I was probably just writing what I was reading – I'm sure it was very derivative and not very good. It may have involved masturbation or the word 'f**k'. Back then that was enough to cause trouble.

There was maybe an element of deliberate provocation involved in writing that story, an aspect of, 'How am I not going to end up with just this? With these people being the rest of my life? How am I going to get out?' Perhaps I wanted it torn up. It's difficult to be definitive, because that time is such a confused maelstrom of emotions and hormones and fears, but the only skill I had was the skill of the imagination, so I think there's a self-styling that went on. A few years on I would probably have been a goth.

I would do people's homework for them, actually, to get liked. It was one of my strategies. I was really good at essays, so some of the kids who weren't doing well, including some of the boys who hated me because I was a 'wog' and a 'poofter', would come to me because I could write their assignments. I had currency. It didn't make me more popular, of course, but it meant that I could negotiate, and that's all I really wanted at that stage – to be in my own world and not have to engage with any of them.

By the end of school there were only ten of us in my art class. I just used to live for those classes. All of us were outsiders, one way or the other, and it was the space where we discussed feminism and sexuality and movies. That's where I found my tribe. My life got a bit easier after Year 10 because the coterie of boys that were just cruel, who'd made the walk to school and the walk back so hard, most of them left for the Tech school down the road. I was so glad about that, having them out of my life.

What I remember of high school is loneliness. The time went so slowly and the aching was so deep. School seemed never-ending. My friendships with the girls were literally lifesavers. But part of loneliness is that you can't speak your truth to anyone, and there were aspects of my emotional life that I was terrified of revealing to my girlfriends. So there was just a longing, I think, for a male best friend. Someone who you could share something with about who you are and what you're experiencing.

I was leading a double life, basically. I'd started experimenting with sex since I was like fifteen, and it was always with older men, because I felt that if I revealed myself to anyone at school, I'd be ostracised. I had one sexual relationship with a boy who was in the class above me. We'd gone to a party, and coming back we'd got onto the subject of David Bowie. Now, I loved David Bowie, but basically 'David Bowie' was code for 'I'm bisexual'. That relationship lasted a little while. So there'd be a Chris Tsiolkas at school, and then a sexual being that was completely unknown to his friends and family. I wasn't knowable back then. I was just so careful, because I didn't want to be attacked, or undermined, or threatened, or to do the wrong thing, or be found out.

What was bizarre was that the boys thought I knew all about straight sex because I was a wog. In Year 9, right, this kid came and up and said, 'How do you get a prostitute? We know that when you're fifteen, Greek fathers take their sons to prostitutes.' Which, for the record, doesn't happen, but I ended up almost, like, studying sex because that knowledge seemed to give me kudos. I remember one of toughest kids took me aside and asked about protection. It was a very strange moment, but because I'd read about it, I could tell him. In terms of my development, the most important moment wasn't something that happened to me, it was something I witnessed. There was one boy, Martin, who was a very gangly, clumsy, physically awkward kid. He wasn't smart either, and the teachers would humiliate him publicly in front of the class. The boys would bully him physically, and the girls teased him mercilessly about how ugly he was. He spat, he had a stutter, but he loved birds, just loved them, and because the oval was my escape I'd see him out there too, making bird sounds. Talking to the birds.

And one day, at the end of Year 8, these boys went out with slingshots. They killed all these birds and stuffed them in Martin's locker. So the poor kid opens it, and these maggies and sparrows fall out, and he loses it, goes ballistic, just howling and howling. I wasn't laughing, I wasn't teasing, I was with a group who were obviously shaken by it, but we didn't intervene. That is still one of the most shaming occasions of my life. I'm still ashamed by that moment. I knew that what was happening was … I'm gonna use the word 'evil' because I can't think of anything else. I knew in my gut what that boy was experiencing and I wasn't brave enough to do anything about it. You know you can't make excuses for it, you know that the right thing to do is stand up. But there's a pecking order, and if you befriend this person, you'll be bullied yourself. So we stayed silent. And no matter how much you pretend that that's not acquiescence, you know it is.

That moment impacted on me as a man, and as a storyteller. The 'taken-for-grantedness' of that kind of cruelty has shaped some of the ways I see thfe world. As I've got older, I believe you've got to speak up. You can't remain silent when you see such evidence of inhumanity. And now I write about those moments, when people don't have the courage to follow their moral convictions. It taught me something about human failure, and it was a really important lesson to learn.

In terms of my writing that emotion of shame comes up again and again, about how sometimes we fail ourselves and others in what we do. I also think those long periods of being on my own were crucial. Walking around and around and around the oval. And I'd just beat a ball against a wall, you know, for hours. What that did was exercise my imagination. Those hours were part of my training to be a writer. Certainly I had an obsession with the desire to write, to be an artist. But those long hours alone were the path that led me there. Spending so much time on my own meant that I created a sense of myself and, really importantly, I'm not scared of not being around other people. It doesn't terrify me, it doesn't make me anxious and, because my mind was so active, it actually became pleasurable for me. There is something about being alone that I really, really love.

It's interesting but because the fantasy world I created for myself was a place I felt safe, I've been able to learn to be comfortable with saying, 'I don't have to please everyone.' Unfortunately, I think one of the ways I tried to fight people's contempt or dislike was trying to be nice. It was part of the way I coped, and it's taken a long time to try and unlearn. Whenever I see a prison film I know exactly who I am. I'd be offering people cigarettes and blow jobs. It sounds like such an extreme metaphor, but school really was like being in a prison. I'd just go, 'Alright, can I make it through this day without being picked on? Without someone commenting on me?' Writing is an escape from that. I'm not nice there. I can be brave in my writing.

I always feel like a bit of traitor to my class by becoming educated, by being artistic. But those working-class boys made it quite clear that I didn't fit there either. If I'd finished high school in Richmond, I'd maybe feel a greater possession around a working-class identity, but the fact is I'd still have been an outsider because of my sexuality. I would have had to wrench myself away anyway. As it was, I moved out of home at eighteen to pursue the life I wanted. My parents were distraught because that wasn't what you did, but I couldn't be the good Greek kid and stay home until I got married. I loved my parents dearly, but there was no way that I could live the life I wanted to live and be in their home.

I'm actually grateful that I never felt quite at home now. I met my partner, Wayne, when I was nineteen, and we've been together ever since. So I got my best male friend. But I would never have met him if I hadn't had to get out of where I was. As a writer I can't separate the influence of my experiences from school, the writers that made an impression on me, and cinema. They were all equally important. That world of the suburbs that I experienced also had a big part to play; it's very strongly part of the Australian environment.

As, for that matter, was my desire to run away from it as fast as I could. I think that being an outsider gives you the beginning of empathy. If you're feeling this way, if you're so isolated, if the world's not working for you, well, maybe it's not working for someone else? Maybe they're Bully for Them not a freak or a loser. Maybe they're also going through shit that is meaningful and important. This was another good lesson.

It's very difficult to imagine that artists can be made without the experience of not fitting in. It's part of what allows you to see beyond yourself. There must be an element of saying, 'I can see the world from another character.' And to make that claim, to observe, you have to have been outside.

But that experience, no matter how difficult the living through of it was, is something I am completely grateful for.

Because it gave me an appetite to begin to explore what was outside the worlds I knew. Outside the migrant family world, but also the world of suburban Australia. I was so hungry that there had to be more.

My relationship to the world is so very different to most people. I'll sometimes be at the dentist or the doctor's and there's the *Women's Weekly* or *New Idea* or *Sports Illustrated* and I'm looking at these people going, who are they? In a sense the 'real world' seems so weird, I have no relationship to that anymore. I live in the world I've created, and that is more than okay.

Reproduced with kind permission of Christos Tsiolkas and Fiona Scott-Norman from the anthology *Bully for Them*, published by Affirm Press 2014

DEAR AUSTRALIA, I LOVE YOU BUT …

Candy Bowers

Dear Australia,
I love you but …
You've been a really shit foster parent.
I thought I'd just lay that out flat, like that, like I
practised in therapy.
You. Are. Not. My. Real. Dad.
But we are family, so here's what I need you to know:
This sister with her fat booty found it difficult to grow
up in a country where beauty was exclusively based
on blonde hair and white skin,
Where long skinny legs were the thing,
And flat, board-like bums awkwardly swung. The
invisibility stung.
In high school, *Home and Away* beach babes haunted
my dreams.
That's what you let me watch on TV?
And then at fifteen you bought me that subscription to
Dolly magazine.
I desperately wanted to look like an Aussie cover
girl, Caucasian, freckled, stick-skinny and sweet
like strawberry cream.

But every teenage part of me was the opposite of that.
I was brown, coconut-round, afro, hands-on-curvaceous-hips fat.
My adolescent subconscious did the maths, Australia,
Dad,
You set me up.

What I'm talking about here is a consistent attack on my body image and self-esteem.
How's a little afro-black girl meant to identify or visualise when she can't see herself reflected:
Booty,
Hips,
Or goddamn thick thighs?
How can she feel comfortable when she doesn't fit into jeans at Sportsgirl or Surf, Dive 'n Ski?
Like her mama and her mama's mama and a large part of her community,
This afro-black girl had a naturally fat body,
Since day one of primary school,
Since 1983.
Your message was consistent,
White and thin equals beautiful,
Black and fat equals unimportant and ugly,
Or simply put
It was unacceptable to look like me.
The constant othering damaged my soul.
Australia, you stole years as I tried to be smaller and whiter and less bold.

So fuck you, Dad,
Why would I be interested in hugging it out or waiting for you to get it?

I grew up feeling like my body was wrong and the pants were right.
No matter how hurt,
I had to fight,
For my womanhood and my worth,
Which tips into a whole other letter about your bullshit misogyny
Because from parliament to hip-hop to film to media to boardrooms
Australia is nowhere near gender equality,
As white men dominate and colonise daily in your toxic image.
But right now,
Let's stick to this particular bullshit, shall we.

You like to call yourself the lucky country,
And yet I had to excavate and travel through mazes and break through walls to find guides to keep me from drowning in the sea of toxicity you built around me.
The authors I was looking for didn't exist in Australian bookshops or libraries.
Growing up African in Australia before black Google, black Twitter and black Instagram was oppressively cruel.
Music pointed the way,
Referencing the higher black female thought I needed to fill my plate.
Lucky for Adeva, Monie Love, Queen Latifah, Salt-N-Pepa
And TLC.
Lucky for Alice Walker, Audre Lorde, Lebo Mashile, Angela Davis, Maya Angelou
And Suzan-Lori.
Lucky for Tiddas, Oodgeroo, Christine Anu
And KillaQueenz.

And lucky for Candy B.
Lucky for me,
Hijacking the stage and fucking with your system,
Rewiring,
Reclaiming,
Rewriting herstory.

Re-parenting myself was tough,
Like any sort of domestic violence, the rebuild is plagued with self-doubt, pain and confusion.
But I did it.

So Dad,
You racist oppressive dangerous colonising misogynist soul-destroying piece of shit,
As I detach from this embedded attachment in which my identity is tangled with yours and I feel like a visitor in my own family and I can't stand people who celebrate the day you invaded and stole this land and
I feel sorry for those trying to reconcile with you because you might have said sorry but what's sorry without accountability, or action, or treaty, and I can't feel comfortable anywhere and I don't even know why
I'm telling you all this because you're not listening and you don't care.

Like anything one ever writes to a perpetrator,
It's more for themselves than the reader;
Like fancy food eaten quickly by hungry children was to the cook or the feeder.

I am no longer your child or student.
My teachers are black women,

Poets, musicians, writers, artists, activists and
philosophers from across the world,
First peoples,
And me.

To all those little afro-black girls still growing up
invisible,
Still seeking reflection,
I see you.
My triumphs will change you
More than my hurt,
I didn't write this for him,
Little sisters feel it,
For you are my words.

THE ELEVENTH HOUSE

Sam Drummond

Mum came up to us, holding a limp figure. 'She's still breathing,' she said.

The mountain looked down at us with pity. The surrounding orchard gathered around to watch the drama. House Eleven had known all along that trouble was coming.

She was alive but motionless. Blood trickled out of her nose.

Tears streamed down my face. I thought back to everything that had led to where we were.

Surgery One

A picture can tell a thousand lies. My inaugural school photo shows a couple dozen middle-class white kids surrounded by suburban bush, smiling with the innocence that comes with embarking on a journey of every opportunity. Front and centre is a beaming kid. The only perceivable difference between him and the others is that he is a bit smaller and sitting in a wheelchair.

'Keep smiling, Sam,' people would say. So I did, hiding my confusion at the transformation that had just occurred.

I don't remember my parents' initial worry and confusion at my diagnosis.

I don't remember the arguments they had about whether there was something wrong with me.

I don't even really remember what life was like before they got divorced, except for the birth of my brother.

All I remember is wanting to chase a ball around. Like a neurotic dog who drops a slimy tennis ball at your feet and then, on being ignored, picks it up and puts it slightly closer to your feet, I was obsessed with anything vaguely spherical.

By the time the letter from the Royal Children's Hospital arrived, Mum, my younger brother and I had moved into House Four – a two-bedroom unit on a main road, built from dark-brown brick that looked as if it could have been cardboard. For all I know, it was. The letter confirmed a date for surgery to both legs. While there was no question in my newly separated parents' minds about whether to go ahead, there was also no explanation of what was going to happen in a way that a five-year-old could understand. At least, not that I can remember.

Even now, when I look through photos with Mum from before Surgery One, we see different images. Mum sees my bowed legs. I see my untouched innocence.

In the slideshow of my memories, that carefree kid woke from a general anaesthetic, legs encased in plaster, at the same time that he began to wake from his childhood.

I screamed from unimaginable pain. Our family quickly discovered that if you want your own room in the public system, the best way is to break decibel records. The doctors said everything was fine. But the screaming didn't stop.

It didn't stop for food or drink. It didn't stop for well wishes from family – sympathetic but ultimately pointless phrases like 'You're being so brave' and 'We wish we could go through the pain instead of you'. It didn't even stop for a celebrity visit from *Full House*'s John Stamos, who was in town for the Logies and pulled an I'll-just-sign-this-photo-and-move-on manoeuvre on me.

It wasn't until my feet went purple that the doctors started taking notice of their patient. The plaster was cutting off my circulation. They wheeled me straight back into surgery for something that should have been done right the first time.

The second round of plaster came off after six weeks. Recovery consisted of sitting in the lounge room of House Four and kicking a balloon over and over again.

I found solace in handling our pet budgerigar, Budge. We had found Budge strolling along our driveway in House Three. I would later walk out the back of House Eight to find Budge in his cage with his head mysteriously severed from his body. He wasn't a real pet like the other families had. For now, though, he was my friend. Animal friends didn't make assumptions or judgements.

I returned to school with a brave face.

'You've been through all this and you're still smiling,' the adults said. 'Keep smiling, Sam.'

So I did. I learnt how to smile like a five-year-old. But my eyes grew the weariness of someone who knew pain earlier than they should have.

Surgery Two

One theory of why time speeds up as we age is that our perception changes in proportion to the time we have already spent alive. So four years for a ten-year-old is the equivalent of twenty years for a fifty-year-old.

Any way you look at it, a lot happened over the next four years. After Husband Two and Divorce Two, we made it to House Seven. House Seven was showing signs of years of neglect. The weatherboards had greyed from exposure to endless peak-hour traffic jams out front. The willow tree in the backyard was felled after its roots began to strangle the sewerage pipes. The home was held together by rotting wooden stumps, Centrelink, child support payments and Mum's five casual jobs.

The back room began to smell after I started making a bit of pocket money from breeding mice and selling them to the local pet store. The cost of the upkeep was probably more than the pittance I received for the litters, but Mum didn't let on. I stopped the business after I learnt that my tiny friends weren't being sold as pets but dropped into heated glass tanks as food for snakes.

House Seven had the advantage of being over the road from school. It was just on the wrong side of the road for our unconventional family to be fully accepted into the established classes.

The houses on the right side of the road didn't run out of petrol on the hill down to the petrol station. The houses on the right side of the road could leave their doors open without fear of burglary, even though their belongings were worth much more. Our thieves were fools. The houses on the right side of the road didn't have to put up with surgery.

I can't remember walking to school on weekdays, but I clearly recall the click of plastic studs as I ambled down to the school oval on Saturday mornings, dressed as a miniature James Hird, for Auskick.

Doctors had always recommended non-weight bearing exercise. They would suggest swimming and cycling. Every time. Swimming and cycling. Swimming came naturally but required regular access to a pool. Putting me on a bike was a bit like trying to get a penguin to fly. I dreaded the school's annual bike ed day like most kids dread the dental van.

Later in life, when I had finally found a bicycle that vaguely fit my design, I would triumphantly announce to a doctor that the torn muscles in my knee and hips were from the very non-weight bearing exercise of riding a bike.

But for now, I was set on ball sports. Aussie rules, in particular. I might have only got a kick here, a handball there, but I was doing what I loved.

At the time, a lot of change was happening in the Victorian school system. While nearby schools were closing because of Kennett's cutbacks, my school was reaping the benefits. Its population boomed with students from increasingly diverse backgrounds, and the extra funding brought the best teachers and facilities from around the leafy suburbs.

We got the news that Surgery Two was needed just after Mr Howard started the stint of conservatism that would shape the progressivism of my generation.

To distract me from what was to come, Dad used his share of the school holidays to drive my brother and me to the Red Centre in an old mustard Ford Falcon. Our young minds were aware of the cultural contrast, as people who had been there for millennia waved at us from shopping centres in Alice that had only just popped up. A hundred kilometres from Uluru, Dad pointed to a rising red mound in the distance. Astonished that we could see the famous landmark from such a long way away, we pulled over to take pictures with our disposable Kodak.

Dad started talking to a fellow traveller.

'You know, some of the international tourists think this is Uluru itself,' said the traveller. 'Unbelievable.'

Dad nodded his head in agreement. 'Unbelievable,' he repeated while sidling over to us.

'Come on, kids,' he said out of the side of his mouth. 'Let's get going.'

Once we got to the real thing, we could not escape the feeling that we were simply an inconsequential blip in the Earth's long story. Despite this insight, it still seemed like the years since Surgery One should have been long enough for doctors to figure out a few things. It helped that only one leg needed to be operated on this time. Also, that no plaster would be required, meaning there would be no chance of the circulation being cut off.

As I left for the hospital, I was confident about the next steps. I had endured countless appointments being poked and prodded by dozens of doctors and medical students. They seemed excited by the opportunity I presented, using words like 'abnormality' and 'mutation'. I knew it wasn't like *X-Men* or *Teenage Mutant Ninja Turtles*, but the message got through: my body needed fixing, and I was ready.

There is something about doctors and normality. Doctors are trained to identify abnormality and to problem-solve until it vaguely resembles their understanding of its reverse. It is little wonder that parents who have always been surrounded by depictions of what is normal are seduced by the idea of fixing abnormality. It is no surprise that children who are taught about the doctrine of abnormality want to satisfy their adults by getting rid of it.

From the very first breath, one might enquire 'Is the baby healthy?'

'Ten fingers, ten toes,' might come the answer. Why, though, but for normality?

Several hours after arriving at the hospital with the goal of resembling normality, I woke with a medieval torture device on my left leg. Seven metal pins held the broken limb together.

Over the months to come, our family woke from any delusions that the normal world was designed for us.

For Mum, life's difficulty level was raised, as if we were playing the outdated version of *Donkey Kong* I had been given as a get-well present. Adding full-time carer to full-time worker and full-time parent needed a circuit breaker.

That circuit breaker came with a knock from a door-to-door salesman, who gave us the cursed gift of pay TV. The first month of the six-month subscription was free, but the screen addiction affected our lives for the next decade.

The TV became our entertainment, our educator and parent. The ability to quote every episode of *The Simpsons*' golden era is a given for many millennials. But knowledge of cartoons that have ended up in animation graveyards, such as *Wacky Races* or *Dastardly and Muttley*, has limited use outside the occasional trivia night.

We would also flick on the news and see Pauline Hanson blaming our national predicaments on my newly arrived schoolmates and the nice locals from our Centralian adventure. But even a ten-year-old could see through that, and we would quickly change the channel back to the Cartoon Network.

Minimal exercise and poor diet left me unhealthy and laid the groundwork for my brother's childhood of obesity.

One night, as Mum lifted me from my chair to the couch, she heard the crack in her back that would put her on the Disability Support Pension fifteen years later. Disadvantage continues and compounds for years and generations.

The entry of the pins into the skin needed constant cleaning. My blanket became soaked with a deathly mixture of blood, Betadine and pus. The wounds became infected.

Once, I screamed at the world, 'Why me?', tears soaking my pillow.

The world did not answer.

At the age of ten, that would be the last time I let myself cry from physical pain.

Surgery Three

Mum found a path to escape Husband Two by following the father she had spent twenty years also escaping, who in turn had spent his adult life escaping the horrors of World War II. We moved to the country – our soundtrack 'Peaches' by The Presidents of the United States of America. We didn't see any peaches, though, just apples and eucalypts starting to feel the effects of the Millennium Drought.

Mum wanted a slower lifestyle and that is what we got.

We were confronted by a choice of schools: the sentimentality provoked by the gold rush–era school buildings had protected them from being consolidated like their city siblings. While teachers' strikes had been a rarity in the city, they were common in the regions.

I survived the change of pace at school by joining a Grade 5/6 composite class and finishing the more senior work a year early.

My final year of primary school was defined by strikes, coursework I had already completed, and constant jibes, comments and laughter about my disability from younger students who had never seen anything like me outside fairytale portrayals.

I entered the maturity of high school with a sigh of relief. Husband Two returned, Houses Eight, Nine and Ten went by,

Husband Two left again.

House Eleven was meant to be another new leaf for our compact family. The yellowed weatherboard farmhouse was surrounded by apple orchards on three sides and a road too close for comfort in such a rural setting. This all stood at the foot of a mountain, whose face was contorted with the colonial tension between ancient eucalypts and the invading, enchanting oak forest. Mum's love of mysticism intensified – perhaps she was trying to find a permanent escape route. Candles and oils filled the rooms. There was a natural remedy for everything. One day, a man with a sword came around, claiming he was Arthur reincarnated and his artefact was Excalibur itself. My brother and I simply shrugged.

House Eleven left no doubt about our isolation, with the road our only connection to civilisation.

Still, Mum fought hard for us to stay connected, even convincing the school bus company to move the designated stop to our driveway. It saved me the walk but forced Jane from down the road to walk an extra 200 metres.

By House Eleven, a fourth member of our family had arrived: Maggie.

There is every chance Maggie had been planned for a while.

For us kids, though, her entry into our lives seemed magical.

A labrador–cocker spaniel, she had a dopey smile, long black hair with a white front and a single white paw. She did not judge any scale of normality. She was the real pet I had longed for.

But a competition began between brothers to be Maggie's favourite. Aged nine and thirteen, the four-year gap between us had never felt so wide. The fighting intensified. A younger brother was a convenient scapegoat. I blamed him for everything, even for life itself. Maggie became the rope in our tug of war.

He would feed her a fish finger from his dinner plate.

I would sneak her into my bedroom and hide her under my doona on the bitter winter nights.

He would walk her through the orchards.

I would throw a ball for her to fetch until after dark.

He would call her for pats. I would call her for more pats. Back and forth it went.

A truce was called the day that dreaded letter with 'RCH' printed in the corner came in the mail. A date had been set for the next surgery.

Health care for a disabled kid in the country adds another level of disruption. Just a simple appointment requires a full day off for both child and parent. The cost of travel skyrockets. Operations require complex logistics to find accommodation for parents as well as finding minders for siblings.

The entourage of medical staff assured me they had some ideas to make the process easier, but it was little comfort.

My trepidation was profound, and I was surprised to wake from Surgery Three without any external apparatus holding my leg together – just a large chunk of metal inserted along my thigh bone. I was given the autonomy of a button to release morphine.

After I refused to press the button enough for their liking, the doctors took that option away and prescribed regular doses.

I returned to House Eleven to find blossoms on the apple trees. On the Saturday after returning, I sat in the sun in my wheelchair as two contests with seemingly foregone conclusions took place: the Victorian state election and the AFL first preliminary final between Essendon and Carlton.

I was far more invested in the latter.

As the day progressed and inevitability was replaced by incredulity, commentators were asking two questions: why had no one seen the Kennett backlash that was coming from the bush, and why, oh why, did Dean Wallis try to take on Fraser Brown in the dying seconds?

The Bombers lost by one point. Steve Bracks's Labor would eventually form government by one seat.

I listened on the wireless as Carlton's Justin Murphy marked and the final siren sounded. I stared at the foot of my wheelchair with a tear in my eye.

Watching me inquisitively was the black-and-white furball of Maggie.

'What are we going to do?' I asked, only half rhetorically.

She turned to look down the path that led past the verandah, then back at me.

I released the chair's brake and put the radio on a nearby table. She got up, wagging her tail expectantly. She looked again down the path.

I pushed along from the side door, rolled down the path, followed the verandah, did a 180-degree turn at the water tank, and came back around the verandah to the side door.

Maggie followed the whole way, barking with the pure joy of someone dancing with nobody watching.

And so began our races.

Out the side door, down the path, follow the verandah, 180 at the water tank, back around the verandah, touch the side door, with Maggie going paw-to-wheel with the chair.

I started timing it. 1 minute, 20 seconds. 1 minute, 10 seconds. 1 minute, 5 seconds. I broke the minute with a 58-second run. Then down to 53 seconds – world records falling thick and fast.

Maggie and I would get our exercise every day I was at home in the wheelchair. At the end of each session, she would lap up some water, go inside and sit at the foot of my chair for the rest of the night. I would sit smiling to myself. It wasn't the fresh air, or the exercise, or the quicker recovery, although those were probably factors. But I had won the battle – I was Maggie's favourite.

*

Once my wounds had healed and I was out of the wheelchair, we were posed with a quandary.

'Maggie's looking a bit pudgy,' said Mum, pointing out what we had all been thinking. She turned to my brother. 'Can you take her out on your bike for some exercise?'

I'll give my brother this: he tried. But as soon as he started pedalling, his bike started moving, Maggie would bark and chase the wheels to the point of forcing him to fall.

She had developed a love of running alongside the wheelchair, but when we swapped four wheels for two, she went into attack mode. Her hatred of bikes was Orwellian: four wheels good, two wheels bad.

Eventually, my brother reluctantly got off his bike and walked her through the orchard.

*

Human memory is a remarkable thing.

My brother and I had not talked about that morning in detail for two decades. It turns out we remember each moment with parallel precision.

Each moment, that is, except for how it begins.

In my mind, we are standing out the front of our house, waiting for the bus with Jane from down the road. A cyclist rides by. Maggie takes chase. She starts to return with a look of triumph.

In my brother's mind, we are also standing out the front of our house, waiting for the bus with Jane from down the road. One of us throws a tennis ball over the road. Maggie takes chase. She picks it up and starts to return with a look of triumph.

From there the memories align.

A tiny car comes speeding around the corner. We yell at Maggie, begging her to stop.

She is completely unaware of anything but her success. Time, for a fleeting moment, stands still.

Time resumes as the car hits her at full speed.

I stand frozen as Mum runs out on the road. The car pulls up 50 metres downwind. A woman gets out and walks towards us.

'I'm sorry,' she says. 'I have to get to work.'

The woman gets back into her car and speeds off. Mum comes up to us, holding a limp figure. 'She's still breathing,' she says.

The mountain looks down at us with pity. The surrounding orchard gathers around to watch the drama. House Eleven had known all along that trouble was coming.

Maggie is alive but motionless. Blood trickles out of her nose.

Tears stream down my face. I think back to everything that has led to where we are.

It is the smell that sticks with you the most. The smell of fear.

The smell of trauma. The smell of impending death.

We put her on a tarpaulin in the car boot and race into town to the vet.

As we lie her down on the surgery table, the vet gives us the news we have been dreading: there is no saving her. She mentions the price of euthanising her. It is more than Mum has in the bank.

Mum looks into Maggie's eyes. She looks back. And, as if giving one final gift, she takes a drawn-out final breath.

The vet puts her stethoscope to Maggie's heart. 'She's gone,' she confirms.

But then, as if on a hunch, she places the stethoscope on Maggie's stomach. She looks up with astonishment. 'Did you know she's pregnant?'

We stare at each other, not knowing what to say.

She feels the belly. 'There are four. They're very young.'

'Can we save them?' Mum asks.

'We could operate,' says the vet, 'but they won't survive.'

Mum looks at us. We shake our heads.

'No,' Mum says. 'Let them go.' tear rolls down my cheek.

It is the final tear of my teenage years.

FIRST, SECOND, THIRD, FOURTH

Tara June Winch

First, looking up, there is the dance. How long ago? A long time ago. Growing up, I knew my father's family came from *a long time ago*. All time, from time travel, yet we were severed from the knowledge of the dance – where the feet go, the arms bent, the hips, the line of spine. We didn't have the *carriberrie* or *corroboree*, nor the song with it. We were living on saltwater country, not freshwater, not from those rivers and lakes where history sat beyond the escarpment in a slouched pose, defeated. There was no dance handed down, it had been cast into the four winds, yet I saw the dance. My cousin is the dancer still and there, that early memory is of her at a family gathering – in one of those blip moments, I am looking up at an impromptu modern dance, fluid, mad, yet articulate. I think she'd just graduated from dancing with the Martha Graham School in New York and returned to our slip of coast. I looked up from where I sat and saw all the possibility in the world. My cousin evoking a dance long buried. From those child's eyes she was the most incredible person I knew. I wondered how it was that she salvaged the dance? I wondered, had she read about it, had someone whispered it to her, did she time travel to find the moves, did the ancestors visit her in her dreams? Would they visit me too?

*

Second, looking down, is the street. Childhood in my mind is that street seen from a bird's-eye view. I recognise the Pizza Hut roof, back and front yards, wire squares of clotheslines, identical tin letterboxes. Perhaps I remember it this way, looking down, because it's too hard to stand there at the front steps and peer through the flyscreen door. In the 1980s children wore fluorescent-coloured clothing; you couldn't miss us. From high up I can see the town pervert who lived opposite our house; I can see me in fluorescent pink bike shorts; I'm sat on the steps at my place, number 15, licking a lemonade ice-block during the time when summer was an entire childhood. If I looked across the road to where he was sitting on his elderly parents' front step, his legs would be wide, his shorts loose, no underwear beneath. He'd often be hidden in the dunes, watching girls and women, and only his arm moving with the lap of tide. I might see the lady who lived next door, and knitted dolls, in her backyard where she picked chokos from the shared vine. I might see the single mother on the other side who cried a lot and tried to befriend my mother, who never wanted friends. Next to the pervert was the girl's house; her mother was alone too, and was bubbly and bronzed; she might be working in the garden. The other house, diagonally from my front steps, was where the drug dealers lived. I can't remember the kids' names; their mother yelled a lot, yet most people yelled. Fights spilt into front yards like the broken toys waiting all year for the town council's rubbish pick-up. Scavengers who drove the streets at that time, looking for thrown-out solid furniture and working electronics, didn't check our kerbside rubbish for bargains; they knew on our street there lay only broken things, bent hopes.

On the street there were bicycles everywhere. The smell of salt outside, inside: cigarette smoke and fly spray in the air. The sound of waves some nights, or cars doing burnouts and night-time arguments. It was night-time when adults made all their loud-voiced *money trouble* arguments, fights that clapped like firecrackers at sunset. Looking down at the cruel intersection, I wonder what it was exactly that the neighbours noticed about us at number 15. Was it class I felt so keenly summed up by, or race? Or both?

At school we learnt explorers. In tablets of milk chocolate, kids could collect an entire set of explorer trading cards. For a brief moment in history class we were presented with archival drawings of Indigenous men, standing one-legged, their rude parts red-clothed, spears in hand; the women were savage and noble, never dressed. *That's all?* I thought. *Well, that's not me*, I realised. We wore jeans, and lived in the commission house, not a humpy. I grew up with a brother, whose father is Torres Strait Islander; a sister, whose mother is my father's sister and is Wiradjuri and whose father is Barkindji; and another brother, who is my cousin. They are darker than me. They are more Indigenous than me. I think I saw life through the lens of a writer from a young age: I never knew how I felt, but wondered how it felt for them. Race was the paradigm that I didn't fit. But we were proud. We are still proud.

I'm still looking down, and I want to yell out to the young girl with bucked teeth, in fluorescent bike shorts; I want her to *look up*! Let me count the ways I love thee. Count the ways I was Aboriginal even if no one is playing AFL on our NSW street. Count the ways you belong somewhere. I'd get dropped off at the Aboriginal Medical Centre for teeth pulling, cavity filling, for painting workshops in the old garage shed out back. I have friends there; it's where I completed my first dot painting, experienced my first kiss, smoked that first cigarette. We got to go on Aboriginal camp once a year, celebrated NAIDOC day annually. Sometimes it feels as if I don't remember anything. I remember almost nothing. Memories are cryptic, translucent blimps rising and bursting, a slice of a life without the details coloured in.

Salvage … I'm standing with Dad at the little shop manned by no one at the local garbage dump – we'll find treasures there.

Dad worked one year as a bricklayer for the botanic gardens' pond; there is a photograph of him somewhere – my mum turned up and brought him lunch perhaps, caught him mid-work or had him pose and laugh for the camera; there are rhododendron flowers in bloom. He's giving me lifts to the beach during his smoko another year when he's a taxi driver. The beach owned us, but the street owned us more. I can see everyone on the street, but we aren't neighbourly. The neighbours argued, our parents argued. I pleaded to have the surf-brand schoolbag, to invite my friends over in the afternoon. I still feel guilty for wanting more than my parents could offer. We went bushwalking. Dad went away working in the bush – he brought back gifts. We went to Lightning Ridge, slept in tents, mattresses beside the fire pits. Those were our holidays.

Salvage … There are no artefacts. Not a *guluman* or *coolaman*, not the one that my grandmother bought on a bus trip to Alice Springs. Her souvenir is at my aunt's house, the last time I saw it she had the *guluman* in the kitchen, high on a shelf. She took it down for me: it used to be in our house growing up; its design was for carrying babies, or collecting berries, or for digging at tuber roots, but this one was a souvenir that was now collecting dust. Quiet truths, unspoken history, that's what lurks growing up, that's what's never dredged up straight from the mouths of rivers. No one is dancing except my cousin.

*

Third, in some middle distance, some certainty, something to look forward to when you're young, is the confluence. The junction of those two rivers, the gush of an estuary. Past and possibility and the knowledge that, if nothing else, I could make my own dance.

And then I left as quick as I'd grown: out into the wide highways, the yonder and blue, all not as brutal as they warned. I was seventeen, high school dropout, wannabe poet, professional hitchhiker. I left because all life is risk; if I stayed, surely that was the bigger risk? I wanted to get to where my sister and cousin were, I wanted to send postcards, to map my country and then the world and figure out exactly how I fit in it all. I think I learnt something early on: that I belonged and didn't belong everywhere. That I was from the world and of the world, and I could move, I could make that extinct dance anywhere, any way I wanted.

Recently my mother left Australia on holiday for the first time. Together we sat in a bed and breakfast in Brittany, France, and watched the TV. *Eurovision* was on, and framed by the screen was a young Aboriginal singer, representing Australia. He didn't win that night, but between where I sat at the end of the bed and the TV is where my daughter sat, a fist raised in the centre of the room. She'll inherit the world, and that place, that *long time ago* place, where her grandfather comes from. I knew then that she too would interpret her own dance, salvage our dance from the wreckage.

*

Fourth, there is the future.

CONTRIBUTORS

INTRODUCTION

ALICE PUNG is an award-winning writer based in Melbourne. She is the bestselling author of the memoirs *Unpolished Gem* and *Her Father's Daughter*, and the essay collection *Close to Home*, as well as the editor of the anthologies *Growing Up Asian in Australia* and *My First Lesson*. Her first novel, *Laurinda*, won the Ethel Turner Prize at the 2016 NSW Premier's Literary Awards. *One Hundred Days* is her most recent novel.

STORIES

FAUSTINA AGOLLEY is a television host, an actor, a DJ, a producer and a writer. She has hosted *Video Hits*, *The Voice* and *The Sydney Gay and Lesbian Mardi Gras*. She made her stage debut in the Molière award-winning play *The Father*, and toured Australia and New Zealand as Oprah Winfrey's resident DJ on her 'An Evening with Oprah' tour. Faustina is a graduate of Media and Communications at the University of Melbourne and Media Studies at RMIT University.

ALISTAIR BALDWIN is a writer and comedian based in Naarm/ Melbourne. He's written for *The Weekly with Charlie Pickering*, *Hard*

Quiz and *Get Krack!n*, developed a play – *Lame* – for MTC First Stage, was a Wheeler Centre Hot Desk Fellow and has been published in *ACMI Ideas*, *un. Magazine*, *Art + Australia*, *Archer* and more.

LECH BLAINE is an award-winning writer from Toowoomba, Queensland. He is the author of the memoir *Car Crash* and the Quarterly Essay *Top Blokes*. His work appears widely, including in *The Best Australian Essays*, *Meanjin*, *The Guardian*, *Griffith Review* and *The Monthly*. An inaugural Griffith Review Queensland Writing Fellow, he won the 2017 Queensland Premier's Young Publishers and Writers Award and the 2019 Brisbane Lord Mayor's Emerging Artist Fellowship.

CANDY BOWERS is a radical theatre-maker, director, lyricist, playwright, actor, teacher and filmmaker. She has starred on screen and stage across the country, and her original plays include *Hot Brown Honey*, *Australian Booty*, *Sista She*, *One the Bear* and *Twelve* (a soul musical from the streets after William Shakespeare's *Twelfth Night*).

KATIE BRYAN's great-great-grandmother was born on Jackie White's station, near Naracoorte, in 1855. She was the first light-skinned girl born in the district and, at the age of two, she was taken from her mother and sent to Blackford mission at Murrabinna. Katie is the first generation of her family to grow up without language, culture and connection to kin and country. Her family have been assimilated; she is the only one who remembers their origins.

JOO-INN CHEW is a writer, and a doctor working in general practice and refugee health. She lives in Canberra with her partner and two kids. She loves diving through green waves, zooming along on her bike, and finding words to decipher the world.

SAM DRUMMOND is a lawyer and disability advocate. He has worked in community, commercial and public broadcasting, and written extensively on disability rights. Sam lives in Melbourne's north with his partner and child. He can often be found swimming laps of Fitzroy pool. His family hopes to get a dog soon.

SARA EL SAYED was born in Alexandria, Egypt. She is the author of the memoir *Muddy People*, and her work features in the anthologies *Growing Up African in Australia* and *Arab, Australian, Other*, among other places. She is a recipient of a Queensland Writers Fellowship and was a finalist for the 2020 Queensland Premier's Young Writers and Publishers Award. She has a Master of Fine Arts and works at Queensland University of Technology.

CARLY FINDLAY OAM is a writer, speaker and appearance activist. She is the author of memoir *Say Hello* and has been published in the ABC, *The Guardian*, *The Age*, *The Sydney Morning Herald*, *CNN* and *Vogue*. She is the editor of *Growing Up Disabled in Australia*.

ANNA GOLDSWORTHY is the author of *Melting Moments*, *Piano Lessons*, *Welcome to Your New Life* and the Quarterly Essay *Unfinished Business: Sex, Freedom and Misogyny*. Her writing has appeared in *The Monthly*, *The Age*, *The Australian*, *The Adelaide Review* and *The Best Australian Essays*. She is also a concert pianist, with several recordings to her name.

ADITI GOUVERNEL was born in Mumbai and grew up in Canberra. She is currently in the US working on her novel.

STAN GRANT is the ABC's international affairs analyst, and vice-chancellor's chair of Australian-Indigenous Belonging at Charles Sturt University. He won the 2015 Walkley Award for coverage of Indigenous affairs and is the author of *On Thomas Keneally*, *The Australian Dream*, *Australia Day*, *The Tears of Strangers* and *Talking to My Country*.

PHOEBE HART is a writer, director and producer of documentaries, factual content and children's television. She is also a lecturer in film, television and digital media at the Queensland University of

Technology, and principal of Hartflicker, a video and film production company. She is known particularly for her autobiographical road trip movie, *Orchids: My Intersex Adventure*.

RAFEIF ISMAIL is a multilingual writer based in Western Australia and the winner of the 2017 Deborah Cass Prize for Writing. Her work has been published by Margaret River Press, Fremantle Press, *Mascara Literary Review*, *Kill Your Darlings* and Djed Press.

ANDY JACKSON is a poet currently living in Castlemaine, Dja Dja Waurrung country. He has co-edited disability-themed issues of *Southerly* and *Australian Poetry Journal*. Andy's most recent collection, *Music our bodies can't hold*, consists of portrait poems of other people with Marfan syndrome.

GAYLE KENNEDY is from the NSW Ngiyaampaa nation. Her poetry collection *Koori Girl Goes Shoppin'* was shortlisted in 2005 for the David Unaipon Award, and she won the award in 2006 with *Me, Antman & Fleabag*. She's published eleven children's books and articles and poems in national and international publications.

BENJAMIN LAW is the author of the memoir *The Family Law*, which he adapted for SBS TV, *Gaysia*, and a Quarterly Essay: *Moral Panic 101*. A columnist for Fairfax's *Good Weekend* magazine, Benjamin has also written for over 50 publications internationally and is a co-host on ABC Radio National's *Stop Everything*. He is the editor of *Growing Up Queer in Australia*.

UYEN LOEWALD was born in Hai Duong, Vietnam. In 1962, while a student at Saigon University, she was detained without trial for her political activism. She married American diplomat Klaus Loewald in 1964; they moved to Australia in 1970. She has worked as a chef, a community worker, a teacher and an interpreter, and is the author of the memoir *Child of Vietnam* (1987).

NATALIE MACKEN is a Sydney-based word tamer. She is the creative director of The Content Folk.

HOPE MATHUMBU is a queer black South African–born woman, who has lived and worked on the sovereign lands of the Kulin Nation since 2003. Her work in public health, radio, arts and various other community development sectors is driven by her belief in the Black African humanist philosophy of Ubuntu.

RICK MORTON is an award-winning journalist and the author of three non-fiction books: *One Hundred Years of Dirt*, *On Money* and *My Year of Living Vulnerably*. He is the senior reporter for *The Saturday Paper*.

OLIVIA MUSCAT is an emerging writer and critic. Her work has appeared in *Meet Me at the Intersection*, and her theatre reviews can be found on *Witness Performance*. She is co-creator and co-host of The YA Page writing community in Melbourne and has worked at the Encounters With Writing festival and the National Young Writers' Festival.

NYADOL NYUON is a commercial litigator and community advocate. She was born in Ethiopia and raised in Kenya, and moved to Australia at age eighteen. In 2011 and 2014, Nyadol was nominated as one of the 100 most influential African-Australians. She is a board member of the Melbourne Social Equity Institute and appears regularly in the media, including on ABC's *The Drum* and *Q&A*.

KERRY REED-GILBERT is a Wiradjuri woman from central New South Wales who has performed and conducted writing workshops nationally and internationally. She was the inaugural Chairperson of the First Nations Australia Writers Network (FNAWN) from 2012 to 2015 and continues today as a Director. Kerry is a former member of the Aboriginal Studies Press Advisory Committee, and her poetry and prose have been published in many journals and anthologies nationally and internationally, including in the *Macquarie PEN Anthology of Australian Literature*.

OLIVER REESON is an essayist and screenwriter. They co-created and wrote *Homecoming Queens*, a web series on SBS about chronic illness in your twenties.

MAGDA SZUBANSKI is one of Australia's best-known and most loved performers. She began her career in university revues, then appeared in a number of sketch comedy shows before creating the iconic character of Sharon Strzelecki in ABC-TV's *Kath and Kim*. She has also acted in films (*Babe*, *Babe: Pig in the City*, *Happy Feet*, *The Golden Compass*) and stage shows. She is the author of the multi-award-winning memoir *Reckoning*.

MIRANDA TAPSELL is an actor best known for her roles in the multi-award-winning feature film *The Sapphires* and for the phenomenally successful TV series *Love Child*. Her recent work includes *Newton's Law*, *Secret City*, *Redfern Now*, *Wolf Creek*, *Cleverman*, *Get Krack!n* and *Play School*. Miranda has appeared in the Sydney Theatre Company's *Secret River* and *Gallipoli*, Griffin Theatre's *The Literati*, Sydney Festival's *I Am Eora*, Riverside Theatre's *Rainbow's End*, Yirra Yakin's *Mother's Tongue*, and played the lead in Belvoir Street's *Yibiyung*. She is the author of the memoir *Top End Girl*.

THINESH THILLAINADARAJAH is a Tamil Canadian lawyer whose views on queer identity and multiculturalism were shaped by his upbringing in Toronto, where he never felt like he had to pick between his Tamil and Canadian identities. He has found Australian culture more monolithic, and his work focuses on creating space where people can embrace and present all facets of their identity.

CHRISTOS TSIOLKAS is the author of six novels: *Loaded*, *The Jesus Man*, *Dead Europe*, *The Slap*, *Barracuda* and *Damascus*. He has published the short story collection, *Merciless Gods*, and co-authored *Jump Cuts: An Autobiography* with Sasha Soldatow. He has published a monograph on Fred Schepisi's *The Devil's Playground*, for the Australian Screen Classics series, and one on Patrick White for the Writers on Writers series. Many of his works have been adapted for the stage and the screen. He is also a playwright, essayist, screenwriter, and film reviewer for *The Saturday Paper*. Christos is a patron of Writers Victoria and an ambassador for the Asylum Seeker Resource Centre. He lives in Melbourne, and alongside Clem Bastow and Casey Bennetto is a co-host of *Superfluity* on community radio station, 3RRR.

TARA JUNE WINCH is a Wiradjuri writer living between Australia and France. Her first novel, *Swallow the Air*, won numerous literary awards, including the Dobbie Award and the Victorian Premier's Award for Indigenous Literature. In 2009 she was awarded the International Rolex Mentor and Protégé Award that saw her work under the guidance of Nobel Laureate Wole Soyinka. She is also the author of the multi-award-winning novel *The Yield*, and a collection of short fiction, *After the Carnage*.

TIM WINTON has published twenty-nine books for adults and children, and his work has been translated into twenty-eight languages. Since his first novel, *An Open Swimmer*, won the *Australian* Vogel Award in 1981, he has won the Miles Franklin Award four times (for *Shallows*, *Cloudstreet*, *Dirt Music* and *Breath*) and twice been shortlisted for the Booker Prize (for *The Riders* and *Dirt Music*). He lives in Western Australia.

VANESSA WOODS is an award-winning journalist and author. She has written three children's books and is the author of the travel memoir *It's Every Monkey for Themselves* (2007), about her experiences chasing wild capuchin monkeys through the Costa Rican jungle. She currently lives in North Carolina.

www.ingramcontent.com/pod-product-compliance
Ingram Content Group UK Ltd.
Pitfield, Milton Keynes, MK11 3LW, UK
UKHW040604210726
13854UKWH00009B/2423

9 781760 643188